CAROLINE MUNRO,
FIRST LADY OF FANTASY

ALSO BY ROBERT MICHAEL "BOBB" COTTER
AND FROM MCFARLAND

Ingrid Pitt, Queen of Horror: The Complete Career (2010)

*A History of the Doc Savage Adventures in Pulps,
Paperbacks, Comics, Fanzines, Radio and Film* (2009)

The Mexican Masked Wrestler and Monster Filmography
(2005; paperback 2008)

*The Great Monster Magazines: A Critical Study of
the Black and White Publications of the
1950s, 1960s and 1970s* (2008)

Caroline Munro, First Lady of Fantasy

A Complete Annotated Record of Film and Television Appearances

Robert Michael "Bobb" Cotter

Foreword by Caroline Munro

McFarland & Company, Inc., Publishers
Jefferson, North Carolina, and London

LIBRARY OF CONGRESS CATALOGUING-IN-PUBLICATION DATA

Cotter, Bobb.
Caroline Munro, first lady of fantasy : a complete annotated record of film and television appearances / Robert Michael "Bobb" Cotter.
　　　　　　p.　　cm.
Includes bibliographical references and index.

ISBN 978-0-7864-6882-9
softcover : acid free paper ∞

1. Munro, Caroline, 1950– [sic; 1949–]　2. Motion picture actors and actresses — Great Britain — Biography.　I. Title.
PN2598.M85C58　2012　　791.4302'8092 — dc23　　[B]　　2012020389

BRITISH LIBRARY CATALOGUING DATA ARE AVAILABLE

© 2012 Robert Michael "Bobb" Cotter. All rights reserved

No part of this book may be reproduced or transmitted in any form or by any means, electronic or mechanical, including photocopying or recording, or by any information storage and retrieval system, without permission in writing from the publisher.

Front cover image: Caroline Munro in *At the Earth's Core*, 1976, directed by Kevin Connor (Photofest)

Manufactured in the United States of America

*McFarland & Company, Inc., Publishers
Box 611, Jefferson, North Carolina 28640
www.mcfarlandpub.com*

To Dad and Brownie and Ingrid Pitt — RIP;
Mum; my loving wife Cheryl and Lucky the Wonder Dog;
Bobby Darin, Joe Bob Briggs, Raoul Duke,
Jack Lambert (#58) and Count Floyd.

ACKNOWLEDGMENTS

Special thanks: Tami Hamalian, Paul Gooding, Gary Svehla, Gary Dile (R.I.P.), Eide's Entertainment, Richard Klemensen, Bruce Timm, Patrick Desmond, the Fin, the Whizzer, and the Usual Gang of Idiots.

Very special thanks: John Del Margio, the Rare Horror/Sci-Fi Movie Collector Extraordinaire for Hire (jddmld@aol.com); Paul "Cookie-Head" Riggie, the Master of Sound and Vision, and, of course, Caroline Munro, the First Lady of Fantasy!

Table of Contents

Acknowledgments vi
Foreword by Caroline Munro 1
Preface 3

Films and Television 5

Documentary and Guest Appearances,
Archival Footage and Other Works 119

Bibliography 161
Index 163

Foreword by Caroline Munro

What you hold in your hands began life at the wonderful Monster Bash in Pittsburgh in 2011. It's one of my favorite events, and taking a break from guest duties I took a wander through the dealers room, intrigued to see what was on offer, when the beautiful face of dear Ingrid Pitt immediately caught my eye. She was on the cover of Bobb's previous book, *Ingrid Pitt: Queen of Horror*, so I stopped and we chatted about my recently departed and still much, much, missed friend.

Toward the end of our conversation Bobb asked if I would like to have a book similar to Ingrid's. I thought it would be a wonderful idea but had to explain that after thinking about it for a while, earlier in the year I had actually started working on my autobiography, with all the scripts and contracts, clippings and photographs that I'd kept over the years finally being retrieved from storage only a month or so before I'd left for this event. Still, because of his boundless enthusiasm and knowledge of my work, I got a really good feeling talking to Bobb and because I knew he would have my best interests at heart, didn't see why he shouldn't go ahead with his own book since it would be less personal than mine, concentrating on the casts and crews, accompanied by his own critiques of the various films and television programs I've been in over the years.

What I particularly liked was seeing the cast and crew getting the recognition they deserve. If the director is the beating heart of every production, it's the invaluable input from all the people from the various departments that provide the blood and muscle and sinew that helps bring each project to life. Even if we didn't always have a particularly generous budget, for me as an actress they did their very best to help create the many different worlds — through the costumes, make-up, sets and lighting — that my characters inhabited, and the more real they made it, the easier it was for me to play the part. Because audiences don't always pay attention or even stay around to read the credits there's a wealth of talented artists and craftsmen who, outside of the industry, don't always get the recognition they rightly deserve. Since a number of those talented people have sadly passed away over the years since we all worked together, as well as remembering them with great affection I'm very pleased to see them recorded here so fans unfamiliar with some of the names might take the opportunity to seek out their other work.

So I thank them for all the effort they put into all the productions I worked on, and I thank Bobb for all his hard work putting this all together. Hopefully, when I eventually finish writing my own book the two can sit side by side and enhance each other. So, nice one, Bobb!

Preface

Yes, that's her real name. Although Caroline Munro has a name which seems like a press agent's play on the name of a certain golden-tressed screen icon, it was given to her by her own mom and dad when she was born in 1949, the year Marilyn Monroe played a bit part in the Marx Brothers film *Love Happy*, and a year before Hollywood started to sit up and take notice of her in *The Asphalt Jungle* and *All About Eve*. So unless they were just extraordinarily prescient, there was no underlying motive in giving their daughter a name that would recall the name of the screen's most famous sex symbol, just as they could not have known that their daughter would grow up to be a pretty famous sex symbol in her own right. In fact, "Munro" is Scottish for a mountain over three thousand feet tall, which is entirely appropriate for a woman whose presence is indeed towering.

The fact that Caroline was born January 16, 1949, in a "wee little town" by the sea is one of the few biographical details that will be offered in this book, because that was the agreement between Caroline and me: When I told her about my idea for a book, she gave it her blessing—as long as it wasn't to be a biography, since she is close to finishing her autobiography. And so I'll try to keep that promise, or at least 99.5 percent of it, because, as I said in *Ingrid Pitt, Queen of Horror*, it's rather odd to write a book about someone and not say anything about their real life. So, other than reiterating that she was launched on her legendary career by her parent's submission of her photo to a "Face of the Year" contest held by Britain's *Evening News* in 1966 and that she won and started modeling for *Vogue* at the tender age of 17, which led to that career (and to cite one or two other items as they relate to the context of the film or show being discussed) and note that she herself is an avid fan of fantasy films, the rest is history—a history she will soon be relating at a bookstore (or Kindle, or whatever) near you.

Like my previous book about Ingrid Pitt (God rest her soul), this will be a reference guide to Caroline's appearances in film and on television. While modeled on that book in terms of structure, there are differences. The synopses have been shortened considerably; in many instances, the original pressbook has been utilized, and the others have been done in that spirit and mostly in the spirit of fun. And while as many technical credits as possible have been listed for the projects that she has been involved with, there will not be an attempt to treat them all equally; in some cases, there will be the technical credits and little or nothing else, simply because very few people want to read about a game show as much as they want to read about, say, *Captain Kronos, Vampire Hunter*. So there will be much more space for information and cracker-box philosophizing about the films.

Like Ingrid, Caroline achieved her iconic status on the basis of a relatively small number of films, but her impact in those films is what earned her that status. It's not my aim to deconstruct that impact, but rather to report on it, to provide as much information as is possible, in as entertaining a way as is possible, to celebrate that impact because it deserves to be celebrated; to, in the words of Joseph Addison, "dwell rather on excellencies than imperfections ... and communicate to the world such things as are worth their observation." And, of course, Caroline has done much worthy of observation: "The Wink," Margiana, Carla, Dia, and the indomitable Stella Star; made integral contributions to movies of three of filmdom's most enduring franchises (Dracula, James Bond, and Sinbad) and one by an acknowledged "Master of Adventure," Edgar Rice Burroughs; and appeared in one of the wackiest takes on yet another enduring franchise, *Star Wars*.

These and more have earned her the title "First Lady of Fantasy" (a term first coined by a New York journalist). It's not a term she uses to promote herself, but rather has been bestowed upon her by her legion of fans. And they're fans not simply because of her roles and stunning beauty, but because, darn it, she's just so nice! Personally, I don't think I've ever met any celebrity as devoid of airs as Caroline, and this is the thing that comes across in her performances, a genuine modesty and desire to give the best performance possible. There's no sense of the diva, no overweening narcissism and transparent opportunism, just a very regular person — who just happens to be a beloved pop culture icon. She's grateful for the opportunities her status has provided, yet never loses contact with Planet Earth or its inhabitants: "Yes, 'First Lady of Fantasy' ... well, it's a big title to live up to, isn't it, really? ... I mean ... it's a lovely thing to have said; it's very flattering and this, that and the other, but in real life, it couldn't be further from the truth, really, because it's just little me ... but maybe through the films I've done, or been involved with ... it's a lovely label to have put on me; I'm very flattered." Thank *you*, Caroline, for being a genuinely sweet and wonderful person, thank you for the joy your roles have given all of us, and thank you for the opportunity to celebrate them all under one roof ... or, as it were, between two covers. You're the First Lady of Fantasy — I hope you don't mind that you've been elected to the post for life!

FILMS AND TELEVISION

This main section contains information about the films and television shows which feature Caroline Munro in starring or supporting roles. Although every attempt has been made to provide as much information as possible, there are still certain appearances whose details managed to elude me. The first film listed, in fact, is one of those: *Smoke Over London* is listed as her first screen appearance on both the Internet and her fan club video documentary *Caroline Munro: First Lady of Fantasy*, is extremely difficult to locate, and it's the one film she consistently does not mention in interviews or seem to have any memories of. The listing of films in the documentary cites the David Bowie appearance, although it is not included in any of his other filmographies.

Smoke Over London (Fumo di Londra)— 1966, Fono Roma

Crew: Executive Producer: Giorgio Bianchi; Director: Alberto Sordi; Screenplay: Alberto Sordi, Sergio Amidei; Music: Piero Piccioni; Photography: Benito Frattari; Film Editor: Antonietta Zita; Sets: Elio Costanzi; Makeup: Alan Brownie; Hair Stylist: Rosemary Diamond; General Organization: Baccio Bandini; Production Manager: Romano Cardarelli; Assistant Director: Vana Caruso; Sound Engineers: Vittorio De Sisti C.S.C., Taffy Haines; Songs: Julie Rogers.

Cast: Alberto Sordi (Dante Fontana), Fiona Lewis (Elizabeth), Amy Dalby (Duchess of Bradford), Alfredo Marchetti (Count Bolla), Clara Bindi (Dante's Wife), Michael Trubshawe (the Colonel), Massimo Ungaretti (A Friend), Romano Giomini C.S.C. (a traveler), Bart Allison (the Vicar), Mr. Chance (Auctioneer), Sara Colmer (Lady Charlotte), Pamela Hollyer (Lady Rachel), George Jones (Chauffeur), William Mostin Owen (Reginald), Elizabeth Rutter (Angel), Jean St. Clair (Headmistress), Philip John Trihble (the Scotsman), Pad John Wells (Diana's guest), Caroline Munro, Dana Gillespie, Carlo Forti, Lucy Hill, David Bowie.

SYNOPSIS

Dante Fontana, an Italian man who wants to be British worse than Eric Burdon wanted to be a black man. So he hops on a plane and flies into a series of "zany" adventures of mistaken identities and clashes, with both culture and bikers, ultimately discovering there's no place like Rome.

REVIEW AND NOTES

Alberto Sordi was an Italian comedian and was the star of Federico Fellini's early films *Lo sceicco bianco* (*The White Sheik*) and *I Vitelloni*. His appeal is hard to see from this distance; he was rather plain-looking, did not really have a distinctive voice or delivery, and bore no particular gift for physical comedy; the humor in the film comes from the situations he finds himself in, rather than his reactions to them. For instance, he hails a cab with his bumbershoot, only to get it caught in a rail on a passing bus, which in theory should lay the groundwork for zaniness, but he only registers mild surprise and then sort of strolls along until the bus comes to a stop. There's a sequence that uses a fox hunt as its setting, so if you find upper-class twits in funny coats participating in a barbaric sport funny, you'll find that sequence hilarious. Caroline has a very small, uncredited, although fairly visible bit part as one of the swinging young Chelsea set, somewhat a harbinger of her role in *Dracula A.D. 1972*, but she doesn't appear until there are only about twenty minutes left in the film. Her big moment comes in the climactic "Mods vs. Rockers"–type battle in which she gets to belt a biker! The credits thank "Prince" Rupert Lowenstein, the merchant banker who would later become the manager of the Rolling Stones. For more Stones connections, see "G.G. Passion" and *Dracula A.D. 1972*.

"G.G. Passion" (short) — 1966, Cadre Films

Crew: Producer: Gene Gutowski; Co-Producer: Roman Polanski; Associate Producer: Arnold Miller; Director: David Bailey; Screenplay: Gerard Brach; Photography: Stanley A. Long; Film Editor: John Beaton; Production Design: Michael Haynes; Ladies' Wardrobe: Maxine Haynes; Song: "G.G. Passion" by Phil Dennis/Terry Roberts.

Cast: Eric Swayne (G.G. Passion), Chrissie Shrimpton (G.G.'s Main Girlfriend), Caroline Munroe (groupie), Marianne Faithfull, Rory Davis, Janice Haye, Greta Rantwick.

SYNOPSIS

(From the British Film Institute screening notes): "G.G. Passion (Eric Swayne) is a successful pop star whose life is a whirlwind of adoring fans, beautiful women (including Caroline Munro and Chrissie Shrimpton) and expensive cars. But while he enjoys the fruits of his celebrity lifestyle, a secret group of observers is judging whether his fame and influence is beneficial to society as a whole. Soon they will make their decision — and it will be final!"

FILMS AND TELEVISION: *Casino Royale* (1966)

REVIEW AND NOTES

Scripted by Gerard Brach, filmed by Stanley Long and produced by Gene Gutowski and Roman Polanski, this ultra-rare short was directed by celebrated photographer David Bailey. Chrissie Shrimpton, the younger sister of fellow fashion model Jean Shrimpton, was one of the many girlfriends of Mick Jagger, and was also featured in Hammer's science-fiction opus *Moon Zero Two*. Caroline had a very small bit as a groupie, which she remembered for *Caroline Munro, First Lady of Fantasy* (the DVD; see next section): "Through the photography, through winning the 'Face of the Year,' and having met David Bailey, he was doing a film called 'G.G. Passion'; shot in black and white, and it was with no known actors at all.... [He] used ... a very well-known photographer as a pop singer, and he had ... girls or groupies or whatever, and I was one of them.... There were lots of models of the day, I think Marianne Faithfull was in it, and I remember the Rolling Stones coming to the set because Mick Jagger was going out with Chrissie Shrimpton, the lead in the thing, and it was kind of very 'Sixties,' I suppose; that was one of my first bits in film." (And yes, in the opening credits they spell Caroline's surname incorrectly.)

Casino Royale—1966, Columbia Pictures Corporation/Famous Artists Productions

Crew: Producers: Jerry Bresler, Charles K. Feldman; Associate Producer: John Dark; Directors: Val Guest, Ken Hughes, John Huston, Joseph McGrath, Robert Parrish, Richard Talmadge; Screenplay: Wolf Mankowitz, John Law, Michael Sayers; Additional Dialogue: Woody Allen, Val Guest, Ben Hecht, Joseph Heller, Terry Southern, Billy Wilder, Peter Sellers; Suggested by the novel *Casino Royale* by Ian Fleming; Music Composer-Conductor: Burt Bacharach; Orchestrators: Jack Hayes, Leo Shuken; Main Title Theme: Herb Alpert and the Tijuana Brass; Photography: Jack Hildyard; Film Editor: Bill Lenny; Casting: Maude Spector; Production Design: Michael Stringer; Art Direction: Ivor Beddoes, Lionel Couch, John Howell; Costume Design: Julie Harris, Anna Duse; Chief Makeup Artist: Neville Smallwood; Chief Hairdresser: Joan Smallwood; Makeup Artist for Ursula Andress: John O'Gorman; Production Managers: Barrie Melrose, John D. Merriman, Douglas Pierce; Assistant Directors: Roy Baird, Carl Mannin, John Stoneman; Second Unit Directors: Anthony Squire, Richard Talmadge; Assistant Art Directors: Norman Dorme, Tony Rimmington; Construction Manager: Bill MacLaren; Set Dresser: Terence Morgan; Sound: Sash Fisher, Bob Jones, Dick Langford, John W. Mitchell; Sound Editor: Chris Greenham; Dialogue Editor: James Shields; Special Effects: Cliff Richardson, John Richardson, Roy Whybrow; Special Matte Work: Les Bowie; Matte Painter: Gerald Larn; Stunts: Gillian Aldam, Bob Anderson, Peter Brace, Ken Buckle, Jack Cooper, Tex Fuller, Rusty Hood, Arthur Howell, George Leech, Jimmy Lodge, Peter Munt, Keith Peacock, Terence Plummer, Dinny Powell, Joe Powell, Nosher Powell, Terry Richards, Tony Smart, Terry Yorke; Stunt Rider: Richard O'Brien; Stunt Driver: Mike Reid; Stunt Double for David Niven: Jimmy Lodge; Additional Photography: Nicolas Roeg, John Wilcox;

Films and Television: *Casino Royale* (1966)

Camera Operators: Gerry Fisher, Alex Thomson, Ken Worringham; Camera Trainee: Trevor Coop; Focus Pullers: Wally Fairweather, Anthony B. Richmond; Focus Puller — "A" Camera: Ted Deason; Still Photographers: Pamela Green, Douglas Webb; Supervising Electrician: Maurice Gillett; Wardrobe Supervisor: Betty Adamson; Assistant Film Editor: Alan Strachan; Technical Advisor: David Berglas; Presenter: Charles K. Feldman; Choreographer: Tutte Lemkow; Titles and Montage Effects: Richard Williams; Continuity: Renee Glynne; Runner: Michael Murray.

Cast: David Niven (Sir James Bond), Orson Welles (Le Chiffre), Peter Sellers (Evelyn Tremble/James Bond 007), Ursula Andress (Vesper Lynd/James Bond 007), Joanna Pettet (Mata Bond/James Bond 007), Daliah Lavi (The Detainer/James Bond 007), Woody Allen (Jimmy Bond/Dr. Noah), Deborah Kerr (Agent Mimi/Lady Fiona McTarry), William Holden (Ransome), Charles Boyer (Le Grand), John Huston ("M"/General McTarry), Kurt Kasznar (Smernov), George Raft (Himself), Jean-Paul Belmondo (French Legionnaire), Terence Cooper (Cooper/James Bond 007), Barbara Bouchet (Moneypenny), Angela Scoular (Buttercup), Gabriella Licudi (Eliza), Tracey Crisp (Heather), Elaine Taylor (Peg), Jacqueline Bisset (Giovanna Goodthighs), Alexandra Bastedo (Meg), Anna Quayle (Frau Hoffner), Derek Nimmo (Hadley), Ronnie Corbett (Polo), Colin Gordon (Casino Director), Bernard Cribbins (Taxi Driver), Tracy Reed (F.A.N.G. Leader), John Bluthal (Casino Doorman/MI5 Agent), Geoffrey Bayldon ("Q"), John Wells (Q's Assistant), Duncan Macrae (Inspector Rene Mathis), Graham Stark (Cashier), Chic Murray (Chic), Jonathan Routh (John), Richard Wattis (British Army Officer), Vladek Sheybal (Le Chiffre's Representative), Percy Herbert (First Piper), Penny Riley (Control Girl), Jeanne Roland (Captain of the Guards); Jennifer Baker, Susan Baker (Le Chiffre's Assistants), R.S.M. Brittain (Sergeant-Major), Richard Burton (Himself), Geraldine Chaplin, Richard Talmadge (Keystone Kops), Erik Chitty (Sir James Bond's Butler), Frances Cosslett (Michele), Alexander Dore (Extra), Valentine Dyall (Vesper Lynd's Assistant/Dr. Noah's Voice), Hal Galili (USA Officer at Auction); Veronica Gardnier, Yvonne Marsh (Bond Girls), Bob Godfrey (Scottish Strongman), Jack Gwillim (British Officer at Auction), John Hollis (Fred), Anjelica Huston (Agent Mimi's Hands), Burt Kwouk (Chinese General), John Le Mesurier (M's Driver), Stirling Moss (Driver), Caroline Munro (Guard Girl), Peter O'Toole (Scottish Piper), David Prowse (Frankenstein's Monster), Milton Reid (Temple Guard), Robert Rowland (MI5 Agent), Nikki Van der Zyl (Vesper Lynd's Voice), Barrie Melrose.

Synopsis

Sir James Bond 007 (David Niven) is retired, living in a world of his own making on a palatial country estate. When the heads of the world's top spy agencies implore him for help, he refuses — until they blow up his house.

SMERSH wants to destroy Bond's reputation, and if they can't corrupt him, they will kill him. Bond, now head of Her Majesty's Secret Service, tries to find an agent immune to the charms of female spies, and decrees that from now on, all agents and trainees, including the women, shall be referred to as James Bond 007 in an effort to confuse the enemy.

Sir James Bond 007 recruits former spy Vesper Lynd (Ursula Andress), now a millionaire businesswoman, as a James Bond 007, to recruit baccarat expert Evelyn Tremble (Peter Sellers) as a James Bond 007, and she offers to stake him in a game against the mysterious Le Chiffre (Orson Welles) at Casino Royale.

SMERSH also operates a covert spy school that supplies babysitters to important households. Sir James' daughter by Mata Hari, Mata Bond (Joanna Pettet), is recruited as a James Bond 007 to infiltrate the organization, and discovers that Le Chiffre is selling his "unique" art collection in order to cover his debt to SMERSH. If he does not pay, he dies.

James Bond 007 and James Bond 007 take their places at the baccarat game while Le Chiffre performs magic tricks. James Bond 007 beats Le Chiffre, who in turn kidnaps James Bond 007. James Bond 007 gives chase, but is captured by Le Chiffre, who tortures him until James Bond 007 kills James Bond 007 with a machine gun concealed in a set of bagpipes. Le Chiffre, in turn, is killed by SMERSH.

A UFO lands in Trafalgar Square, where James Bond 007 is kidnapped and taken to Casino Royale. Sir James Bond 007 and Moneypenny (Barbara Bouchet) are captured and taken to the leader of SMERSH, Dr. Noah, who turns out to be Sir James' sexually frustrated nephew, Jimmy Bond (Woody Allen). He plans to replace all heads of state with robot doubles under his command and release a virus that will wipe out everyone except beautiful women and all men taller than himself.

Jimmy has kidnapped MI5's "secret weapon," "The Detainer — James Bond 007" (Daliah Lavi), and shows her his greatest invention: a capsule that contains 400 tiny time pills that will create an atomic chain reaction and explosion. She tricks him into drinking it, and Jimmy begins hiccupping his way to Armageddon.

Sir James Bond 007, Moneypenny, James Bond 007, James Bond 007, and James Bond 007 escape captivity and get directions from the Frankenstein Monster to the melee which is taking place in the casino. James Bond 007 gets the drop on Sir James Bond 007. The cavalry arrives. The Indians arrive. The French arrive. The Keystone Kops arrive. But Jimmy hiccups his last, and the island is blown to smithereens. Which James Bond 007 survives?

REVIEW AND NOTES

Chicago Sun-Times reviewer Roger Ebert called *Casino Royale* a "definitive example of what can happen when everybody working on a film goes simultaneously berserk. This is possibly the most indulgent film ever made. The five directors were given instructions only for their own segments, according to publicity, and none knew what the other four were doing. This is painfully apparent. I suppose a film this chaotic was inevitable. There has been a blight of these unorganized comedies, usually featuring [Peter] Sellers, [Woody] Allen and/or Jonathan Winters, in which the idea is to prove how zany and clever everyone is.... Peter Sellers was the funniest comedian in the movies when he was making those lightly directed low-budget pictures like *I'm All Right Jack*. Now he is simply self-infatuated and wearisome. Ebert salutes the hilarious bits by Woody Allen, Orson Welles and others, and shares the opinion of many film fans in wishing that Welles would have been allowed to play Le Chiffre straight. (Welles' personal dislike of Peter Sellers gives his performance an edge which might have been lacking otherwise.) Val Guest, in an interview in *Scarlet Street* No. 15 (Summer 1994) explains: "Orson Welles and Peter Sellers could not get on. Orson Welles said one day, 'Call me when that fucking amateur is finished.' That gives you an idea of how they got on." John Brosnan (in *James Bond in the Cinema*, The Tantivy Press, 1972) opined: "Overblown and unnecessarily extravagant though it may have been, it was still a very funny film. A few of the sequences failed, but the majority of them worked — most successfully. *Casino Royale* may have been a failure, but it was a most enjoyable one."

Of course, time and changing mores of many types have a way of changing the perceptions of films, and that has been the case with *Casino Royale*, which has developed something of a cult following, seemingly *because* of its very bizarre patchwork nature and incoherence. Simon Winder (*The Man Who Saved Britain*, FSG, 2006) is decidedly not part of that cult; he deems it a "disaster," a "horror," and "not even a mad cousin locked in the attic" because "it has nothing to do with Bond — or with anything." But really, does it have any less to do with Bond or the source novel than, say, *The Spy Who Loved Me* or *Octopussy*? And it's still miles ahead of either the awful 1954 American television version (which managed to feature Peter Lorre as Le Chiffre in another missed opportunity) or the modern version with Daniel Craig, in a performance which made one nostalgic for Roger Moore. The patchwork nature, of course, can be attributed to the number of cooks with their hands in the broth, and the chaotic production has become the stuff of Hollywood legend; in *Scarlet Street* No. 15 (Summer 1994), Guest elaborated when asked if he had a favorite story about the making of the film:

> It was an unbelievable experience! I went on it under contract for eight weeks, and I was still under contract nine months later! [Producer] Charlie Feldman was a madman. There were days when you loved him ... and then other days you could throttle him! An extraordinary man, who would change his mind overnight — *during* the night, mostly — and call you at all hours. They had bought *Casino Royale*, which was a Bond book, but when they went through it, they found that every single sequence in that book had been used in the other Bond pictures. This was the only book that had "gotten away," the only one Cubby Broccoli and Harry Saltzman didn't have. But they had used all the bits out of it, including the card game!
>
> [When asked if he worked with the other directors, Guest said,] Only to say "Hey, don't use such-and-such a star on Wednesday, 'cause *I* need her!" It was a very strange set-up. At the beginning, it was just John Huston and me. One day, John said to me, "Is Feldman as mad as I think he is?" I said, "Oh, he's madder!" Huston said, "He's talking now about having a compendium of directors." I didn't know that. "Oh, yes, it's not just us! There's a compendium coming along!" Then Charlie said he wanted a compendium of stars as well — a lot of stars, different segments, and a compendium of directors. He gave me a script by Terry Southern, a script by Ben Hecht, a script by Richard Maibaum — and he said, "Take all these away and see if you can get *one* out of 'em."

Caroline's role in the film is minuscule but it was her first official role as a Bond Girl (she was one of an elite few that did it twice). She can be seen in the climactic scene where David Niven confronts Woody Allen, which in itself is an accomplishment, given the cornucopia of scenery-chewing stars. Hollywood still makes plenty of overblown and unnecessarily extravagant films, but rarely with the kind of wall-to-wall star power we get here, and in other sprawling '60s comedies like *A Funny Thing Happened on the Way to the Forum* and *It's a Mad Mad Mad Mad World*. In *The Beauty Behind Faceless* (DVD extra, 2004), Caroline describes her role as "a tiny-weenie, flash of a pan bit ... I mean, not even a bit, a spot...." In *First Lady of Fantasy* she said, "I played a Guard Girl, and there were about 150 Guard Girls in this particular scene, and I think I was stuck at the very back of the line ... and in this particular scene, I think it was Woody Allen that was coming through, and we had to fire these machine guns that contained ping-pong balls at him, and it was ... sort of bizarre, and I seemed to be on the film for weeks doing these scenes at the back of the line...."

Another immense pleasure is the soundtrack; the title track is a virtual aural definition of "The Sixties" and the "Now Sound." But ultimately, the main pleasure must come from the situations and performances. Woody Allen is indeed hilarious, at the height of his nebbishness, and Deborah Kerr is absolutely mad. Val Guest, who directed Allen's segment, said, "Woody and I sat down and wrote it together. Then we took it over to Charlie Feldman, who would go through it and send it back with all the gags cut out, having left all the buildups! Woody'd say, 'How can a guy do this?' I'd say, 'Look, don't worry about it. Let him think he's cutting something. We can put 'em back in when we shoot'—which is exactly what we did."

Anna Quayle is wonderfully weird in the movie, and David Niven is charming as the stuttering, retired James Bond, complaining about the "sexual acrobat" that has taken his place. When "M" has Bond's palatial country estate blown to smithereens in order to coerce his cooperation, the look on Bond's face is priceless. Ian Fleming felt that Niven was the perfect actor for the role, considering Sean Connery a "Glaswegian truck driver." Vladek Sheybal (Kronsteen in *From Russia with Love*) has a great scene trying to chase down Joanna Pettet and emptying his rifle at her while a policeman stands right next to him. When the clip is emptied, Sheybal looks over at the policeman, shrugs his shoulders and walks away. Derek Nimmo plays Sir James' male secretary; his wonderfully unctuous description of various liquidated agents being "stabbed to death in a ladies' sauna bath," "burnt in a blazing bordello" and "garroted in a geisha house" is an aural treat. Bondian gadgets are given their ridiculous due, and there are some great sight gags, such as when Sir James and his lot break into a room of the casino where there is nothing but gold-painted girls. There are some "hip" drug references: Mata Bond asks Sir James if he "wants a drag" off of her hookah, to which he replies, "No, thanks, I'm trying to give that up," and later offers him some poppy tea, two cups of which will get him "stoned out of his mind." Frankenstein's Monster is essayed by David Prowse, who would tackle the role again, in quite different form and fashion, in *Frankenstein and the Monster from Hell*. And therein lies the key to appreciating the film. Firstly, get over the fact that it is not going to be a "straight" Bond flick (they often skidded quite close to parody themselves), and secondly, don't attempt to see it as a coherent whole, which it never was to begin with. Simply derive pleasures from the disparate parts that make it something other than just a sum total of those parts.

Joanna—1968, Laughlin–20th Century–Fox

Crew: Producer: Michael S. Loughlin; Director-Screenplay: Michael Sarne; Music: Rod McKuen; Photography: Walter Lassally; Film Editor: Norman Wanstall; Production Design-Art Direction: Michael Wield; Costume Design: Sue West, Virginia Hamilton-Kearse; Wardrobe Supervisor: Shura Cohen; Makeup: Gordon Kay; Production Manager: David Anderson; First Assistant Director: Antal Kovacs; Third Assistant Director: Nicolas Hippisley-Coxe; Dubbing Editors: Mike Le Mare, Jim Roddan; Additional Photography: David Muir; Camera Operator: Ronnie Fox Rogers; Conductor-Arranger-Musical Director: Arthur Greenslade; Sound Recording: Delta Sound; Continuity: Ann Edwards; Assembly Editor: Lucy O'Sullivan; Shoes: Charles Jourdan.

Cast: Genevieve Waite (Joanna), Christian Doermer (Hendrik Casson), Calvin Lockhart (Gordon), Donald Sutherland (Lord Peter Sanderson), Glenna Forster-Jones (Beryl), David Scheuer (Dominic Endersley), Marda Vanne (Granny), Geoffrey Morris (The Father), Michelle Cook (Margot), Manning Wilson (Inspector), Clifton Jones (Black Detective), Dan Caulfield (White Detective), Michael Chow (Lefty), Anthony Ainley (Bruce), Jane Bradbury (Angela), Fiona Lewis (Miranda De Hyde), John Owens (PC Dove), Michael Sarne (Film Director), Carlos Baker (Critic's Child), David Collings (Critic), John Gulliver (Art Dealer), Jenny Hanley (Married Woman), Richard Hurndall (Butler), Sibylla Kay (Critic's Wife), Brenda Kempner (Woman with Glasses), Elizabeth MacClennan (Nurse), Peter Porteous (Taxi Driver), Annette Robertson (Maid), Jayne Sofiano (Teacher), Caroline Munro.

SYNOPSIS

From original pressbook:

Joanna (Genevieve Waite) arrives in London from her home in the provinces to live with her grandmother (Marda Vanne), while attending art school. There she becomes friendly with her teacher Hendrik (Christian Doermer).

Joanna immediately becomes involved with the free-swinging young set in London. She moves from her grandmother's house and has a series of amorous adventures. She meets a Negro girl, Beryl (Glenna Forster-Jones), a hustler who sleeps where she can and hunts for rich men.

Beryl becomes Joanna's mentor, teaching her how to make her way in the world. Joanna meets Beryl's brother Gordon (Calvin Lockhart) for whom she feels an attraction, but being in the midst of an affair with Dominic (David Scheuer), she takes no action.

At a party Dominic and Joanna run into Beryl who has come with wealthy Lord Sanderson (Donald Sutherland). After several parties in London, they go to Peter's home in Tangier, where their good times are marred only by Peter's spells of illness. Although he loves Beryl, Peter confides in Joanna that he has only a short time to live. He explains that his illness has taught him to believe in people. He stresses his belief that everyone needs to be committed in order to fulfill himself.

Back in London, Dominic stops seeing Joanna because of her promiscuity. She become involved with Gordon, who runs a nightclub which Peter has helped him acquire. She becomes his mistress. When Peter is taken to the hospital, his friends visit him and find that, to the end, Peter remains optimistic, courageous, and terribly proud of having helped people.

Gordon gets in trouble with a gang of hoodlums who want him to pay "protection" for his club. One of the gang is killed, and Gordon has to flee. Aware at last that commitment is desirable, Joanna seeks to help Gordon to escape, but he is apprehended and sentenced to 10 years in prison. Joanna fully commits herself by returning to her parents to have Gordon's baby.

REVIEW AND NOTES

TV Guide called *Joanna* "[s]lightly surreal, with sunshine-and-roses songs by poet McKuen, the film is most notable for its attempt at dealing openly and honestly with miscegenation. However, the rest of the film falters, particularly from the confusion between what is real and what is imagined. Sutherland steals the film as the dying man."

Joanna is the Mod version of *Guess Who's Coming to Dinner*; it was self-consciously arty at the time, and so it is unintentionally campy now. Sarne, who would soon direct the epic bomb (and subsequent cult classic) *Myra Breckenridge*, had done a similar film two years earlier, *A Road to Saint Tropez*, in which a woman drives to scenic spots in Europe and has sex with different men, including Udo Kier. After her love scenes with Calvin Lockhart, Genevieve Waite was blacklisted in her birthplace of South Africa and moved to the United States, where she married and subsequently divorced John Phillips, leader of the Mamas and the Papas, and in between became the mama of Bijou Phillips. Sarne would remember Lockhart for *Myra Breckenridge*; Lockhart went on to star in the classic of Blaxploitation films, *Cotton Comes to Harlem* (1970). He also appeared in *The Beast Must Die* (1974) (with Peter Cushing and Anton Diffring). Anthony Ainley came from a distinguished acting family, and had quite the distinguished career as well; he had roles in, among many others, *You Only Live Twice*, *The Blood on Satan's Claw*, *The Land that Time Forgot* and 31 episodes of *Doctor Who* as the Doctor's arch-nemesis, the Master. Fiona Lewis had been in Caroline's first film, *Smoke Over London*, and would later appear with her in *Where's Jack?* and *Dr. Phibes Rises Again*. She only did one other genre film, but it was excellent: the underrated Dan Curtis production of *Dracula* with Jack Palance (sometimes called *Bram Stoker's Dracula*, which only serves to confuse it with the one where Dracula's head looks like a butt).

A Talent for Loving (a.k.a. *Gun Crazy*)—1969, Walter Shenson Films/American Broadcasting Company (ABC)

Crew: Producer: Walter Shenson; Associate Producer: Leon Becker; Director: Richard Quine; Screenplay: Jack Rose, based on the novel by Richard Condon; Music Composer-Conductor: Ken Thorne; Photography: Clifford Stine; Film Editor: Eric Boyd-Perkins; Art

FILMS AND TELEVISION: *A Talent for Loving* (1969)

Director: Ramiro Gomez; Costume Design: Yvonne Blake; Production Managers: Walter Shenson, Manuel Perez; Sound Re-Recording Mixer: Gerry Humphreys; Camera Operator: Dennis C. Lewiston; Title Designer: Maurice Binder; Script Supervisor: Esther Stephenson; Associate Editor: Barrie Vince; Sound: George Stephenson, Gerry Humphries; Sound Editor: Les Wiggins; Assistant Directors: Tony Fuentes, Gil Carretero; Set Dresser: Rafael Salazar; Makeup: Carman Martin; Hairdresser: Carmen Sanchez.

Cast: Richard Widmark (Major Patten), Topol (General Molina), Genevieve Page (Delphine), Cesar Romero (Don Jose), Fran Jeffries (Maria), Derek Nimmo (Moodie), Max Showalter (Franklin), Joe Melia (Tortillaw), John Bluthal (Martinelli), Mircha Carven (Benito), Judd Hamilton (Jim Street), Caroline Munro (Evalina), Jack Brami (Mexican Bandit), Marie Rogers (Marylyn Ridgeway), Janet Storti (Florita), Libby Morris (Jacaranda), Milo Quesada (Don Patricio).

SYNOPSIS

Major Patten (Richard Widmark) wins 150,000 acres of land in a poker game with Mexican "freedom fighter," "General" Molina (Topol), the worst shot in Mexico. Before Patten can claim the land, he must first clear up some land grants with Don Jose (Cesar Romero), the richest man in Mexico. Don Jose has a large cache of rifles, which both the "freedom fighters" and a hostile Indian tribe would like to get their hands on. His daughter, Maria (Fran Jeffries), cannot wait to get her hands on Major Patten. Don Jose, eager to marry her off to Patten, tells him their family suffers from an ancient Aztec curse: "A talent for loving!"

Four days later, an exhausted Patten visits a friend, a widower with a daughter and two sons, Benito and Jim. The Indians kidnap the daughter; the father gives pursuit, never to return. The boys become Patten's adopted sons. Patten also has a daughter of his own by this time, Evalina. When Don Jose arranges a circus to celebrate her birth, Maria runs off with four Hungarian acrobats. The strain is too much for Don Jose, but before he rides off to that big ranchero in the sky, he makes Patten promise never to tell Evalina about the curse. She is sent to a convent.

Twelve years later, Evalina (Caroline Munro) returns from the convent; she does not know about the "curse" but she is beginning to experience the symptoms! Benito and Jim and their sister have grown up as well. Jim has met Marylyn Ridgeway, who dresses as a deer and shows him the ways of love. Benito meets Molina's daughter, who doesn't. Their sister has married the chief of the tribe. Molina and the Indians still want those guns.

After Evalina learns about the curse, Patten discovers her in bed with Benito (eager to learn those ways of love) and Jim (along for the ride), and says one of them must marry her. A British snake-oil salesman, Moodie, who also has eyes for Evalina, suggests a horse race between the two; whoever reaches Mexico City first will have her hand (and everything else, in spades) in marriage. Patten will meet them on a train which also carries the guns.

Molina's "freedom fighters" attack the train. The Indians decide discretion is the better part of valor. The bullets from the guns, which are now rusted, are thrown into the fire and the train attacks the "freedom fighters." When Molina's ill-costumed cohorts regroup, the Indians attack them, saving the train from Molina's "cavalry"! After the smoke clears, Patten and Molina discover they share a terrible secret. Who will be the next "victim" of the "curse"?

REVIEW AND NOTES

This was originally conceived as a film for the Beatles; they backed out due to the fact that by this time, they could barely stand to make music together, much less a movie (witness *Let It Be*). Although it premiered on U.S. television, it was not a TV movie *per se*; it simply failed to receive a theatrical release in the U.S. One is tempted to speculate that the reason for this is the almost casual racism and sexism on display. Gender and racial equality in movies took a long time to evolve; some would say that it still is evolving, and that in some cases, some stereotypes have merely been replaced with others. But it seems slightly cruel to dismiss an entire film because of these assumptions; some can and some won't, and those who can make it past the lazy and treacherous Mexicans and the Borscht Belt (and treacherous) Native Americans and the nymphomaniacal females will find some spots of amusement, especially in the dialogue, which is pregnant with innuendo and double entendre: Don Jose wistfully recalls his "mother's pucker," and the unctuous Englishman Moodie tells the owner of a rough-and-tumble saloon, "You certainly keep a gay bar!" Sometimes it's even mildly insightful, as when Delphine observes: "If all soldiers had to fight in their underwear, there wouldn't be any wars."

Although the credits say "Introducing Caroline Munro," it obviously wasn't her first film, but it was her first substantial part, and she does not disappoint, in the role of the boy-crazy daughter which doesn't require much else than looking beautiful and, well, boy-crazy. Topol, however stereotypical his role, is hilarious, glazed ham all the way, and Richard Widmark, in a comedic variation of his roles in films like *Cheyenne Autumn*, generates a smile or two. It's kind of hard to figure how the Fab Four would have fit into this folderol, although one can easily see Ringo ending up with Caroline; and while perhaps not the normal Caroline fan's typical bill of fare, still good for having a laugh. And on a personal level, Caroline got a little more out of the film than a paycheck and a featured role; while on the set, she met Judd Hamilton, whom she would marry in 1974.

Where's Jack?—1969, Oakhurst Productions/Paramount Pictures (PP)

Crew: Producers: Stanley Baker, James Clavell; Executive Producer: Michael Deeley; Associate Producer: Robert Porter; Director: James Clavell; Screenplay: David Newhouse,

Films and Television: *Where's Jack?* (1969)

Rafe Newhouse; Music-Conductor: Elmer Bernstein; Photography: John Wilcox; Film Editor: Peter Thornton; Casting: Lesley Pettit; Production Design: Cedric Dawe; Costume Design: Cynthia Tingey; Makeup: Jill Carpenter, Wally Schneiderman; Assistant Makeup Artist: Sean Berry-Weske; Hair Stylist: Gordon Bond; Production Supervisor: Ron Carr; Assistant Director: Patrick Clayton; Construction Manager: John Paterson; Property Master: Mickey O'Toole; Chargehand Prop: Tommy Ibbetson; Sound Mixer: Laurie Clarkson; Assistant Sound Editor: Alan Jones; Dubbing Editor: Dino Di Campo; Dialogue Editor: John Ireland; Stunt Arranger: Terry Plummer; Camera Operators: Ernie Day, John Stannier; Chief Electrician: Bernie Prentiss; Best Boy: Roy Rodhouse; Wardrobe Master: Jimmy Smith; Assistant Editor: Richard Hiscott; Choreographer: Malcolm Goddard; Puppeteers: Paul Page, Peta Page; Continuity: June Randall; Production Secretary: Rosemary Wright; Historical Consultant: Alan Dent; Special Consultant: Maurice Zuberano.

Cast: Tommy Steele (Jack Sheppard), Stanley Baker (Jonathan Wild), Alan Badel (The Lord Chancellor), Dudley Foster (Blueskin), Fiona Lewis (Edgeworth Bess), Sue Lloyd (Lady Darlington), Noel Purcell (Leatherchest), Eddie Byrne (Reverend Wagstaff), Ivan Dixon (Naval Officer), Michael Douglas, Danny Holland, Terence Plummer (Constables), Michael Elphick (Hogarth), Roy Evans (Mr. Hind), Howard Gorney (Surgeon), John Hallam (The Captain), Dafydd Havard (Clerk), Fred Johnson (Merchant), Howard Kasket (The King), John Kelly (Proprietor), Esmond Knight (Ballad Singer), Leon Lissek (Deeley), Yole Marinelli (Lady Clarissa), William Marlowe (Tom Sheppard), Skip Martin (Dwarf), John Morley (Judge), Caroline Munro (Madame Vendonne), Cardew Robinson (Lord Mayor), Liam Sweeney (Austin), George Woodbridge (Hangman), Jack Woolgar (Mr. Woods), Bernadette Brady (Ballad Singer's Guide), Rock Brynner (Drunkard), Carla Challoner (Emma), Loretta Clarke (Lady Mayoress), Danny Cummins (Barker), Vernon Hayden (Deputy Marshal), Carolyn Montague (Mistress Barrow), Clare Mullin (Dwarf's Girlfriend), Cecil Nash (Storyteller), Rona Newton-John (Countess Bethune), Rascal Perry (Guard), Norman Smythe (Bosun), Mary Willoughby (Pole Maggott).

SYNOPSIS

From original pressbook:

In 18th Century London, two brothers named Sheppard drift into the seamy, steaming criminal world. One is Tom, the other John (Jack) Sheppard.

Tom (William Marlowe), a fugitive from infamous underworld despot and "Thief Taker" Jonathan Wild (Stanley Baker), flees in manacles and broken chains to Jack's attic room in search of a hiding place. Moments later, Wild and his terrifying henchmen burst in and capture him.

Jack (Tommy Steele), a locksmith's apprentice, realizes that Wild will hang his brother, but there is nothing he can do to help. However, Wild tells Jack he will spare Tom's life — if Jack, with his expert knowledge of locks, will become a burglar and turn his loot over to Wild.

At a Thames waterfront meeting, confederates named Blueskin (Dudley Foster) and Leatherchest (Noel Purcell) are given orders to enter the home of the Count de la Ruisee and steal a jeweled tiara. The precious bauble is stolen so daringly that it is literally snatched by Jack from the bedside of the count, who is sleeping with his mistress.

Jack soon finds a devilishly pretty barmaid, "Edgeworth Bess" (Fiona Lewis), promising him all manner of physical delights. His happiness is short-lived, however, when he learns that brother Tom, rather than being freed by Wild, is to be transported to America as a prisoner. Jack swears to avenge the appalling betrayal and to make Wild suffer for his perfidy.

Jack finds Bess in his attic room and learns that she has the tiara he had stolen from the count. She thinks Jack has given it to her as a present, whereas Wild has deliberately "planted" it to incriminate Jack. Moments later, Wild's men rush in and Jack is hustled off to St. Giles Roundhouse Prison. But Jack can't be contained in the Roundhouse and soon makes his escape. From this point on, Jack can only live by his wits and he turns to highway robbery and audacious burglaries, aided by Blueskin and Leatherchest.

When next Jack shows up at Bess's place, he finds a jealous sweetheart accusing him of "enjoying" his work too much, especially when his "victims" have been pretty women. After Jack leaves, Bess is seized and taken before Wild, who tells her he will use her as bait to attract Jack to his warehouse. Jack upsets that plan with consummate skill by suddenly—and astonishingly—showing up at the warehouse. Through a very brash ploy, Jack forces Wild to release Bess. But he is clamped in irons and hustled off to Newgate Prison, where he is lodged in the supposedly escape-proof Castle Room.

Lady Darlington, who has been robbed by Jack but found the experience to her fancy, passes the prison on several occasions. Finally, she decides on an exquisite way of testing young Jack's mettle. She decides to send him an invitation to dinner. Chided by Wild as he apparently languishes in chains in Newgate, Jack resolves to break out.

He then makes one of the most daring escapes of all time; a feat celebrated in song and story for many years, and becomes the most talked-about man in London. Even King George I finds himself interested and eventually His Majesty bets 1,000 golden guineas that Jack Sheppard could burst into the Lord Chancellor's residence and steal his chain of office. The Lord Chancellor (Alan Badel) takes the bet.

Not long after, Macclesfield Hall, the Lord Chancellor's residence, appears to be on fire. Believing his home to be afire, the Lord Chancellor hands a footman a box containing his chain of office, bidding him to see to its safety. The "footman" is Jack Sheppard.

But Jack soon learns that Jonathan Wild has snared Blueskin and Leatherchest, and is about to hang them. Rather than see his friends die so swiftly and ignominiously, Jack returns the stolen chain of office to the Lord Chancellor and gives himself up to Wild, while his friends are given a chance to ride for their lives.

Wild informs the Lord Chancellor that he will have to hang Jack for theft and a short time later Jack Sheppard is sentenced to be hanged. He will swing from the gallows at Tyburn (London's Marble Arch today). Bess tearfully says goodbye and Jack is hustled off to his rendezvous with the hangman, an event that attracts thousands and is set aside in London as a holiday for the wretched poor. So ends the career of Jack Sheppard. Or does it?

REVIEW AND NOTES

Actually, it does. Although the ending of the film suggests that Sheppard escaped the noose and headed for the States, the reality was that Jack was hanged until he was really most sincerely dead. Tommy Steele plays Jack, which is appropriate; Steele was Britain's first real "teen idol," the UK's answer to Elvis Presley, and Jack Sheppard was the 18th century's Tommy Steele, not just a "teen idol," but a genuine folk hero. Naturally, the film plays a bit fast and loose with the facts; "Edgeworth Bess" (real name: Elizabeth Lyon) was a bit more than a "devilishly pretty barmaid," she was a prostitute, and saucy Jack didn't take to crime out of a sense of brotherly love: The first time he was arrested, it was as a result of a caper gone wrong with Tom and Bess. And then when Tom was arrested again a few months later, he gave up Jack to the authorities in order to save his own skin.

Caroline has a bit part as one of Jack's victims, Madame Vendonne, and had this to say about the experience in an interview in *Filmfax* #83:

> What I recall was going for the interview. The interview was with the late, great Stanley Baker and Tommy Steele. I ended up at the interview crying. I think they felt sorry for this sad little thing and I ended up getting the part. The part was totally incongruous, with me being a crying wimp at the interview. Stanley Baker was there, maybe that was it ... I think I was quite filled with awe and a bit of terror, because he was quite foreboding, actually. That was one of my first forays into film, and we shot the film in Ireland, in a wonderful, baroque stately home. It was fantastic.

Her role is very brief, and she literally sleeps through it: Jack creeps into the room where she lays in bed slumbering, smiling, alongside her heavily snoring husband. Jack smiles as he makes off with the family jewels.

The Abominable Dr. Phibes—1971, American International Pictures

Crew: Executive Producers: James H. Nicholson, Samuel Z. Arkoff; Producers: Ronald Dunas, Louis M. Heyward; Director: Robert Fuest; Story and Screenplay: James Whiton, William Goldstein; Music: Basil Kirchin; Photography: Norman Warwick; Film Editor: Tristam Cones; Casting: Sally Nicholl; Art Director: Bernard Reeves; Makeup: Trevor Crole-Rees; Hair Stylist: Bernadette Ibbetson; Production Manager: Richard F. Dalton; Assistant Director: Frank Ernst; Assistant Art Director: Chris Burke; Set Designer: Brian Eatwell; Construction Manager: George Gunning; Property Master: Rex Hobbs; Painter: Michael Finlay; Recording Director: A.W. Lumkin; Dubbing Editor: Peter Lennard; Sound Recordist: Dennis Whitlock; Sound Assistant: Ken Nightingall; Special Effects: George Blackwell; Camera Operator: Godfrey A. Godar; Assistant Camera: Steve Clayton; Still Photographer: John Jay; Supervisory Electrician: Steve Birtles; Wardrobe: Elsa Fennel; Music Associate: Jack Nathan; Continuity: Gladys Goldsmith.

Cast: Vincent Price (Dr. Anton Phibes), Joseph Cotten (Dr. Vesalius), Hugh Griffith (Rabbi), Terry-Thomas (Dr. Longstreet), Virginia North (Vulnavia), Peter Jeffrey (Inspector Trout), Derek Godfrey (Crow), Norman Jones (Sgt. Tom Schenley), John Cater (Superintendent Waverly), Aubrey Woods (Goldsmith), John Laurie (Darrow), Maurice Kaufmann (Dr. Whitcombe), Barbara Keogh (Mrs. Frawley), Sean Bury (Lem Vesalius), Susan Travers (Nurse Allen), David Hutchison (Dr. Hedgepath), Edward Burnham (Dr. Dunwoody), Alex Scott (Dr. Hargreaves), Peter Gilmore (Dr. Kitaj), Alan Zipson (First Police Official), Dallas Adams (Second Police Official), James Grout (Sergeant), Alister Williamson, Thomas Heathcote, Ian Marter, Julian Grant (Policemen), Charles Farrell (Chauffeur), John Franklyn (Graveyard Attendant), Walter Horsbrugh (Butler-Ross), Paul Frees (Singer of "The Darktown Strutters' Ball"), Caroline Munro (Victoria Regina Phibes).

FILMS AND TELEVISION: *The Abominable Dr. Phibes* (1971)

SYNOPSIS

An eminently respectable surgeon is found shredded to death by bats. One of Scotland Yard's investigating officers remarks that it reminds him of a death the week before: Another surgeon had been stung to death by bees, leaving his body nothing but a mass of boils. Detective Inspector Trout (Peter Jeffrey) thinks there is a connection, but his superiors don't. A mysterious hooded figure burns a wax effigy of the just-murdered doctor's face, along with an amulet bearing a strange symbol.

The hooded figure puts on facial makeup and turns up at a posh masked ball, where he gives an elaborate, bejeweled frog mask to another surgeon. The surgeon has to cancel all future appointments, as the mask becomes a death mask and crushes his skull!

As yet another surgeon, Dr. Longstreet (Terry-Thomas), begins to watch a reel of an exotic snake dancer, he is interrupted by a beautiful silent woman and the mysterious stranger. After the woman ties him to a chair, the stranger drains every drop of Longstreet's blood!

Trout visits a surgeon, Dr. Vesalius (Joseph Cotten), whom all of the dead doctors had been associated with. He also discovers the meaning of the symbol on an amulet that the stranger has inadvertently left behind, and goes to a rabbi for an explanation. The rabbi tells Trout that the symbols stand for each of the plagues of the Curse of the Pharaohs in the time of Exodus: Boils, Bats, Frogs, Blood, Hail, Rats, Beasts, Locusts, The Death of the First-Born, and The Curse of Darkness.

Vesalius finds that the only case that they all had in common was that of Victoria Regina Phibes (Caroline Munro), a woman who died during emergency surgery. Her husband, Anton Phibes (Vincent Price), reportedly died in a car crash while rushing to her side. Someone has condemned the whole surgical team to death — but who?

After another one of the surgeons is pelted to death by hail, Vesalius discovers that his son's music teacher not only knew Phibes, but insists he still visits his shop. Vesalius and Trout's suspicions are confirmed when they invade Phibes' crypt: His coffin contains only unidentified ashes, while Mrs. Phibes' coffin is empty.

Despite the Yard's best efforts, Phibes stays one step ahead: Rats finish off the next surgeon, and the one after that is impaled by a brass unicorn head. The nurse at the operation winds up eaten by locusts! Vesalius' son is kidnapped — will he suffer the Death of the First-Born?

REVIEW AND NOTES

Any searching for an objective critique of this film should probably look elsewhere, as *The Abominable Dr. Phibes* maintains a secure position as one of the author's Top five Favorite Horror Films of All Time. Critics were none too kind upon its original release; *The New York Times* carped: "The plot, buried under all the iron tinsel, isn't bad. But the tone of steamroller camp flattens the fun"; *Variety* dismissed it too: "[A]nachronistic period horror musical camp fantasy is a fair description, loaded with comedic gore of the type that packs theaters and drives child psychologists up the wall."

"Love means never having to say you're ugly." A parody of the banal *Love Story* provided one of the most famous tag lines of all time on this one-sheet poster from the classic *The Abominable Dr. Phibes*.

But they accurately predicted the audience reception. According to the book *Vincent Price Unmasked*: "This neatly handled mock horror tale reveled in its art deco camp ambience, and proved to be a strong audience pleaser."

Although some critics have called it trite, unfunny or smug, the author vehemently disagrees, siding with those who revel in its black humor, wit, style, grand design and impeccable performances. And these are only some of the elements; there are so many fine aspects to the movie, it's difficult to know where to begin. Perhaps we should start, as the film does, with the music; the quite wonderful soundtrack is a mix of classical (Mendelssohn's "War March of the Priests"), the Great American Songbook ("One for My Baby"), and the original score contributed by eccentric British composer Basil Kirchin. Kirchin was a multi-talented musician and composer, and his experience stretched from playing drums with his father's jazz band (providing backing for greats such as Sarah Vaughan) to his experiments with the manipulation of sound and "organic" instruments like hand bells, glass harmonicas, and steel drums, leading some to cite him as "the Father of Ambient music," a style whose most popular public practitioner is the similarly multi-faceted Brian Eno. Eno, at the time a member of the legendary Roxy Music, would contribute the sleeve notes to Kirchin's 1971 Island Records release *Worlds Within Worlds*. Kirchin financed his experiments by writing soundtracks for movies like *Phibes*, and used some of those techniques in those soundtracks.

The grand sense of design, utilizing flourishes of both Art Deco and Art Nouveau, creates a surreal, dream-like atmosphere, which is enhanced by the combination of musical styles. The movie contains many wonderful visual gags, like the telephone in Dr. and Mrs. Phibes' burial chamber, or Phibes' assistant Vulnavia (a surrogate for Victoria) breaking the "fourth wall" and staring out at the audience. Rather than appearing patchwork, the various styles of art and music mesh to create a confluence that is actually more "authentic" and evocative of period than many other period pictures of the time. The quite wonderful ensemble cast plays their roles like Phibes plays his violin; perfectly pitched. Vincent Price is irreproachable in a role that was both a summing up of all that had gone before and a template for roles for years to come. His old Mercury Theater pal, the great Joseph Cotten, had, in association with old pal and Mercury Theater boss Orson Welles, appeared in some of the greatest films of all time: *Citizen Kane* (1941), *The Magnificent Ambersons* (1942), *Touch of Evil* (1958) and *The Third Man* (1949), as well as Hitchcock's classic *Shadow of a Doubt* (1943) as the unforgettable Uncle Charlie ("Do you know that the world is a foul sty?") He also had his fair share of other genre credits: *From the Earth to the Moon* (1958), *Hush ... Hush, Sweet Charlotte* (1964), *Latitude Zero* (1969), *Lady Frankenstein* (1971), *Baron Blood* (1972), *Soylent Green* (1973) and more. Peter Jeffrey ("And if you tell me they all died mysteriously, I'll bloody kill you") did both the original and *New Avengers*, *Doctor Who*, and essentially played Trout in all but name in Hammer's *Countess Dracula* (1971). Virginia North was a Bond Girl in *On Her Majesty's Secret Service* (1969); one of her few other roles was in the Bond-influenced updating of Bulldog Drummond, 1967's *Deadlier Than the Male*. Terry-

Thomas was in over 100 films in almost five decades; his genre appearances include *tom thumb* (1958), *Munster, Go Home!* (1966), *Danger: Diabolik* (1968), and *The Vault of Horror* (1973). Hugh Griffith had been in *Cry of the Banshee* (1970) with Price and would be reunited with Terry-Thomas in what was to be the next-to-last film of both of their careers, the Peter Cook-Dudley Moore version of *Hound of the Baskervilles* (1978). Derek Godfrey, the Crow to Jeffrey's Trout, went on to work for Hammer in *Hands of the Ripper* (1971). Norman Jones, who gives perhaps the most underrated comic performance of the film as Sgt. Schenley, worked with two Bonds, Sean Connery in *You Only Live Twice* (1967) and Roger Moore in *The Saint*. Susan Travers had starred in 1961's *The Snake Woman*, and the year before had a role in Michael Powell's groundbreaking *Peeping Tom*.

Caroline's role as Victoria Regina Phibes, who died young and left a beautiful corpse, required her to do nothing more than lay in state, which she joked about in an interview in *Filmfax #83*:

> That was really one of the most *taxing* parts I've *ever* done [laughs]. Seriously, we had a ball! Vincent Price was so wonderful to work with, and he made me *feel* so special! He was so gentle and so funny, and what a fantastic cook! He used to come into the makeup room. It was about seven o'clock in the morning, and he had made some homemade pâté, so the makeup girl, the hairdresser, Vincent and I stuffed ourselves with pâté. Then I sort of lay there in the coffin, trying not to burp.

She also had to contend with feathers on her stylish negligee that persisted in tickling her nose: "I'm allergic to feathers, and I was attired in this beautiful negligee—but it was covered by feathers! It took a great deal of willpower not to sneeze or sniffle. On occasion, I would simply have to sneeze, and this would result in having to do another take." But her presence hovers over the whole film, and if the movie itself revolves around Phibes, then his actions in the movie all revolve around her. Though he's a murderer, his devotion to Victoria is real and touching, and when he's not busy carrying out his revenge, he is paying homage to the image of Victoria (Caroline in various poses and outfits of authentic 1920s vintage) with unforgettable, eloquent soliloquies: "My love ... sweet queen and noble wife ... I alone remain; to bring delivery of your pain ... severed my darling, too quickly from this life of fires drawn and of memories met ... I shall hold our two hearts again, in single time." There's also his most impassioned, "Where can we find two better hemispheres, without sharp North, without declining West; my face in thine eye, thine in mine appears, and true plain hearts in these faces do rest.... Within 24 hours, my work will be finished, and then my precious jewel, I will join you in your setting ... we shall be reunited forever, in a secluded corner of the great Elysian field, of the beautiful beyond!" Interestingly, neither of the two principal female characters, Victoria and Vulnavia, are able to respond to Phibes when he addresses them; Victoria because she is dead, and Vulnavia because ... well, we've never told why. Perhaps Phibes believes that women, like children, should be seen and not heard; in any case, his connection with Vulnavia, unlike Victoria, is never explored or explained.

FILMS AND TELEVISION: *The Abominable Dr. Phibes* (1971)

The original script states that Vulnavia is not even human, that she is the most successful and lifelike result of Phibes' clockwork wizardry, and even in the finished film, this is certainly still a possibility (given Phibes' obvious success in preserving Victoria), as she returns in the next film intact after the acid shower, but no comment to this effect is made by Vesalius or Trout when they witness the results of the red rain. Victoria's role in Phibes' life is clear; Vulnavia is a riddle wrapped in an enigma.

In an informative article in *MonsterScene* #10 (Summer 1997), William R. Harrison compare the original William Goldstein–James Whiton script and the finished version. The black humor for which the movie is noted is not found in the original; and Phibes is called "Dr. Pibe" (which sort of sounds like a soft drink). Pibe still utilizes the curses of the G'Tach, but in a different order; the death of the first born, instead of being saved for the finale, originally takes place first, prior to the beginning of the movie, and Lem Vesalius dies in that version. Dr. Hargreaves still suffers the curse of frogs but the original has him frightened to death by a large number of frogs, instead of having his skull crushed by the frog mask. The original script also contains more details about Victoria's condition and operation; Vesalius remembers that the operation, unlike the almost in-passing mention of "immediate radical resection" in the final version, was "ten hours of dissection," and that she was suffering from metastic carcinoma of the uterus. For what was a sterilization procedure, Vesalius infers that had it been performed when first diagnosed, Victoria might have survived, but that "in cases like this, it is often difficult to persuade the husband," implicating him in Victoria's death. Vesalius also thinks that a man in Pibe's condition must require constant injections of cocaine and morphine — and there is a scene where a criminal type makes a drop at Pibe's house. Phibes (or Pibe) was a much darker character in the original script, and so they added the black humor and some sympathetic touches for the character, making his devotion to Victoria much more pure, and removing any possibility that he might have been responsible for her death. The name of Vesalius was a constant in both, and refers to Andreas Vesalius, often referred to as the father of modern human anatomy. While it is fairly certain that director Robert Fuest was responsible for the change of the overall tone of the film, but I don't know whether or not he did the actual script doctoring.

Any discussion of Phibes must include a word about its accompanying "soundtrack" album, a psychotronic gem for the ages. The word "soundtrack" is in quotes because in this case, the term is used very loosely. While the album advertises itself as containing "Music from the soundtrack of the American International picture," the actual music from the soundtrack is represented only by a few short pieces by Basil Kirchin. The remaining songs, like "One for My Baby," "Darktown Strutter's Ball," and "Over the Rainbow," *were* featured in the film, but not the versions on this record; here, they have been turned into bizarre set-pieces for the vocal skills of Paul Frees, Hollywood's Master of Voice who camps them up to the nth degree with impersonations of period celebrities. It's the concept itself which brings on the dropping of the jaw. "Darktown Strutter's Ball" was performed by Frees, channeling Al Jolson, in the film, but here it's a different take, and that's where any similarity to the actual soundtrack ends. Johnny Mercer's "One for My Baby," originally a hit for Frank Sinatra in 1947, was performed for the film by Scott Peters, basing his performance on Sinatra's. Here, in perhaps the nuttiest track on the album, Frees does it in the voice of Humphrey Bogart! Close behind is his rendition of "All I Do Is Dream of You" as done by Chico Marx. He does "Over the Rainbow" in the style of Ronald Colman. "What Can I Say After I Say I'm Sorry" is performed in the style of W.C. Fields, "Charmaine" as if by Dick Powell, etc.

The character and image of Dr. Phibes have been perpetuated by musical culture as much as they have been by film culture. Seminal horror-punk band The Misfits did a song called "Dr. Phibes Rises Again" that was released on their 2001 album *Cuts from the Crypt*. The Misfits' spiritual forbears, The Damned, reference the first film in the lyrics of "13th Floor Vendetta," from *The Black Album* (1980). And little did Keith Moon know, when The Who appeared with Caroline on *A Whole Scene Going* (see next section), that she would appear in the film, or that it would be the last one he would start to watch the night he died.

Dracula A.D. 1972—1972, Hammer Films

Crew: Producer: Josephine Douglas; Director: Alan Gibson; Screenplay: Don Houghton; Photography: Dick Bush; Camera Operator: Bernie Ford; Art Director: Don Mingaye; Assistant Art Director: Bill Benton; Film Editor: James Needs; Continuity: Doreen Dearnaley; Sound Editor: Roy Baker; Recording Director: A.W. Lumkin; Dubbing Mixer: Bill Rowe; Sound Recordist: Claude Hitchcock; Casting: James Liggat; Music: Mike Vickers; Music Supervisor: Philip Martell; Songs: "Alligator Man" by Sal Valentino, "You Better Come Through" by Tim Barnes; Production Supervisor: Roy Skeggs; Production Manager: Ron Jackson; Special Effects: Les Bowie; Makeup: Jill Carpenter; Hair Stylist: Barbara Ritchie; Wardrobe Supervisor: Rosemary Burrows; Assistant Director: Robert Lynn; Construction Manager: Bill Greene.

Cast: Christopher Lee (Dracula), Peter Cushing (Prof. Van Helsing), Stephanie Beacham (Jessica Van Helsing), Michael Coles (Inspector Murray), Christopher Neame (Johnny Alucard), William Ellis (Joe Mitchum), Marsha Hunt (Gaynor), Janet Key (Anna), Philip Miller (Bob), Michael Kitchen (Greg), David Andrews (Detective Sergeant Pearson), Caroline Munro (Laura Bellows), Lally Bowers (Matron); Tim Barnes, Sal Valentino, Annie Sampson, John Blakely, Brian Godula, Lynn Hughes, Deirdre La Porte, Cory Lerios, Lydia Mareno, Steve Price (Stoneground), Jane Anthony ("Debby" Girl), Flanagan (Go-Go Girl), John Franklin-Robbins (Minister), Constance Luttrell (Mrs. Donnelly), Michael Daly (Charles), Arturo Morris (Police Sergeant), Jo Richardson (Crying Matron), Penny Brahms (Hippie Chick), Brian John Smith (Hippie Dude).

SYNOPSIS

From original pressbook:

London today. A group of young people are attending a party in Chelsea enlivened only by the Stoneground group. Jessica Van Helsing (Stephanie Beacham), who lives with her

FILMS AND TELEVISION: *Dracula A.D. 1972* (1972)

Christopher Lee, who made a career out of portraying Dracula on the screen, is surrounded by his victims in *Dracula A.D. 1972*: Stephanie Beacham, upper left, and clockwise, Marsha Hunt, Janet Key and Caroline Munro.

grandfather, Professor Van Helsing (Peter Cushing), is there with a number of friends. Among them: Bob (Phillip Miller), Joe (William Ellis), Gaynor (Marsha Hunt), Greg (Michael Kitchen), Laura (Caroline Munro), Anna (Janet Key), and Johnny Alucard (Christopher Neame), a direct descendant of Dracula's disciple.

Johnny's suggestion that they liven things up by keeping a "date with the Devil" at a desanctified church, takes them to St. Bartolph's where he ceremoniously calls up all evil spirits.

The group leaves in fright before Dracula (Christopher Lee) is brought back by the ancient rites, and claims Laura as the first victim of his new reign. Jessica first learns of her death when Police Inspector Murray (Michael Coles) and Sergeant Peterson (David Andrews) visit her home. Professor Van Helsing conveys his first suspicions of vampirism to the startled, pragmatic investigators.

When Gaynor becomes Dracula's second victim, the details of her death confirm Van Helsing's suspicions. He links the name of Alucard with Dracula, and tells the police that the key to the murders lies in him. Jessica is Dracula's main target, and she is eventually trapped when Bob, now a vampire, lures her to a rendezvous where Johnny is waiting to take her to the master.

Van Helsing goes to her rescue, first tracking down Johnny to his flat where a violent fight between the two results in young Alucard's death when he falls backwards into the bath, a vampire killed by water.

On his way to St. Bartolph's Church, where Jessica is trapped by Dracula, Van Helsing finds the dead body of Bob spread-eagled on a tomb. A newly initiated vampire, he had been unable to return to a grave before the sun rose.

Van Helsing rescues Jessica from Dracula's clutches, and kills the monster when he flings a phial of Holy Water in his face. Triumphant in this last battle between the forces of good and evil, he covers the ground over the decaying, shriveled remains, putting to rest the corrupt powers of Dracula.

REVIEW AND NOTES

Castle of Frankenstein No. 19 reviewed the movie, opining,

Though excitement and suspense aren't spared, some fans of the genre may have trouble from flinching at a number of enormous liberties taken to provide this latest vehicle for Count Dracula. Christopher Lee is in usual great form but, again, he becomes more of a cameo than prevalent character, as in other recent Hammer versions, and a growing source of irritation to the many who would like seeing more of this fine artist. Alan Gibson's direction is smooth and vivid enough to make one almost prone to forgive various liberties. Undoubtedly slick, good entertainment all the way through — but impaired by lack of those sensitive touches employed by the late Seth Holt in creating *Blood from the Mummy's Tomb*, which retained a powerful and classic period flavor though in modern setting. Les Bowie's special effects are good, and Stephanie Beacham in the femme lead has already won fame for beauty and her role opposite Marlon Brando in *The Nightcomers*."

"I put a spell on you," Christopher Neame seems to be saying to Caroline in this publicity photo from *Dracula A.D. 1972*.

According to *Variety*'s Whit:

> Count Dracula reappears in this suspenseful folo-up [*sic*] to the series launched many years ago by Bela Lugosi. [F]ilm carries the type of chill ingredients any spectator associates with the living dead and should fare well in its intended market. Gibson's direction is particularly effective in maintaining mood and spirit and editing by James Needs is a strong contributing factor. Mike Vickers' music score also is a definite plus, as is Dick Bush's facile color photography, and production design by Don Mingaye is particularly atmospheric.

Los Angeles Times' Kevin Thomas wrote: "*Dracula A.D. 1972* and *Crescendo*, both directed by Alan Gibson, make a satisfactory horror double feature. Both are somewhat of a departure from Hammer's period gore formula. The first is a witty, successful attempt to bring the old Transylvanian vampire into present-day London. It's a very tricky business to let Dracula go through his flamboyant paces in a modern setting but Gibson, his clever writers and capable cast make it work."

According to *San Diego Evening Tribune*'s Dave McIntyre,

> *Dracula A.D. 1972* returns Christopher Lee to the screen in a role which he has now done many more times than did Bela Lugosi, the granddaddy of all vampires. Lee is very competent in the role; as well he should be considering the practice he has had. And he gets the advantage of good physical production put on by the people at Hammer Studios in England. There's never anything shoddy about their shows, even if they are going over material with slight variations that has been used endlessly. Hammer likes its heroines to be bosomy and all the costumes for Dracula girls are low cut. Miss Beacham fits hers snugly.

Hammer films from 1970 on are an odd, often maligned lot. The chief reason for this was that, at this point, Hammer films were being formed by the times instead of the other way around. Their stylish, blood 'n' bosoms approach to horror had become the gold standard, and imitators of that style ranged far and wide. And by the late sixties and early seventies, other companies took that envelope and pushed it even farther; blood got bloodier, sex became sexier, and all of a sudden, Hammer Films, which had been so groundbreaking, now seemed rather quaint. Instead of initiating trends, Hammer now followed them, with decidedly mixed results — sometimes within the space of a single movie. *Dracula A.D. 1972* is one of those movies.

Hammer's business partner Warner Brothers had seen the success of the *Count Yorga* films featuring Robert Quarry as a vampire operating in the present day, and "suggested" that Hammer juxtapose its most famous monster not with angry villagers with stakes and torches and jigs and reels, but thrill-seeking, dope-smoking hippies grooving to rock music. The film was also inspired by the much-publicized "Highgate Vampire" case, in which a vampire supposedly haunted the Highgate Cemetery.

Oddly enough, the original reviewers were kinder to the film than the original fans. For many years, it seems the film was thought of in the same terms as *Abbott and Costello Meet Frankenstein*: the ignominious near-end to a once-glorious series, the monsters pulled out of their original gothic element to cavort with numbskulls of one kind or another. But in more recent years, the critical pendulum has swung, and now *Abbott and Costello Meet Frankenstein* is rightly considered the premier horror comedy of all time, and *Dracula A.D. 1972* is considered ... well, still not really a premiere film, but it has seen its stature grow. The main reason is the very bizarre combination of the gothic and the topical; or rather a much older person's idea of what was "topical" or "hip," resulting in some gloriously camp scenes. It's the type of camp that acquires the appellation due to changing societal values, not the studied camp of *Dr. Phibes*, although, to be fair, the hippie lingo and the producers' idea of what constituted "rock" music were pretty ridiculous even at the time. (As Caroline recalled in an interview in *Little Shoppe of Horrors* No. 22, "I think they were a little bit out of touch. Some of the dialogue left a bit to be desired, didn't it?"). But what was once viewed with scorn can now be viewed as a compelling period snapshot; not as an accurate snapshot of the period so much as a very telling snapshot of how the creators of the film viewed that period.

Dracula A.D. 1972 is at least as interesting and compelling as, really, any of the sequels to *Horror of Dracula*, and one of the main reasons for this can be explained in two words: Peter Cushing. *The Brides of Dracula* is a classic, stylish movie, and it features Cushing in a smashing performance, but it really does miss Christopher Lee. And so do the next two, in a sense; *Dracula, Prince of Darkness* and *Dracula Has Risen from the Grave* do feature Lee, but in so few scenes that he might as well have been on holiday. This was rectified in *Scars of Dracula* and *Taste the Blood of Dracula*, but there are very few high points in either. So after squaring off against guntotin' monks, atheists, and upper-class hypocrites, Lee's Dracula was finally reunited with the only actor and character that could truly give him a run for his blood money. Still, Lee was typically dismissive of the film when doing a question-and-answer session at the First Fantasy Filmcon in Los Angeles, in 1972: When asked by a fan if he was

Caroline was the first of several victims in *Dracula A.D. 1972*.

pleased with *Dracula A.D. 1972*: "I've not seen it, so I don't know. But I have very grave doubts about the mixing of the styles, and great reservations."

As previously stated, Warners took notice of the success of *Count Yorga* and "suggested" to Michel Carreras that Hammer bring Dracula "up to date," so Carreras contracted Don Houghton to try the new approach. Houghton submitted an outline known alternately as "Dracula in Chelsea" and "Dracula — Chelsea 1971." Production began under the working title of *Dracula Today*, from Houghton's first-draft screenplay, which he had no time to polish or rewrite because Warners wanted to rush the film into production. It was subsequently announced as *Dracula Is Dead and Well and Living in London*, and gained some notoriety because of that title, but it was ultimately released under the title we all know. While it was still being touted under the title *Dracula Is Dead and Well and Living in London*, Lee complained very aggressively to Don Glut about it in a 1972 interview: "I just think it's fatuous. I can think of twenty adjectives — fatuous, pointless, and absurd. It's not a comedy; at least with me it's not a comedy. But it's a comic title. People who go to see a character like this go to see him seriously. They don't laugh at him. That I know. They may laugh at some of the things in the pictures, but they'll never laugh at me, to my knowledge." Actually, they would, when he unveiled his Bela Lugosi impersonation in *The Satanic Rites of Dracula*.

The only thing wrong with Caroline's role as Dracula's first victim is just that — she's his first victim. But although her screen time is short, all eyes were glued to her when she was on screen. Whether fetchingly attired in thigh-high boots or low-cut black gowns, she makes an incredibly sultry victim, and all the more memorable because, unlike most of the count's willing victims, Caroline screams all the way to the "climax" of the scene. Lamb's Navy Rum was responsible for her getting the part: Hammer's Sir James Carreras spotted her in one of their ads on a billboard. She first did a reading, then a screen test, and was then signed to a one-year contract; this was her first assignment. In *Little Shoppe of Horrors* she recalled: "I had done a few films before that, but that was my turning point, when I worked with Christopher Lee, and when I worked with all those young, up-and-coming actors. Suddenly I thought, this is what I want to do, I absolutely know." But life with Drac was not all a bed of blood and roses, as she discovered in her burial scene, where she is covered in rubble: "On the set, it started to rain. The crew all went off on a tea break, but since they'd spent so much effort on my makeup for the scene, and the set-up and so forth, they just stuck a paper bag over my head, left me in the rubble and said ta-ta!" But that wasn't the end of it, as she said in a 2004 interview:

> They had a special kind of blood then, in the '70's, and they called it "Kensington Gore," and it was very dense and very thick and very ... bloody, really, for want of a better word, and so we did the scene ... and I had to cook dinner for people that night, so I had a shower at Pinewood, and it didn't seem to come off and then I had another shower ... and it still didn't come off, and I thought, oh gosh, what am I going to do, I'm going to have to jump in the car and go as I am.... Now I was late ... and sped down the motorway too fast, and then there was a siren ... and it was the police ... and he pulled me over and he looked

at me, 'cause I'd been crying ... and I was covered in blood ... and he actually did let me off.

Stephanie Beacham, as quoted in *Little Shoppe of Horrors*, had glowing words for her co-star: "I thought Caroline was one of the sweetest girls ever. I couldn't believe that anybody so pretty — so beautiful, for Heaven's sake — could possibly be so nice, but she was.... Far too lovely hair; it was just immaculate all the time, and she used to look disgustingly good at six o'clock in the morning!"

Caroline Munro's outfit may have been the best thing about *Dracula A.D. 1972.*

As for the rest of the groovers, Christopher Neame (*Lust for a Vampire, License to Kill*) is suitably and genuinely creepy in the "Ralph Bates–type" role of Johnny Alucard. The name was one of Hammer's nods to the Universal Dracula series: Lon Chaney, Jr., was Count Alucard in 1943's *Son of Dracula*. The still-active Michael Kitchen has had a long and fruitful career, including starring in the BBC's *The Comedy of Errors* with Roger Daltrey and Ingrid Pitt, and, like Caroline, doing time in two Bond movies, the dreary *GoldenEye* and the drearier *The World Is Not Enough*. Marsha Hunt was born in Philadelphia and moved to London; she appeared in *Hair*, had musical stints with the Alexis Korner trio, Ferris Wheel, and played at the 1969 Isle of Wight Festival with her backing band, White Trash (not to be confused with Edgar Winter's White Trash). She gave birth to Mick Jagger's first daughter, Karis, and was the inspiration for the Stones' hit "Brown Sugar." Caroline remembers, "Marsha Hunt had just had a baby with Mick Jagger, and I used to pick her up in my little car and take her to the set. It was a long, cold journey up to Elstree." Hunt, always an activist, is also now an author many times over.

Dr. Phibes Rises Again—1972, American International Pictures

Crew: Executive Producers: James H. Nicholson, Samuel Z. Arkoff; Producer: Louis M. Heyward; Director: Robert Fuest; Story and Screenplay: Robert Fuest, Robert Blees; Characters: James Whiton, William Goldstein; Music Composer–Conductor: John Gale; Photography: Alex Thomson; Film Editor: Tristam Cones; Casting: Sally Nicholl; Art Director: Bernard Reeves; Makeup: Trevor Crole-Rees; Hair Stylist: Bernadette Ibbetson; Production Manager: Richard F. Dalton; Assistant Director: Jake Wright; Second Assistant Director: Terry Hodgkinson; Assistant Art Director: Peter Withers; Set Designer: Brian Eatwell; Construction Manager: Harry Phipps; Property Master: Rex Hobbs; Painter: Michael Finlay; Recording Director: A.W. Lumkin; Dubbing Editor: Peter Lennard; Sound Recordists: Dennis Whitlock, Leslie Hammond; Sound Assistant: Fred Tomlin; Sound Effects Editor: William Butler; Camera Operator: Colin Corby; Assistant Camera: John Golding; Supervisory Electrician: Roy Bond; Costume Supervisor: Ivy Baker Jones; Costumes for Vulnavia: Brian Cox; Choral Music: The Bach Singers; Continuity: Jane Buck; Production Executive: David Sheldon.

Cast: Vincent Price (Dr. Anton Phibes), Robert Quarry (Biederbeck), Valli Kemp (Vulnavia), Peter Jeffrey (Inspector Trout), Fiona Lewis (Diana Trowbridge), Hugh Griffith (Harry Ambrose), Peter Cushing (Captain), Beryl Reed (Miss Ambrose), Terry-Thomas (Lombardo), John Cater (Superintendent Waverly), Gerald Sim (Hackett), Lewis Fiander (Baker), John Thaw (Shavers), Keith Buckley (Stewart), Milton Reid (Cheng), Gary Owens (Narrator), Caroline Munro (Victoria Regina Phibes).

SYNOPSIS

From original pressbook:

Dr. Phibes (Vincent Price), the bizarre evil genius with a diabolical ingenuity in dispensing death and destruction, has risen from his ten-year hibernation to embark on his latest fantastic adventure. He has vowed to restore life to his wife Victoria (Caroline Munro), who died many years before of injuries following an automobile crash.

He knows this can only be achieved through a secret elixir hidden deep in an underground chamber deep below a mountain in the Egyptian desert. He also knows that another scientific genius, Biederbeck (Robert Quarry), plans, for a different reason, an expedition in search of the same wonder-drug.

Both are accompanied by beautiful women: Phibes by his ethereal, non-speaking assistant, Vulnavia (Valli Kemp), Biederbeck by his exotic mistress, Diana (Fiona Lewis). For the two men, superbly matched in brains, knowledge, cunning and villainy, the race for the reincarnating drug becomes a matter of life and death....

Using all his powers of invention and imaginative genius, Phibes sets about destroying the members of Biederbeck's expedition who threaten the success of his mission.

One man, a mighty oriental hunk called Cheng (Milton Reid), who is Biederbeck's bodyguard, is dispatched to his ancestors by means of a diabolical Phibesian gadget. Another, Biederbeck's assistant Ambrose (Hugh Griffith), is sealed inside a gigantic gin bottle and thrown overboard from the luxury liner taking Phibes and Biederbeck to Egypt.

When Ambrose, in his strange container, is washed up on the shores of England, Inspector Trout (Peter Jeffrey) and Superintendant Waverly (John Cater) of Scotland Yard recognize the evil genius of Dr. Phibes. Though they cannot believe he could still be "alive," the bumbling detectives immediately journey to Egypt to begin their search, once again, for Dr. Phibes.

In the desert, Phibes continues his piecemeal decimation of Biederbeck's expedition as one member is stung to death by scorpions; another is clawed raw by an eagle and a third has his flesh ground from his bones by a sand-blasting contraption.

In an ancient sarcophagus Phibes discovers the secret hiding place of a key which opens the gates to his final destination, the secret chamber containing the elixir of life. But Biederbeck, too, discovers the key and the two are now face to face in a struggle for the prize. Phibes captures Diana and, as she is strapped under a ceiling laden with menacing spikes, it begins a descent toward her vulnerable body. Biederbeck surrenders the key to Phibes to save her life.

The artful villain [Phibes] now paddles through the gates of an underground tunnel toward his destination on a raft bearing his dead wife in her elaborate coffin which is the hood of a Rolls-Royce. Screaming in frustration, Biederbeck is behind and, cut off from his goal, his face suddenly ages, revealing he had retained his youth by artificial means and sought the elixir of life to complete his reincarnation.

REVIEW AND NOTES

The British *Monthly Film Bulletin* opined: "It's refreshing to find a sequel that's better than its prototype." A reviewer for *Castle of Frankenstein* No. 19) called it "excellent," adding: "Brisk, imaginative direction by Robert Fuest amid even more splendiferous art deco sets this time." According to the book *Vincent Price Unmasked*: "The art-deco trappings, the nostalgic jazzy music (from the Phibes Clockwork Band), the witty touches in disposing of Price's victims, provided continued zest for the deliberately awful script."

The script's not awful, not by a long shot, but it was certainly a missed opportunity. It was rushed into production and hastily completed to cash in on the success of the brilliant first film, which it didn't, despite the good reviews. Had a bit more care gone into the making, it could have been what its glowing reviews described.

This sequel's pressbook also seems to have been put together in haste. They seem to have forgotten the reason for the first film entirely, stating that Victoria Regina Phibes died of "injuries following an automobile crash." It also refers to Trout and Waverly as the "bumbling detectives," and in the film, they certainly are, but in the first they weren't. They were used for comedic effect, especially Waverly, but the comedy came from their very dedication to their work and hidebound ideas and methods, rather than simply being morons; they weren't necessarily stupid, they were just out-maneuvered at every turn by Phibes. An amusing aspect of the synopsis is when they refer to Milton Reid's character as a "mighty oriental hunk," and I do believe this was supposed to be "hulk," as Reid was the British Tor Johnson, and would qualify on few lists as a "hunk." But the most priceless moment comes from the suggestions for ballyhoo and exploitation. Besides the usual "scary" lobby displays and questionable ideas (one is to stage a "loudest scream" contest and rig a p.a. system to broadcast screams throughout the city), there's a suggestion to stage a "Women's Lib Controversy Stunt":

> The character of Vulnavia, played by Australian beauty Valli Kemp, is an ideal example of female servitude as she plays background music to Dr. Phibes' nasty machinations; pops grapes in his mouth and provides gorgeous feminine comfort in complete silence to the master criminal. Have pretty girls picket your theater with signs stating Dr. Phibes Is A Chauvanist Male Monster ... Free Vulnavia... See A Woman Enslaved In Dr. Phibes Rises Again."

It is certainly not a rule of thumb that a horror movie has to make sense, at least in the context of the "real" world, but it does have to make sense in the context of the world that it's created for itself, and *Dr. Phibes Rises Again* doesn't. Like *The Mummy's Tomb* (1942), which was filmed two years after *The Mummy's Hand* (1940) but takes place "25 years later," this sequel was released the next year, but takes place "three years later." The film opens with about five minutes of clips from the previous film (always a bad sign), but somewhat compensated for by having the prologue narrated by "Space Ghost" himself, Gary Owens. It corrects the pressbook mistake and correctly states that Victoria died on the operating table, but it makes her resurrection seem like something that Phibes had been planning even before her death. No mention is made of Vesalius; Phibes' adversary this time is Biederbeck, who covets the same "Elixir of Life" that Dr. Phibes covets for Victoria. Why Biederbeck wants it is made clear by the climax (he will quickly age and die if he doesn't), but what isn't made clear is how or why he got that way in the first place. The character of Biederbeck is a strange part; he's not exactly a hero, and he's not the main villain, but he's such a bastard that it seems as if he's only there to give the audience someone to hate and to make Phibes seem more sympathetic, which he really isn't. It's also never stated exactly what Biederbeck is or does. He's acclaimed as "one of the most brilliant minds in the western hemisphere," but the movie gives no reason as to why. He obtains Phibes' papyrus from a dealer who got it when

Films and Television: *Dr. Phibes Rises Again* (1972)

A rarely seen ad art poster for *Dr. Phibes Rises Again*.

they "demolished the old house in Maldine Square," and Phibes discovers this when he awakes, which shocks and stuns him — but if he has planned for this many years, surely he would have made provisions for the upkeep of the house in anticipation of this day.

It is Phibes' "nasty machinations" which are both the selling and weak points of the movie. They are certainly inventive, and make for some visually arresting and bizarre set-pieces, but this time around there's no rhyme or reason to them. In *Dr. Phibes*, he had employed his knowledge of the G'Tach to devise an elaborate scheme of revenge on the surgeons he felt responsible for Victoria's death; in *Rises Again*, he is more like a simple, old-fashioned pulp magazine villain like Doctor Death, the Scorpion or the Octopus. And while that's certainly an appealing sensibility in some cases, in this one it somewhat serves to lessen the sympathy for Phibes, making him appear more garden-variety maniac than grieving husband. *Dr. Phibes Rises Again*'s music is by John Gale instead of Basil Kirchin, and it's a much more conventional score; it's not bad at all, but lacks the quirkiness of Kirchin's work and doesn't work with or put its stamp on individual scenes the way Kirchin's did. Again, this is not to say that it's not entertaining or enjoyable; it certainly is, just not in the same way as the first one.

Vincent Price as Phibes is solid; Phibes' devotion and dedication to Victoria is unwavering, his sense of purpose strong, but the character has changed in ways besides the ones noted above. As the *Monsterscene* article cited, just in technical terms, Price's voice has changed, or rather the effect on his voice — it also uses a more conventional reverb effect instead of the harsher, more metallic tone employed in the first, which made it seem as though getting every word out was an effort. But that would have just slowed things up this time around, because it sometimes seems like all Phibes does is talk, talk, and talk some more. In *Phibes*, a great many of his lines were directed toward Victoria, and most of the rest of the time he either let his actions do the talking and let the other characters explain what was going on; in this one, he is constantly explaining his plans to Vulnavia or railing against Biederbeck or the fates. The character of Vulnavia has also lost something; Valli Kemp (1970's Miss Australia) is pretty, but her doe-eyed look carries none of the mystery projected by Virginia North (who was unavailable for the sequel due to pregnancy). Vulnavia had not originally been a part of the screenplay; Phibes was to have a new assistant, but studio executives wanted Vulnavia again (which rather didn't make sense, as she was portrayed by a different actress anyway). She does have one neat scene where, like some posh cigarette girl, she brings Phibes his makeup appliances on a portable tray; but this is also another change in character for Phibes, because he had always done so in private before. Kemp only made one other film, *The Great Muppet Caper* (1981).

The great Robert Quarry's casting as Biederbeck (the name coming from legendary jazz man Bix Beiderbecke) was inspired by his success in the classic *Count Yorga* movies. He's the perfect foil for Price, however nebulous his origins. He's as dispassionate as Phibes is passionate, at least where anyone other than himself is concerned. Like Phibes, he will stop at nothing, but while it's Phibes who actually commits murders, Biederbeck's stunning lack of concern for the fates of his friends and associates makes him seem the less sympathetic of the two. Unfortunately, the antagonism of their on-screen personas was duplicated in real life. Quarry complained that Price was overacting, and Price felt that AIP was grooming the man whom they hoped would become their new Vincent Price right before his eyes.

Peter Cushing is always welcome, although he's completely wasted as a no-nonsense ship's captain. Peter Jeffrey and John Cater *are* funny, even though mostly silly. *The Abominable Dr. Phibes'* sharp dialogue was replaced by outright jokes and more visual slapstick — *dumb* stupid instead of *clever* stupid. Two other members of the "Phibes Stock Company," Hugh Griffith and Terry-Thomas, return in different roles. Gerald Sim was featured in one of the movies Caroline turned down while at Hammer, *Doctor Jekyll and Sister Hyde*, and had also been in Hitchcock's *Frenzy*. Milton Reid was a fantasy film mainstay, working for Hammer (*The Camp on Blood Island*, *The Terror of the Tongs*, *Night Creatures*), Tigon (*The Blood on Satan's Claw*) and Amicus (*The People That Time Forgot*); he also appeared in Caroline's two Bond films (*Casino Royale* and *The Spy Who Loved Me*), and in the *very* first, *Dr. No*.

Caroline still makes a beautiful corpse, but she gets even less respect in this one, removed from her stately surroundings (Phibes' mansion) and shunted around (at one point even being lost) like a parcel at the mercy of the postal service. But at least she travels in style: In one of the few clever visual touches in the film, her coffin-to-go has end panels that look like the grille of a Rolls-Royce. In *MonsterScene* No. 10 (Summer 1997), she had this to say about the additional Phibes films (which were never made) and the role she would have played in them: "There was talk, and the talk that I'd heard, that seemed quite fascinating to me, was that she would actually come back, he would bring her back, and she would be far worse than he was!"

This was another consequence of *Dr. Phibes Rises Again*'s failure at the box office: No more sequels would be forthcoming. And the character had been created for Price with precisely that idea in mind, as revealed by original scripter William Goldstein in the book *The Complete Films of Vincent Price* by Lucy Chase Williams: "[AIP] picked it up with the idea that there would be a series; we were told in the beginning perhaps five pictures." The prospect of Caroline getting to show that Hell hath no fury like a woman embalmed is enticing and fun to speculate about but perhaps, given the direction in which the series was going, it was better that no more sequels were made. But perhaps the ship could have been righted; almost up until the time of Price's death, there was talk of reviving the character and series, but nothing ever came of it.

Although none of the sequels were ever produced, definite details exist for each. In what was supposed to be the first sequel, *The Bride of Dr. Phibes*, Phibes would have battled a man named Emil Salveus, the head of a satanic cult called the Institute for Psychic Phenomena. The twist would be that Salveus was actually Lem Vesalius, who steals Victoria's body, after which Phibes begins murdering members of the Institute in order to recover her. The murder methods, of course, would be inventive — a Colonel

Trenchard would be sealed in amber and then shattered, Charles Carruthers would have the life sucked out of him by leeches in his bathtub, an orchestra conductor would be covered in melted butter and be eaten by a lobster (!), a wheelchair-bound Lady Peune would be whisked into the stratosphere with a balloon attached to the wheelchair, a dirty vicar would have his insides sucked out by a vacuum, a representative of the Abyssinian Embassy in which would end up in a bed full of cobras, and Salveus would have perished in an acid pit he'd originally intended to dunk Phibes. Victoria would have been brought back to life in the sequel, only to have to quickly go into cryogenic hiding when the police once again invade the house. But this idea was rejected by producer Louis "Deke" Heyward, who turned to his friend Robert Blees. Blees' idea for that film, which would have simply been called *Phibes II*, was for Phibes to battle Quarry as Count Yorga; but Heyward switched to the idea of the Egyptian locale, which Fuest then re-wrote. Heyward retained one central idea from *Bride*, that of the adversary who steals Victoria's body and the subsequent killing of his associates, and also retained the idea of casting Robert Quarry.

Dr. Phibes in the Holy Land would have been the third film; Price says there was a "very funny" script, but I don't know the details. *The Son of Dr. Phibes* may have not even had a complete script, but the idea was for Phibes to battle environmental polluters, and his killings would have involved earthquakes and tidal waves. In 1977, *Phibes Resurrectus* apparently got closer to being made than the other sequels, with the idea being sold to Roger Corman's New World Pictures, but this too fell through. It was essentially the same as *The Bride of Dr. Phibes* with some minor changes; for one sequence, set at Wembley, Corman wanted to cast Forry Ackerman (who often called himself "The Poor Man's Vincent Price" in the pages of *Famous Monsters*) as a robot Phibes double that fools Trout. In 1981, Whiton and Goldstein did a treatment for *Dr. Phibes*, which brings the good doctor, Victoria and Vulnavia to America for a New York adventure. In this film, Victoria has not been revived, and Phibes' efforts draw the attention of the "Wormwood Institute," a "think tank of glorious eggheads" who each lead a "strange private life." And those lives are not just strange; they're bizarrely kinky and warped. Bulwark Stanton is an astrophysicist obsessed with little girls; Lester is 12 and is obsessed with trying to disprove the theory of relativity. The Smith Brothers are identical twins — and transvestites. Eighty-year-old Hector Wormwood smashes Victoria's coffin, which causes her to decompose. This is the act that spurs Phibes to his acts of elimination, based on his victims' greatest loves; for instance, Mr. Nim loves chocolate, and so is turned into a chocolate statue. While he is doing away with his victims, Phibes searches for the "essential salts" which will restore Victoria. Three years later, *Phibes Resurrectus* was again resurrected, with a different first act, and prepared for George Romero, but again it did not go anywhere. The most surprising thing about this version of *Resurrectus* was that Whiton and Goldstein did not have Vincent Price penciled in for the role of Phibes! They suggested David Carradine (along with Orson Welles, Paul Williams, John Carradine and Donald Pleasence, among others, in the cast); perhaps Price had balked at the prospect of working with Romero. The last attempt at a Phibes sequel was *The Seven Fates of Dr. Phibes*, a treatment (by Paul Clemens and Ron Magid), that was enthusiastically received by Price. It disregarded the other elaborations on Phibes' adventures and picked up directly where *Dr. Phibes Rises Again* ended. Victoria has been revived, and she and Phibes begin a new quest: to recover seven ivory statues, depicting characters from Greek mythology, that will permit them to join the gods in the heavens. But on their return to London, Phibes and Victoria find the house demolished and the statues sold. Phibes then plans a new set of murders, according to the statue the new owners possess: Dekker has the Cyclops, so naturally, he loses an eye (this sounds like an in-joke, as actor Albert Dekker had starred in the film *Dr. Cyclops*). Thundershaft has Cerberus, so Phibes gives him an even larger statue, with a bonus: This "action figure" has movable parts, specifically the three heads. Azzared has the Arachne statue, so of course she gets a roomful of spiders. Halifax has Medusa, so he winds up set in stone. The last statue has been purchased by yet another Phibes archenemy, Professor Norquist, and this one has fashioned bullets containing the waters of the River Styx, which can kill Phibes. When the statues are joined, Phibes and Victoria are invited to the heavens by Vulnavia, whose true identity has finally been revealed: the goddess Athena!

One last, and truly bizarre, attempt to revive Phibes came courtesy of "Deke" Heyward and Goldstein, who wrote the pilot and tried to sell NBC a TV series in which a completely reformed Phibes has become a crimefighter who uses his makeup and technical skills to catch the crooks! So while it can't be said that the character never lived up to his potential (he had done that quite admirably in the first movie), it was certainly sad to see that no more opportunities to expand that character would materialize. The ultimate victim of the Curse of Darkness was the series itself.

Captain Kronos, Vampire Hunter—1974, Hammer Films, Paramount Pictures

Crew: Producers: Brian Clemens, Albert Fennell; Director-Screenplay: Brian Clemens; Music Composer–Conductor: Laurie Johnson; Music Supervisor: Philip Martell; Photography: Ian Wilson; Film Editor: James Needs; Casting: James Liggat; Production Design: Robert Jones; Makeup: Jimmy Evans; Hair Stylist: Barbara Ritchie; Production Supervisor: Roy Skeggs; Production Manager: Richard F. Dalton; Assistant Directors: Nick Farnes, David Tringham; Second Assistant Director: Terry Hodgkinson; Assistant Art Director: Kenneth McCallum Tait; Sound Editor: Peter Lennard; Recording Director: A.W. Lumkin; Dubbing Mixer: Bill Rowe; Sound Recordist: Jim Willis; Camera Operator: Godfrey A. Godar; First Assistant Camera: David Wynn-Jones; Wardrobe Supervisors: Dulcie Midwinter, Margie Midwinter; Final Colorist: Donald Freeman; Fight Supervisor: William Hobbs; Continuity: June Randall; Stand-in for Caroline Munro: Glenda Allen.

FILMS AND TELEVISION: *Captain Kronos, Vampire Hunter* (1974)

Cast: Horst Janson (Captain Kronos), John Carson (Dr. Marcus), Shane Briant (Paul Durward), Caroline Munro (Carla), John Cater (Grost), Lois Daine (Sara Durward), Ian Hendry (Kerro), Wanda Ventham (Lady Durward), William Hobbs (Hagen), Brian Tully (George Sorell), Robert James (Pointer), Perry Soblosky (Barlow), Paul Greenwood (Giles), Lisa Collings (Vanda Sorell), John Hollis (Barman), Susanna East (Isabella Sorell), Stafford Gordon (Barton Sorell), Elizabeth Dear (Ann Sorell), Joanna Ross (Myra), Neil Seiler (Priest), Olga Anthony (Lilian), Gigi Gurpinar (Blind Girl), Peter Davidson (Big Man), Terence Sewards (Tom), Trevor Lawrence (Deke), Jacqui Cook (Barmaid), Penny Price (Whore), B.H. Barry, Michael Buchanan, Steve James, Ian McKay, Barry Smith, Roger Williams (Villagers), Linda Cunningham (Jane), Caroline Villiers (Petra), Julian Holloway (Kronos Voice).

SYNOPSIS

From original pressbook:

The time is the early nineteenth century. A stranger, sitting proudly on his horse, rides into town, a battle jacket slung over his shoulders, the sleeves swinging loose. Two swords, a rapier and a Samurai, gleam as they rest sheathed on his hips. The stranger is Captain Kronos (Horst Janson), who is accompanied by Professor Grost (John Cater). Grost's intelligence balances well with Kronos' strength.

Caroline and the captain (Horst Janson) get cozy in this publicity still from *Captain Kronos, Vampire Hunter.*

Dr. Marcus (John Carson) has asked the two men, both old friends, to help solve the mysterious deaths that have occurred in the village. Several beautiful young girls have died, seemingly from old age. Fear is rampant throughout the countryside.

Vampirism is suspected, but no one knows who the vampire is. Captain Kronos, who was once a member of the Imperial Guard, has been beckoned to seek out the evil and destroy it. He had been the victim of a vampire once, but survived the evil forces. He knows his enemy.

Kronos is also a man of great passion. He meets Carla (Caroline Munro), who becomes his mistress and companion while he is in the village. With the help of Marcus, Kronos begins tracking down the criminal. As more girls go one by one to their deaths, Kronos sets his trap. The vampire continues to elude him.

A strange turn of events occurs when Kronos' friend Marcus feels blood on his lips, the same flecks of red that have been found on the mouths of the dead girls. As his face stares back at him from the mirror, Marcus knows that he must be destroyed. He asks his friends Kronos and Grost to kill him. They plunge a stake through his heart, but he lives on. Kronos attempts to hang him, but he lives on. Kronos and Grost prepare to burn him, but he suddenly topples and falls. At last he is dead. Strangely it is Marcus' crucifix, usually a vampire deterrent, which has plunged itself into his chest. Blood seeps through the wound.

Dr. Marcus had visited Durward Hall, the home of Lady Durward (Wanda Ventham), her son Paul (Shane Briant), and daughter Sara (Lois Daine), all his one-time patients. Kronos sets his trap, knowing the family is somehow connected.

He recruits Carla to act as a decoy by going to the Durward house. First he must fight against the villagers who suspect he has had something to do with the deaths. That accomplished, he goes to the Durward house, his glinting rapier and Samurai in hand.

The evil is destroyed, finally and forever. Kronos rides off, accompanied by Grost, leaving behind Carla. Maybe he'll return, to fight another evil in another time. Kronos knows that evil is timeless.

REVIEW AND NOTES

Castle of Frankenstein No. 23 (1974) called *Captain Kronos* a "[s]emi-parody, with a strange blend of western, horror and a movie serial approach." The *Los Angeles Times'* Kevin Thomas wrote that *Frankenstein and the Monster from Hell* and *Captain Kronos, Vampire Hunter* "add up to a pretty tepid double feature, certain to satisfy only the most diehard of horror fans.... Writer-director Brian Clemens tries for style and mood, but his lack of wit and lethally languorous pacing do him in most of the way." According to *Variety*'s Murf, "[The] film features a lot of kinky plot lines but never follows through. More bohemian audiences may find all manner of turn-on, but the whole is an uneven tease. Clemens keeps his plot going for 91 minutes with a sincerity which almost makes it work." The reviewer for *Monster Fantasy* No. 1 (April 1975) wrote, "After scripting films like *The Golden Voyage of Sinbad*, *Doctor Jekyll and Sister Hyde*, and countless TVers, Clemens makes his debut as a director on this film. The results are terrific—good suspense, a nice sense of atmosphere, appropriately sexy, and many unexpected turns. The two drawbacks are phony makeup and a disappointing finale. But go see this one—*Captain Kronos* might just become a new cult hero!"

If only that prediction had come true. In 1972, Hammer was in trouble—not just your average, garden-variety trouble, like how low to cut the ladies' blouses, or wondering if Woolworth's had enough rubber bats to film a climax, but T-R-O-U-B-L-E. The British film industry as a whole was in its death throes. In 1969, after several changes in name, ownership and management, Warner Bros. declined to continue their distributorship of Hammer's product, and Hammer was left up the Thames without a paddle. Nineteen sixty-nine was particularly rough, a year of great changes: Anthony Nelson-Keys left the company, forming his own production company with Christopher Lee, Charlemagne Productions; Bernard Robinson also left, as well as company secretary James Dawson. Dawson was replaced by accountant Roy Skeggs, whose own ascent was fairly meteoric: In 1971, he graduated to overall production supervisor of Hammer, and the next year he became a producer. In December 1970, Sir James Carreras' son, Michael Carreras was offered the position of managing director, which he only accepted after urging from his mother, and officially took the job in January 1971. In 1972, in order to avert a take-over bid by Studio Film Labs, Michael bought the company from Sir James, and in January 1973 became chairman and chief executive.

It was in this unstable atmosphere that *Captain Kronos* came to be. Michael Carreras was never behind it — some have said that he "killed" the movie and used it as a tax write-off — and due to the dodgy financing deal, it had not been guaranteed distribution. I didn't see release until 1974, although "released" is perhaps too generous a term; "dumped" is more like it. As Caroline recalled in an interview in *Fangoria*, "It didn't have any publicity at all. Nothing. In fact, we weren't even told it was coming out. It just crept out in Hammersmith; I and my family went to see it one evening. And that was it — we never heard another word about it." In another *Fangoria* interview, Carreras opined, "Clemens' team didn't have the proper expertise with this type of material.... [They] were treating it with tongue-in-cheek. Maybe I didn't understand their style, but I just didn't like it. It may be totally my own failing, but I wasn't in tune with their approach." Time did not soften his stance towards the film, either, as evidenced by this quote from *Little Shoppe of Horrors* No. 4: "I really don't want to discuss *Kronos*. It was so badly mishandled. The conception was very good, but unfortunately it wasn't handled by the Hammer team. The people involved in the making hadn't the Hammer talent, but they had the ideas." Time would also prove Carreras correct: He didn't understand the style, and it was totally his own failing.

But it wasn't just financial and infrastructure problems that helped to bring Hammer down; they had begun to flounder from a lack of direction and creative instinct. No doubt this had a lot to do with the old hands being replaced by new ones, but in a way, the old hands were part of the problem. They made wonderful movies, the same kind of wonderful movies they had made since Hammer had first reared its bloody head, but as already noted in the *Dracula A.D. 1972* section, they had started to be bypassed by both audience tastes and the horror movies that had been made in the meantime. Hammer had made blood redder and bosoms fuller, but, predictably, after a time the ante had to be upped, and it was, by films like *Night of the Living Dead*, *The Exorcist*, et al. Hammer responded with more blood and more breasts, but was still losing ground. Perhaps, in retrospect, given the ruinous financial condition of the country as a whole and the British film industry in general, they were doomed anyway. But even if they could read the writing on the wall, they can be forgiven, and admired, for thinking that a few tweaks to the formula here and there could change the message. But, as shown by Michael Carreras' statements, Hammer did not necessarily recognize or approve of the elements that could have provided the change they were so desperately seeking. *Captain Kronos* sought to turn the conventions of the vampire film on their head, which it mostly successfully does, especially since it does this within the confines of its own universe. Dracula was a prisoner within the confines of his conventions, and so any changes to that series were not so much to the character, merely his situation or opposition. *Kronos* was free to experiment; Dracula was free to meet hippies and kung fu.

Kronos "experiments" from the very first scene on. The initial vampire attack takes place in broad daylight, as do the subsequent killings. This adds immensely to the overall dread, as well as removing one of the most time-honored conventions of vampiric vulnerability, in that the characters of this film do not have the luxury of seeking out the vampires in the daytime and staking them in their coffins. The vampires' victims in this film are not simply drained of blood and left to lay with puncture marks in their necks, their looks essentially unchanged, but are drained of the very essence of life itself, leaving withered corpses. Generally a vampire's victims would pop up at some point later in a film to further pile grief upon the protagonists (as well as providing an opportunity for more sexualized behavior and clothing), but not so here.

Kronos also breaks with tradition in that the vampires are not the central characters. Here the focus is on the hero — who, in another break with tradition, is actually heroic, athletic and extremely capable, unlike the usual, ineffectual ninnies and twits who must always bow to the knowledge of an older, wiser man. The older, wiser men in this film, in fact, get the short ends of their respective sticks: Kronos' old friend Dr. Marcus becomes a vampire, forcing Kronos to kill him, and Kronos' friend and partner Grost is a hunchback. And Kronos and Grost really are partners, not a traditional hero-sidekick team; there is a kind of duality to them, as if they are two parts of the same being, Kronos performing the actions that Grost cannot.

Kronos is not merely the "brawn" of the operation; there's a mystical aspect to his character that would have been explored more fully had there been sequels. Kronos was to have been more or less ageless and timeless, appearing in different eras of history to combat vampires. Kronos can also be likened to another screen icon, Clint Eastwood's "Man with No Name" character in *High Plains Drifter et al.*, and indeed, Clemens has claimed those films as inspiration for the structure of Kronos: the mysterious hero who rides into town, wipes out the bad guys, and then leaves again. It's another experiment in structure that works.

The tone of the film has been described as tongue-in-cheek, and indeed it is, but that quality is mostly relegated to dialogue and characters, rather than the physical

FILMS AND TELEVISION: *Captain Kronos, Vampire Hunter* (1974)

The always-beautiful artwork of Bruce Timm graced the cover of *Little Shoppe of Horrors* #18, which has been autographed by members of the cast of *Captain Kronos, Vampire Hunter* (courtesy Richard Klemensen and Bruce Timm).

FILMS AND TELEVISION: *Captain Kronos, Vampire Hunter* (1974)

John Cater and Caroline prepare a serving of Toad-in-the-Hole in this publicity still from *Captain Kronos, Vampire Hunter* (courtesy Paul C. Riggie).

action, although there is one scene that is most definitely handled very lightly. It reminds me of the scene in *Blazing Saddles* where Cleavon Little is sitting on his horse with his arms folded; cut to twenty bad guys getting their guns shot out of their hands, then cut back to Little still sitting with his arms folded. In this film's version, Kronos is accosted by three pug-uglies in a bar. He draws his sword; cut to the three villains slashed to ribbons almost simultaneously; then cut back to Kronos sheathing the sword. One of the more memorable bits of dialogue involves a traditional (and most horrible) British entrée known as "Toad in the Hole" (a dish consisting of sausages in Yorkshire pudding batter, generally served with vegetables and onion gravy). One of the new bits of vampire lore in this movie involves the planting of dead toads in a circle around the area where a suspected vampire lurks; if the boxes are dug up, and a toad is now alive, then a vampire has indeed passed that way. As Grost and Carla are planting the toads (no actual toads were harmed during the making of this film), John Cater looks up at Caroline and gleefully exclaims "Toad in the Hole!" Perhaps it's funnier if you've eaten it.

Caroline was not Clemens' first choice. He had envisioned the role of Carla as a red-haired gypsy firebrand, but when Caroline was suggested by Hammer, Clemens reconsidered and then rewrote the part to suit her more demure personality. This is not to say she's a shrinking violet: She readily accompanies Kronos into harm's way, and even acts as bait for the vampires in the climax. Her "entrance" is rather auspicious. She is first glimpsed locked up in stocks in the center of town, her hair dripping with the tomatoes and eggs she has been pelted with (for dancing on a Saturday). *Kronos* remains one of her favorite roles and films, and she explained why in *Little Shoppe of Horrors* No. 18: "It has its own very natural, very human feel to it. I know that we were dealing with vampires and things, but it was so grounded in every way. It had a very real feeling to it. It was earthy. And the actors were absolutely right. You couldn't see anybody else in John Cater's role, or in Horst's role. They *were* the characters. I loved it." And she, in turn, is absolutely right, particularly in the case of John Cater, whose talent had recently been on display in the Phibes sequel.

Cater is one of many people involved in *Kronos* who had also been associated with *The Avengers*, another major reason that the tone of *Kronos* is so different from other Hammer films. Brian Clemens had produced and written many of the most memorable episodes of the classic series; Laurie Johnson had composed the music for nearly all of the original episodes (plus all 26 episodes of *The New Avengers*, an episode of which, "Angels of Death," would feature Caroline), and Robert Jones had done production design on the series. Ian Hendry was featured in the first 25 episodes as Dr. David Keel. Veteran John Carson was featured in three *Avengers* episodes, and provided a veteran Hammer presence as well, having already served in *Taste the Blood of Dracula* and the classic *The Plague of the Zombies*.

Kronos received the graphic-story treatment in issue No. 20 of Britain's legendary *Halls of Horror* (formerly *House of Hammer*) magazine, with a cover by Bill Phillips (it took a bit of artistic liberty by having Kronos attacked by a horde of huge, vampire-bat-demon-monsters). The inside adaptation was written by Steve Moore, with good artwork by Steve Parkhouse. The adaptation is serviceable enough, if necessarily brief; in fact, so brief that it nearly ignores Carla, who does not even get a proper introduction, simply appearing here and there, and is not even mentioned by name until a page or two from the end. *Kronos* also gets a mention in one of the feature articles, "Those Fearless Vampire Hunters": "In 1973, there seemed to be some hope in getting another Van Helsing–like vampire-hunter off the ground with *Captain Kronos*, but any follow-up series has yet to appear.... [W]here Kronos and associates fail is in the action department; their operations are all deeply prepared and methodical — they lack the sudden sprints of activity that made Peter Cushing/Van Helsing's hectic days much more exciting." (Numerous sword-fights and beheadings fail to qualify as "sprints of activity"?)

Captain Kronos and Grost did rather better in the comics than they did on film: The very first issue of *House of Hammer* featured the first sequel to the film, which takes place immediately after the film has ended. Accompanied by a one-page recap of the movie, the five-page, untitled strip (written by Steve Moore, art by Ian Gibson) took the dynamic duo to Bavaria. As it happens, that is where Carla now lives and works as a maid in the employ of a Count Balderstein, who employs an army of vampire security guards and is trying to contact the Lords of Chaos. Curiously (or perhaps conveniently), the characters now adhere to the strict rules of vampirism, which allows Grost to stake all of them in their coffins. True, he does this at night, but he and Kronos have carved a large cross to hold them in their graves. But in the meantime, Balderstein escapes, with Carla in tow. The second strip appeared the next issue, advertised with the title "The Terror of Walpurgis Night!" Kronos and Grost finally track down Balderstein, who plans to seal his deal with the Lords of Chaos with the sacrifice of Carla. Kronos slices and dices a path through Balderstein's minions to save her, but her wish to accompany the vampire hunters is denied by Kronos, who leaves her at a local convent for safekeeping. The mother superior tells Kronos the nuns will be pleased to take her in: "Only too pleased," she tells Kronos and Grost as she turns away from them and smiles — revealing her fangs.

The character that Captain Kronos recalls most is not Van Helsing but Solomon Kane, Robert E. Howard's "grim Puritan adventurer," a man devoted to God who, clothed in a dark cloak and slouch hat, roamed the 18th century world, ridding it of monsters and godless barbarians. (Like Kronos, Kane wears two swords.) Kane's quest takes him to all corners of the Earth, and he faced off against vampires in "The Moon of Skulls," in which he encounters Nakari, the vampire queen of Negari. In "Hills of the Dead," he finds a city of vampires in the jungle. Kronos, of course, is the opposite of Kane in important ways, such as Kronos's willingness to engage in some extra-marital sex with Carla, and his propensity to light up what looks like a big spliff (it seems to have the same effect). Both Solomon Kane and *Captain Kronos* would seem to have been an influence on 2004's awful *Van Helsing*, in which Hugh Jackman dresses like Solomon Kane, fights vampires and other assorted monsters, and has the general overall disposition of his most famous characterization, that of Marvel Comics' Wolverine from the X-Men comics.

The Golden Voyage of Sinbad—1974, Columbia Pictures

Crew: Producers: Ray Harryhausen, Charles H. Schneer; Director: Gordon Hessler; Screenplay: Brian Clemens; Story: Brian Clemens, Ray Harryhausen; Music: Miklos Rozsa; Orchestrator: Lawrence Ashmore; Photography: Ted Moore; Creator of Special Visual Effects: Ray Harryhausen; Film Editor: Roy Watts; Casting: Maude Spector; Production Design: John Stoll; Art Director: Fernando Gonzalez; Costume Design: Verena Coleman, Gabriella Falk; Makeup: Jose Antonio Sanchez; Production Supervisor: Roberto Roberts; Assistant Director: Miguel Gil; Second Assistant Director: Carlos Gil; Set Dresser: Julian Mateos; Assistant Art Director: Benjamin Fernandez; Construction Coordinator: Francisco Prosper; Sound Recordists: George Stephenson, Doug E. Turner; Dubbing Editor: Peter Elliott; Camera Operator: Salvador Gil; Assistant Editor: Jeremy Thomas; Special Masks: Colin Arthur; Continuity: Eva Del Castillo; Assistant Continuity: Lesley J. Silver; Production Executive: Andrew Donally.

Cast: John Phillip Law (Sinbad), Caroline Munro (Margiana), Tom Baker (Koura), Douglas Wilmer (Vizier), Martin Shaw (Rachid), Gregoire Aslan (Hakim), Kurt Christian (Haroun), Takis Emmanuel (Achmed), John David Garfield (Abdul), Aldo Sambrell (Omar), Robert Shaw (The Oracle of All Knowledge).

SYNOPSIS

The legendary Captain Sinbad (John Phillip Law) comes into possession of a fragment of a mysterious golden tablet. He keeps it, against the wishes of his crew, and begins to see visions of a beautiful woman (whose hand seems to bear the evil eye) and a masked figure who calls his name. He awakens just in time to keep the ship from crashing on the jagged rocks in a savage storm.

Once ashore in the kingdom of Marabia, Sinbad encounters both the evil sorcerer, Prince Koura (Tom Baker), whose masked face he saw in the dream, and the benevolent Grand Vizier (Douglas Wilmer), whose face has been horribly burned by Koura's magic.

Sinbad also meets the girl of his dream, Margiana (Caroline Munro), whose hand bears the symbol of the eye. With two pieces of the golden tablet in hand, both they and Koura set sail in a furious race for the third and final piece of the tablet, which promises more power than any mortal has ever known.

The prize they seek rests in the Fountain of Destiny in the lost land of Lemuria. When Sinbad tries to outrun Koura's vessel in treacherous waters, Koura brings the figurehead of Sinbad's ship to life. It steals Sinbad's charts and floats back to Koura, who ages with every use of his power.

In Lemuria, they make haste to the multi-faced temple of the Oracle of All Knowledge. But before they can begin their quest for the golden piece, Koura traps them in the temple with a calamitous cave-in. Sinbad and crew escape, in the process killing Koura's bat-winged homunculus. Koura feels its pain.

Green-skinned savages capture Koura and his henchman, but Koura brings the six-armed stone statue of Kali to life and becomes their master. When Sinbad finds the cave, Koura sends the statue, now armed with six swords, to fight with Sinbad. When the idol is shattered, it reveals the missing golden piece.

The green men capture Sinbad's band, and are just about to sacrifice Sinbad when they see the symbol of the eye on Margiana's hand. They seize her and proclaim that she is the chosen one of the God of the Single Eye, a cyclopean centaur. Margiana is lowered into the pit of the monster. Koura, rapidly aging, finds the Fountain of Destiny. He drops a piece of the tablet into it, and the Fountain's golden shower returns youth to the sorcerer. Sinbad grapples with the one-eyed monster, which is then attacked by a winged gryphon, which loses its life in battle. The noble beast is avenged when Sinbad sinks his dagger into the back of the centaur.

Sinbad can't stop Koura from putting the remaining pieces of the puzzle into the Fountain. One of the powers that Koura receives is the Shield of Darkness, and Sinbad finds himself in battle with an invisible man. When Koura takes respite in the Fountain, he is made visible, and Sinbad penetrates him with a mighty thrust!

German one-sheet poster art for *The Golden Voyage of Sinbad*.

FILMS AND TELEVISION: *The Golden Voyage of Sinbad* (1974)

When the waters calm, Sinbad sees in them a reflection of himself as a king. But he returns the crown to the rightful ruler of Marabia, the Grand Vizier, whose face and kingdom are restored. Sinbad and Margiana are free to marry and sail the seas in search of new worlds.

REVIEW AND NOTES

Cinefantastique (Vol. 3 No. 2, 1974) called the movie "one of the better fantasy films in recent years," adding "On the distaff side, we are given Caroline Munro. Although she has little to do in the film, her presence is often a welcome diversion.... The film, despite its faults, does entertain and reaffirms the fact that any film undertaken by Ray Harryhausen is worth seeing." According to *FXRH Magazine* No. 4, Spring 1974: "*The Golden Voyage of Sinbad*, Ray Harryhausen's latest film, is the kind of entertainment that only he could have devised — a richly atmospheric, exotic motion picture which reunites his technical wizardry with the magical fantasy realm to which his talents are best suited.... All factors considered, *The Golden Voyage of Sinbad* is one of the most satisfying fantasy films ever made. [T]his visit into the fanciful world of the imagination is a stunning technical achievement seldom encountered on modern movie screens."

The problem with reviewing movies by Ray Harryhausen has always been one of practically reviewing two separate movies: the scenes where Harryhausen works his inimitable magic, and then all the others in between those set-pieces. The directors are almost interchangeable; it is Harryhausen's vision which dominates the picture, and even the actors (sometimes literally) become puppets in Harryhausen's hands. Occasionally, both directors and actors manage to rise above the situation, as in the classic *The 7th Voyage of Sinbad*, and all of the elements contributed an equal share in making that film a fantasy masterpiece. Others, like

Tom Baker and Caroline look to see if there's a Doctor in the house in this publicity still from *The Golden Voyage of Sinbad*.

49

FILMS AND TELEVISION: *The Golden Voyage of Sinbad* (1974)

The Valley of Gwangi, just leave you wishing for the allosaurus to show up again real quick and chow down on some cowboy lunch meat. And very occasionally, as in the case with this film, the humans actually outshine the special effects.

Harryhausen's creations in this film were his best to that date, and their movements and interaction with the live actors are some of his most skilled ever; it's just that the creations themselves leave a bit to be desired in terms of design and inspiration. The best one here is the Kali statue come to life; a nice variation on the man-vs.-skeletons swordfights from previous films. The centaur–Cyclops and the gryphon in this film's Kong–T. Rex tribute are both sculpturally well-executed (particularly the centaur–Cyclops), but they lack the classic, magical look of the Cyclops or the Dragon from *7th Voyage* or the Ymir from *20 Million Miles to Earth*.

But the cast and crew more than make up for the lack of truly classic creatures. Director Gordon Hessler, whose first work was for the *Alfred Hitchcock Presents* television series, had a proven track record coming into the film, having already lensed *The Oblong Box*, *Cry of the Banshee*, *Scream and Scream Again* (all starring Vincent Price), and the 1971 version of *Murders in the Rue Morgue*. He had also directed the TV movie *Scream, Pretty Peggy*, which had immediately preceded his work on *Golden Voyage*. TV is where

Ray Harryhausen's Centaur-Cyclops gets the point in this autographed theater still from *The Golden Voyage of Sinbad*. The swordsman is John Phillip Law (courtesy Paul C. Riggie).

the majority of his future would lie; his CV would come to include the good (episodes of *Kolchak: The Night Stalker, Kung Fu,* and *Wonder Woman*), the bad (*CHiPs*), and the ugly (*KISS Meets the Phantom of the Park*). Screenwriter Brian Clemens had written and been story editor for many episodes of the classic television series *The Avengers*, as well as writing and producing Hammer's *Doctor Jekyll and Sister Hyde*. He produced, directed and wrote *Captain Kronos, Vampire Hunter* with Caroline, and worked on many episodes of the TV series *The New Avengers*, including the entry featuring Caroline, "Angels of Death." Miklos Rozsa was an Academy Award–winning composer. His score for *Golden Voyage* is reminiscent of his Oscar-nominated *The Thief of Bagdad* (1940). While beautiful, it lacks the panache of Bernard Herrmann's instantly recognizable music for *The 7th Voyage of Sinbad*.

John Phillip Law was already very familiar to genre fans as the cunning master thief Diabolik in *Danger: Diabolik* (1968) and from his best-known role, the blind angel Pygar in the seminal sci-fi spoof *Barbarella* (1968). He would continue to act up until his death in 2008. Another very familiar face was that of Douglas Wilmer, who had already worked with Harryhausen, in *Jason and the Argonauts*. He also opposed Christopher Lee twice, as Nayland Smith, in *The Brides of Fu Manchu* (1966) and *The Vengeance of Fu Manchu* (1967), staked out a role in *The Vampire Lovers* (1970) with Ingrid Pitt, and portrayed Sherlock Holmes in both his own television series (1964–65) and Gene Wilder's *The Adventure of Sherlock Holmes' Smarter Brother* (1975). Tom Baker's first big break was a showy part as Rasputin in *Nicholas and Alexandra* (1971). An even bigger break came about as a result of his role in *Golden Voyage*: He was hired to play the title role in Britain's landmark television sci-fi series, *Doctor Who*. Baker also portrayed Sherlock Holmes, in a 1982 mini-series version of *The Hound of the Baskervilles*. The uncredited Robert Shaw (*From Russia with Love, Jaws*) had been keen to play Sinbad, but settled for a cameo as the Oracle of All Knowledge; heavily made-up, with an electronically distorted voice, he is virtually unrecognizable.

Caroline, who plays one of her signature roles, recalled for interviewer Graham Groom:

> I had been signed by Hammer, for one year, for a contract, out of which I did two films, one being *Dracula A.D. 1972*, and the second one being *Captain Kronos, Vampire Hunter*, which kind of would come full circle to *Sinbad*. [*Captain Kronos*] was written and directed by Brian Clemens, who wrote the screenplay for *The Golden Voyage of Sinbad*, so I was lucky enough to have been chosen for *Captain Kronos*, and they were searching for somebody to do *Sinbad*, and they wanted a big name, somebody American or well-known, but Brian said "No." He kept lobbying Charles Schneer and Ray Harryhausen, saying, "I think you should come and look at the rushes and see what you think, because I think she's right." So they said "No," but eventually Brian persuaded them to do that, and they saw the rushes, and that was how I got the part. So it was lovely, like work-out-of-work. I was very lucky to have done that."

Interviewer Graham Groom was so taken with her performance that he devoted an entire website to it, "Margiana: Caroline Munro and *The Golden Voyage of Sinbad*"

FILMS AND TELEVISION: *The Golden Voyage of Sinbad* (1974)

(http://www.margiana.freeservers.com/index.html). It's quite a detailed and lovely site and, among its other features, it offers the definitive interview with Caroline on the film.

Caroline said in an interview in *Famous Monsters* No. 182: "Ray draws a beautiful picture of the beast you'll be confronting, to give you an idea of its appearance and height. He then directs a technician to wave a stick to simulate the beast's motion. He directs all the special effects sequences himself." To prepare for these scenes, she did not imagine the beasts Harryhausen had drawn for her; she imagined what frightens her: "Spiders. Silly things, really. I'm not too keen on heights either. Being a Capricorn, I am drawn to the earth." The *Golden Voyage* coverage in the magazine *FXRH*, although primarily concerned with the special effects, nevertheless had a kind word for Caroline: "[A]lthough given relatively little to do, [she] is blessed with an uncommonly pleasant smile over and above her more pronounced attributes." The issue itself is a wealth of Harryhausen information, and features an interview with the star of *7th Voyage*, Kerwin Mathews, conducted by Mark Hamill (along with Anne Wyndham) three years before Hamill's biggest break. Amusingly, the issue also contains a letter from Hamill (Caroline's future co-host of the Seventh Annual Science Fiction Film Awards show in 1980), who confesses that he still does not know what a matte is. That's something he would presumably learn in the very near future, in a galaxy far, far away.

Caroline has her eye on this horde of godless savages (actors unidentified) in this publicity photograph from *The Golden Voyage of Sinbad.*

52

FILMS AND TELEVISION: *The Golden Voyage of Sinbad* (1974)

Cinefantastique Vol. 3 No. 2 (1974) featured an interview with *Golden Voyage of Sinbad* producer Charles Schneer. The interviewer asked, "In the scene where Sinbad's party is landing on the beach, there seemed to be a rather revealing shot of Miss Munro's cleavage."

> Schneer replied, "I guess I've seen this picture a thousand times, and we looked at it on a Movieola, which you know is a positive picture about 8 × 10, and we looked at it for well over a year and never saw it until we put it on a big screen. And then when we put it on the big screen, we had as much revelation as you did. We were quite surprised to see what we saw. Much to my surprise, the UK censor, if he saw it, ignored it, because no mention was made of it at all. I don't even think that Miss Munro was aware of it. But you did see what you thought you saw. It's there."

An editor's note then informs us: "It *was* there. A brief scene exposing Caroline Munro's breast as she jumps from a landing boat has been trimmed at the request of the Code and Rating Administration, otherwise the G-rated film would have received an R rating." If it was indeed trimmed at some point, then the footage has been restored: In a long shot, the boat hits the beach and then she swings into Sinbad's arms, with a jump cut to a medium shot of the group wading up onto the beach, and when she swings down, she is oh-so-briefly exposed, her hair immediately falling down to provide cover.

Golden Voyage was the cover feature for *Castle of Frankenstein* No. 21 (1974), which featured a very serviceable painting by Marcus Boas depicting Caroline, Law, and the Vizier along with Harryhausen's creatures. Caroline's was the issue's "Slay-Mate of the Month" but it contained this bit of misinformation: "Caroline is the daughter of the late Janet Munro, a fine actress whom fans will remember from *The Day the Earth Caught Fire*." This was surely a revelation to Caroline and her mom and dad, as well as to Janet Munro's real two daughters, Sally and Connie.

Golden Voyage was more than three years in preparation, and Harryhausen did over 1,000 diagrams. One of the early sketches depicted the centaur–Cyclops in battle with a huge, brutish Troglodyte, but there was not that much contrast in the forms, so Harryhausen replaced the Troglodyte with the Gryphon. The locations were all shot in Spain. "They were real caves in Arta, in Majorca," Caroline recalled. "The main bits were done in Madrid — Sevia Studios, Madrid, outside in the mountains and things and then we went to Majorca and did the insides in the caves. But we could only film at night because, of course, the caves were used as a tourist attraction, and in the nighttime they had all these bats and things. It was quite extraordinary — we shared with the bats! It was wonderful." Harryhausen had been keen to use the Alhambra palace, but the authorities asked for a rental fee that would have blown the budget sky-high. With all of the location shooting, time and work on the animation, salaries, etc, the film was still delivered at a shade under a million dollars — $982,351. The viewer may experience a sense of *déjà vu* when Sinbad, Margiana and company hit the beach at Lemuria; it's the same beach at Torrente de Pareis in Spain that was used for *The 7th Voyage of Sinbad*.

FILMS AND TELEVISION: *I Don't Want to Be Born* (1975)

The Golden Voyage of Sinbad was adapted for the comics in the seventh and eighth issues of Marvel's *Worlds Unknown* (June and August, 1974), with a script by Len Wein, pencils by George Tuska, and inks by Vince Colletta. Issue No. 8 featured a particularly dynamic cover by Gil Kane. An amusing blurb advertised the story as "Sword vs. Sorcery in the Titanic Tradition of CONAN!"

I Don't Want to Be Born (a.k.a. *The Devil Within Her; Sharon's Baby; It Lives Within Her*)—1975, Unicapital Production's, The Rank Organization, AIP

Crew: Executive Producer Story: Nato De Angeles; Producer: Norma Corney; Director: Peter Sasdy; Screenplay: Stanley Price; Music Composer-Conductor: Ron Grainer; Photography: Kenneth Talbot; Film Editor: Keith Palmer; Art Director: Roy Stannard; Makeup: Eddie Knight; Hairdresser: Stephanie Kaye; Production Supervisor: Christopher Sutton; Assistant Director: David Bracknell; Assistant Art Director: Ted Ambrose; Sound: Dushko Indjic; Sound Editor: Don Challis; Sound Recording: Kevin Sutton; Sound Re-Recording Mixer: John Hayward; Dubbing Mixer: Gordon K. McCallum; Special Effects: Bert Luxford; Camera Operator: Bob Kindred; Wardrobe Supervisor: Brenda Dabbs; Assistant to Director: Jill Bender; Continuity: Renee Glynne; Choreographer: Mia Nardi.

Cast: Joan Collins (Lucy Carlesi), Eileen Atkins (Sister Albana), Ralph Bates (Gino Carlesi), Donald Pleasence (Dr. Finch), Caroline Munro (Mandy), Hilary Mason (Mrs. Hyde), John Steiner (Tommy Morris), Janet Key (Jill Fletcher), George Claydon (Hercules), Derek Benfield (Police Inspector), Stanley Lebor (Police Sergeant), Judy Buxton (Sheila), Andrew Secombe (Delivery Boy), Susan Richards (Old Lady), Phyllis McMahon (Nun), John Moore (Priest), Floella Benjamin (First Nurse), Penny Darch (Second Nurse), Maria Lopez, Susie Lightning (Strippers), Val Hoadley, Janice Brett (Dancers).

SYNOPSIS

From original pressbook:

For Lucy Carlesi (Joan Collins) and her husband Gino (Ralph Bates), the birth of their first child should be a happy event; instead, it's the beginning of a nightmare.

The birth is extremely difficult since the boy is exceptionally large and even Dr. Finch (Donald Pleasence) is disturbed by the baby's size and strength and especially by the infant's almost violent behavior.

Gino is relieved when his sister, Albana (Eileen Atkins), a nun, arrives from Italy, hoping she will be some comfort for Lucy. Though she tries to keep up appearances with their friends, life with the baby has become a nightmare. The child becomes increasingly violent, almost as if it were born with an inbuilt hatred for its parents.

Once, while Lucy is visiting with Mandy (Caroline Munro), an old friend from her days as a nightclub dancer, they are interrupted by angry noises from the nursery. When they rush upstairs they find the room a complete wreck ... and the cherubic-looking infant is the only one there.

FILMS AND TELEVISION: *I Don't Want to Be Born* (1975)

When the nursemaid dies mysteriously while airing the baby in the park, Lucy is convinced her death was no accident. She remembers a sinister dwarf (George Claydon) who used to work with her at the club and she remembers the blood-curdling curse he shouted at her when she left. But surely that sort of thing couldn't affect her or her baby.

Albana approaches Dr. Finch with Lucy's belief that the baby is "possessed" by some evil force. She reminds him that violence is an expression of evil. Could the infant's violence reflect some kind of "possession," a revenge against being born?

Awakened one night by the baby's eerie howling, Gino goes to the nursery to investigate ... it is an investigation from which he never returns. Before Gino's disappearance, Lucy had been worried and concerned but now begins the blind panic of absolute terror.

REVIEW AND NOTES

Chicago Sun-Times' Roger Ebert wrote, "At the beginning of *The Devil Within Her* [Donald Pleasence] is a doctor assisting at a delivery. A face mask hides everything but his eyes, but they're enough; they look sinister as he says, 'This baby doesn't want to be born!' Well, I'd gone expecting a third-rate rip-off of *The Exorcist*, but for just a few minutes there, I'd permitted myself some hope. When it comes to trashy horror exploitation movies, the British are about the best, and more often than not, Pleasence is one of the reasons ... and so I thought maybe he'd bring a little class into *The Devil Within Her*, but no, it was precisely as I feared, a third-rate rip-off of *The Exorcist*." In *British Horror Films*, Chris Wood opined, "There are some films that just defy description.... There are brutal killings galore, including drowning, hangings, a spectacular beheading and a comedy sweaty dwarf heart attack that seems to go on forever. Plus you get to see a (dubbed) Caroline Munro, and hear some fantastically bad dialogue. Tat, thy name is *I Don't Want to Be Born*."

Success breeds imitators like flies, and *The Exorcist* was no exception, spawning more than its share of "third-rate rip-offs." This film does indeed belong in that category. Each reviewer seizes on different reasons for its banality; but it seems the one complaint they all share is that Joan Collins, in her stripper flashback, never gets her kit off. (Caroline's a stripper, too, but don't get your hopes up, she doesn't either; although she does get to sport some sexy knickers.) One of the funniest aspects is that Collins is immaculately coiffed in every scene, whether she's giving birth or getting felt up by a dwarf, or getting killed. And despite being made at Pinewood, the picture has a grainy, "made-for-TV" look to it, giving the impression that Collins' makeup occupied more of the budget than quality film stock.

Caroline as Mandy Gregory plays somewhat of a variation on her usual damsel-in-distress role; she's sympathetic enough towards her friend Lucy, but she also thinks nothing of sleeping with her boss, a right sleazy bastard, with whom Lucy has also had an affair, or flirting with the dwarf who cursed Lucy. (For some odd reason, even though the baby's mom's name is Lucy, one of the alternate titles was *Sharon's Baby*. Huh?) She is not spared in the awful dialogue category: "I need to find myself someone like Gino before I bump-and-grind myself to death"; "They always say Italians make the best husbands—if you can get them away from their mothers." She manages to make it

FILMS AND TELEVISION: *I Don't Want to Be Born* (1975)

The Devil Within Her was a terrible rip-off of *The Exorcist*, as might be suspected from this poster.

through the film unscathed, being one of the few people the baby doesn't decapitate, hang, or otherwise mutilate. Another humorous aspect is the disconnect between the baby and the killings; oh, of course, he's always there and he's obviously the one who done it, but every time somebody dies, director Sasdy (*Countess Dracula, Taste the Blood of Dracula, Hands of the Ripper*) keeps intercutting shots of the evil dwarf's face, almost giving the impression that he's committing the murders and trying to frame the baby, which might have been more interesting. Surely the shots of mayhem, contrasted with immediately following shots of the tot goo-gooing away in his crib, are intended to illustrate the banality of evil or something like that, but they just come off as banal. And even if you don't find heart attack scenes entertaining, Wood is right, the dwarf's is hilarious; he dies slowly while Gino's sister, the nun, performs the exorcism, but he does so while on stage in the middle of a bunch of strippers, who think his wobbling is part of the show, and blithely pass him around until he keels over.

Donald Pleasence (*The Flesh and the Fiends, Fantastic Voyage, You Only Live Twice*, so many more), like Caroline, does add a touch of class to the proceedings; this genuinely lovely man managed to invest even his most benign roles (of which, admittedly, there were few) with an undercurrent of creepiness, so well conveyed through his well-modulated voice and intense gaze. The same could be said of Hammer veteran Ralph Bates (*Doctor Jekyll and Sister Hyde, The Horror of Frankenstein, Lust for a Vampire*), here playing an Italian businessman with an outrageous accent. And even Joan Collins, who is hardly identified primarily with genre credits, nonetheless had an impressive résumé of them, both before and after this film: *Star Trek, Batman, Tales that Witness Madness, Tales from the Crypt, Space: 1999* and *The Fantastic Journey*.

So even though it's a third-rate *Exorcist* rip-off, at least it's fun to watch, and has no pretensions to being anything other than it is, and it has the one thing that other *Exorcist* rip-offs don't have, and that's Caroline. She recalled the movie for *Filmfax* #83:

> Joan Collins became like a sister to me — unlike what people have heard about her, she was so sweet. She was very protective, and we'd go off and sip our coffee, and I'd be doing my knitting, and there she'd be, chatting away. And there was Ralph Bates; I didn't, unfortunately, have any scenes with him. I play a very second-rate stripper, a sad case, really. I was Joan Collins' friend in it. Joan Collins gets lucky, she gets Ralph Bates. I get a rather seedy character....
>
> [I]n one of the scenes, we were actually in a strip club. I didn't have to take anything off, but I had to dance with some professional dancers. There was a choreographer, and I said, "You know, I'm not a dancer." "Don't worry, don't worry," they said. So I was put in the back, and, boy, did I look bad in it...."

The movie found new life on DVD in 2011, courtesy of Scorpion Releasing's "Katarina's Nightmare Theatre" series (hosted by pro wrestling celeb Katarina Leigh Waters)—but the time between has done little to change the critical perspective, as evidenced by the Shane M. Dallmann review in Darryl Mayeski's excellent *Screem* magazine No. 23: "If more people had seen this film, perhaps the widely-circulated 'Worst Of' movie lists wouldn't automatically start with better-known films ranging from *Plan 9 from*

Outer Space to Battlefield Earth.... [I]t's a prime candidate for the worst film ever made by a talented director ... working with a potentially terrific cast. The picture is spiced up with some ... topless cabaret dancing (Caroline Munro ... doesn't participate in the latter, but she and her showgirl outfit are still quite appealing) ... *The Devil Within Her* is jaw-droppingly abysmal from beginning to end — and of course, is not to be missed."

At the Earth's Core—1976, American International Pictures/Amicus Productions

Crew: Executive Producer: Harry N. Blum; Producers: John Dark, Max J. Rosenberg, Milton Subotsky; Director: Kevin Connor; Screenplay: Milton Subotsky; Based on the novel by Edgar Rice Burroughs; Music: Mike Vickers; Photography: Alan Hume; Film Editors: John Ireland, Barry Peters; Production Designer: Maurice Carter; Art Director: Bert Davey; Makeup: Robin Grantham, Neville Smallwood; Hairdresser: Joan Carpenter; Production Manager: Graham Easton; Executive in Charge of Production for Edgar Rice Burroughs Inc.: Robert Hodes; First Assistant Directors: Jack Causey, Guy Travers; Construction Manager: Vic Simpson; Set Dresser: Michael White; Scenic Artists: Bill Beavis, Frank Graves; Sound Editor: Jim Atkinson; Sound Mixer: George Stephenson; Dubbing Mixers: Ken Barker, Gordon K. McCallum; Special Effects Supervisor: Ian Wingrove; Process Photography: Charles Staffell; Stunt Arranger: Joe Powell; Camera Operator: Derek V. Browne; Camera Focus: Mike Frift; Second Unit Focus Puller: John Golding; Wardrobe Supervisor: Rosemary Burrows; Assistant Editor: Rita Burgess; Production Administrator: Arthur Cleaver; Production Executive: David Shelton; Continuity: Doreen Soan.

Cast: Doug McClure (David Innes), Peter Cushing (Dr. Abner Perry), Caroline Munro (Dia), Cy Grant (Ra), Godfrey James (Ghak), Sean Lynch (Hoojah the Sly One), Keith Barron (Dowsett), Helen Gill (Maisie), Anthony Vemer (Gadsby), Robert Gillespie (Photographer), Michael Crane (Jubal), Bobby Parr (Sagoth Chief), Andee Cromarty (Girl Slave).

SYNOPSIS

From original pressbook:

A huge burrowing machine nicknamed "The Iron Mole," brainchild of scientist Dr. Abner Perry (Peter Cushing), is all set for an experimental run prior to its main task — that of piercing the Earth's core and exploring the mysteries deep beneath the surface of our planet.

With David Innes (Doug McClure), the rich young American backer of the project, on board, Perry sets the giant machine in motion for a test bore through a mountainous outcrop. But something goes wrong ... the machine takes a downward trek and, tunneling out of control at a ferocious speed, cuts clean through into the center of the earth.

Perry recognizes the eerie, twilight world into which they emerge as Pellucidar, a fabled land lost in the mists of antiquity. As the explorers emerge bewildered from their machine, they are captured by the Sagoths, a tribe of loathsome, half-human creatures who have under their yoke primitive human slaves.

The land is ruled, the explorers discover, by a dynasty of giant, lizard-like birds called

FILMS AND TELEVISION: *At the Earth's Core* (1976)

Caroline is at the core of the pressbook cover for *At the Earth's Core.*

FILMS AND TELEVISION: *At the Earth's Core* (1976)

Mahars. They are all female, since having discovered the way to propagate their kind without recourse to the male of the species. The Mahars communicate their orders to the Sagoths by means of mental telepathy.

Davis manages to establish contact with Dia (Caroline Munro), a beautiful slave girl. But even within the hapless slave army there is dissension, and David soon incurs the wrath of others who want Dia for themselves.

David manages to escape from the slave gang and begins to formulate a daring plan by which he will rid the land of the Mahars and the Sagoths and set the humans free.

But his bequest is beset with dangers from the giant animals who roam the tortured landscape; from voracious man-eating plants which pluck into their clutches anything coming within reach; and, above all, from the all-seeing, all-hearing Mahars themselves which seek to destroy him at every turn.

In an awesome climax, David manages to destroy the Mahar citadel, set the Sagoths to rout and release the slaves. But as Perry prepares to launch the "Iron Mole" back to the surface of the earth, David is faced with an agonizing choice: does he return with Perry or remain to make a new life with Dia in the land of Pellucidar "AT THE EARTH'S CORE"?

REVIEW AND NOTES

Chicago Sun-Times reviewer Roger Ebert wrote:

You remember Peter Cushing. His dialogue usually runs along the lines of "But good heavens, man! The person you saw has been dead for more than two centuries!" This time all he says is "David!" David is played by Doug McClure. You remember Doug McClure. Good. I don't. Pellucidar is inhabited by Dia, the beautiful slave girl with the heaving bodice, and Ra, her boyfriend, and the evil Ghak, not to mention the impenetrable Hoojah. All of these people speak proper English, you understand, except when it comes to the matter of proper names. Well, anyway, Doug and the professor step out into this sinister underworld, which is filled with telepathic giant parrots and next thing you know, they're on the chain gang. About here, we begin to notice the Captain Video effect. You remember Captain Video. He and his trusty sidekick were forever landing on strange planets and sneaking around rocks. After three weeks, you realized that the rocks were always the same. Doug and the professor sneak around one strange man-eating vegetable, and there's another one — which is the original vegetable, photographed from a new angle. Meanwhile, the telepathic parrots, wander by, opening and closing their beaks by spring action. It's along about here we begin to really zero in on Dia's bodice.

Ebert's review is somewhat painful, in that it's, for the most part, correct; the one thing Ebert fails to note is that it's a pretty darn entertaining movie. As discussed elsewhere, time has a way of changing perspectives, for better or worse; and at the time of its release, many fans were too busy being sniffy about the fact that the creatures were not animated by Ray Harryhausen or Jim Danforth (in fact, they weren't animated at all, they were the old standard men-in-suits, and cheap suits at that), or that the creatures didn't look like the wonderful monsters envisioned by Roy Krenkel or Frank Frazetta for the paperback covers, to notice the other good things about the movie. The creature suits are still quite risible, as are some of the makeups, but other, intangible factors make it work — the inherent good nature and heart of the picture, the sense of fun and the presentation of the material itself, which is never patronizing or condescending.

FILMS AND TELEVISION: *At the Earth's Core* (1976)

Sometimes you just need forty more years of wading through increasingly cynical and dreadful filmmaking to put things in the proper light.

At the Earth's Core was originally published as a four-part serial in the pulp magazine *All-Story Weekly* in April of 1914, and was first published in book form by McClurg eight years later. One of Burroughs' most popular series, it would spawn six sequels: *Pellucidar* (1915), *Tanar of Pellucidar* (1929), *Tarzan at the Earth's Core* (also 1929), *Back to the Stone Age* (1937), *The Land of Terror* (1944), and *Savage Pellucidar* (1963). Caroline's character of Dia was called Dian in the novel, changed presumably because Dia sounded more exotic. Caroline is the living embodiment of the women that Burroughs, Krenkel and Frazetta wrote and drew, although her characterization seems to have been subtly altered in keeping with Caroline's more demure personality. In the novel, she is more imperious, and much more resistant to David when they are reunited, constantly telling him how much she hates him (before she finally tells him she really loves him). In the film, her character is less haughty and, although she still resists David a bit when they are reunited, she succumbs to his charms much more quickly. The assignment was not without its little hazards: "One of the beasties — a flying Mahar, I believe it was called — clonked me on the head. They flew it in on a wire, a Mahar suit with a very hot man inside it."

Peter Cushing (who did all his own stunts, and as usual, supplied his own props)

Peter Cushing, Caroline and Doug McClure amidst the trees of Pellucidar in *At the Earth's Core*.

is often cited as playing Abner Perry just as he did The Doctor in Amicus' two Doctor Who movies, and this is true, but the characterization of Perry in the first half of the novel does not differ too greatly from this interpretation — and he says "David" in the novel as much as he does in the film. Interestingly, in both the second half of the novel and the movie, Perry's personality undergoes a change, but with quite different results. In the novel, he becomes consumed with a missionary-like zeal to raise the humans above their ignorance, introduce them to modern weapons, and defeat the intellectually superior Mahars; in the movie, he still acts the same, but becomes Action Man with a bow and arrow, even killing a fire-breathing dragon-like creature that menaces David and Dia (well, in the novel it was very dragon-like, but here it's more like an overgrown komodo lizard with a Zippo in its throat). The personality of David Innes is somewhat changed as well, but this may have been for the better. Many of Burroughs' heroes had an annoying tendency to find that new worlds or environments made them virtual, if not literal, supermen, a fact which they never got tired of telling us, and they inevitably rose to the rank of warlord of Barsoom or emperor of Pellucidar or some similar imperial nonsense. Doug McClure was a serviceable action hero who made a less-super but still plenty brave Innes (as well as Bowen Tyler in *The Land That Time Forgot* and *The People That Time Forgot*). Despite reports of his being difficult on the set due to personal problems, Caroline had nothing but good words for him and Peter Cushing: "There was Peter Cushing, Doug McClure and myself, and throughout the six weeks of the shoot, we worked solidly together ... became like the Three Musketeers, so that was fantastic" (*Caroline Munro: First Lady of Fantasy*). The character "Ja the Mesop" from the novel has been changed to "Ra" in the movie, and no mention is made that he is from another part of Pellucidar. It is in this part of the inner world that David first encounters Ja, saving him from an ichthyosaur-like sea monster; in the film, David saves him from a more cost-effective man-eating plant. The movie is more or less faithful to the major plot elements of the novel, delivered in a more linear manner than the original story, which has David Innes spending much more time among the flora and fauna of this strange land. The scene where the young women are sacrificed to the Mahars has been rendered less gruesome; in the film, they simply fly down, abduct them and carry them off; in the novel, the Mahars hypnotize the girls and then devour them one body part at a time. The film introduces a plot element not in the story: a river of lava which runs underneath the Mahar city which, if it is not kept under control, will destroy the city, which of course it does in the fiery finale. The character of Ghak is essentially unchanged from the novel, and his fur boots are filled admirably by Godfrey James, who had already appeared with McClure in *The Land That Time Forgot* (1969).

In the book, David takes Dian as his bride in the customary fashion of Pellucidar, there is a terrific battle with the Sagoths and Mahars, and then David and Abner make their plans to return to the surface, in order to accumulate enough modern technology to take back to the people of Pellucidar to help them defeat the Mahars. Dian is eager to make the trip to the surface, but her placement on the Iron Mole is left to the provinces

FILMS AND TELEVISION: *At the Earth's Core* (1976)

of Hoojah the Sly One, and he substitutes a Mahar for Dian, which David does not discover until they are on their way back. This only gives him more resolve to return, and in the finale, Burroughs himself helps Innes gather what he will need, but provides the hook for the sequel by saying that he doesn't know if Innes actually got started back, or whether he was murdered by desert marauders. In the movie, there is the terrific battle with the Sagoths and Mahars, and then the Mahars and their city are destroyed. Hoojah the Sly One gets eaten by a dinosaur. Then, as David and Abner prepare to make the journey back, Innes announces that he will take Dia as his bride and return to the surface. But Dia tearfully informs him that she must stay with her people, and David

Caroline strikes a pose on this French lobby card for *At the Earth's Core*.

and Abner make the trip themselves (with not so much as a hint that they'll return), and jokily come up through the White House lawn.

This was Caroline's only appearance for Amicus. *At the Earth's Core* was one of the very last gasps for the much-loved production company of Milton Subotsky and Max J. Rosenberg. The company that made its entrance proper into the genre with *Horror Hotel* (*City of the Dead*) and carried on with classics like *The Skull*, *The House That Dripped Blood*, and *Tales from the Crypt* to create an indelible legacy, put the finishing touches on that legacy with a pair of films based on works by Burroughs, *The Land That Time Forgot* and this film. (The sequel to *The Land That Time Forgot*, *The People That Time Forgot*, is officially a "Max J. Rosenberg Production.") *The Land That Time Forgot* had been the company's highest-grossing film to date, and *At the Earth's Core* would do even better: The last official Amicus Production was also its most financially successful ever.

The Howerd Confessions (television series, 1976; 6 episodes) Thames Television, Independent Television (ITV)

Episode # 2, September 9, 1976

Episode Crew: Producer/Director: Mike Mills; Writers: Peter Robinson, Hugh Stuckey; Production Design: Robin Parker; Composer/Theme Music: Peter Knight.

Episode Cast: Frankie Howerd (Frankie), Caroline Munro (Captain Latour), Alex Scott (Pierre), Hans Meyer (Lieutenant Gruber), Cyril Appleton (Sergeant), Mike Grady (Kaufman).

SYNOPSIS

From the UK's *TV Times*: "More comic confessions as Frankie reveals: 'My secret work with the French Resistance.... How I hood-winked the Germans.... How my George Formby impressions helped to win World War Two.'"

REVIEW AND NOTES

Courtesy of Paul Gooding:

Starring Frankie Howerd, an English comedian whose career spanned over six decades, *The Howerd Confessions* featured six playlets that were supposedly related to different episodes from his past.... Volume two features Howerd's unlikely exploits during the Second World War.

Finding himself a prisoner of war, having made his "daring escape" while being transported to Stalag Luft III — which entailed being thrown out of the truck by the guards who couldn't put up with his George Formby impersonation — Howerd finds himself in a French farmhouse occupied by members of the Resistance. Taken by the Resistance and first interrogated by Captain Latour to prove his veracity before they plan his return to England, the French make a speedy exit once the Germans appear, leaving him in the hands of the enemy. When British troops arrive the two sides argue over who is going to take responsibility for Private Howerd, with neither side wanting anything to do with him.

The Howerd Confessions [used Howard's] trademark double entendres and sexual innuendo, as well as addressing the studio audience and even stopping to jokingly berate them when one of the more dreadful puns didn't receive the laughter he thought it deserved. At the time Caroline said in the press: "It's the first time I have appeared in a television programme with a live audience and it was a marvellous experience for me."

The Spy Who Loved Me—1977, Danjaq/Eon Productions, United Artists

Crew: Producer: Albert R. Broccoli; Associate Producer: William P. Cartlidge; Director: Lewis Gilbert; Screenplay: Christopher Wood, Richard Maibaum; Suggested by the novel by Ian Fleming; Music: Marvin Hamlisch; Composer of James Bond Theme: Monty Norman; Photography: Claude Renoir; Film Editor: John Glen; Casting: Weston Drury Jr., Maude Spector; Production Design: Ken Adam; Art Director: Peter Lamont; Assistant Art Director: Ernie Archer; Set Decorator: Hugh Scaife; Makeup: Paul Engelen; Hairdresser: Barbara Ritchie; Production Manager: David Middlemas; Unit Manager: Stefan Zurcher; Assistant Director: Ariel Levy; Second Unit Assistant Director: Chris Kenny; Second Unit Directors: Ernest Day, John Glen; Second Assistant Directors: Terence Churcher, Michael Stevenson; Construction Manager: Michael Redding; Props: John Chisholm; Sound Recordist: Gordon Everett; Sound Re-Recording Mixers: Graham V. Hartstone, Nicolas Le Messurier; Dubbing Mixer: Gordon K. McCallum; Dubbing Editor: Allan Sones; Special Effects: John Gant; Special Optical Effects: Alan Maley; Special Visual Effects: Derek Meddings; Stunt Arranger: Bob Simmons; Stunt Performer (Ski Jump): Rick Sylvester; Ski Stunts: Stefan Zurcher; Stunt Skiers: John Eaves, Ed Lincoln, Jake Lombard; Stunt Driver: Jack Cooper; Stunt Pilot: Marc Wolff; Stunt Double for Barbara Bach: Dorothy Ford; Stunt Double for Richard Kiel and Roger Moore: Martin Grace; Stunt Double for Bryan Marshall: Terry Walsh; Stunts: Ray Alon, Marc Boyle, David Brandon, Tim Condren, Jack Cooper, Gerry Crampton, Bill Cummings, Clive Curtis, Jim Dowdall, Eddie Eddon, Dorothy Ford, Nick Gillard, Martin Grace, Richard Graydon, Fred Haggerty, Reg Harding, Nick Hobbs, Billy Horrigan, Jazzer Jeyes, George Leech, Jimmy Lodge, Terence Maidment, Mark McBride, Terence Plummer, Dinny Powell, Eddie Powell, Greg Powell, Nosher Powell, Doug Robinson, Roy Scammell, Ken Shepherd, Bob Simmons, Colin Skeeping, Tony Smart, Roy Street, Rocky Taylor, Terry Walsh, Chris Webb, Bill Weston, Paul Weston.

Cast: Roger Moore (James Bond), Barbara Bach (Major Anya Amasova), Curt Jurgens (Karl Stromberg), Richard Kiel ("Jaws"/Zbigniew Krycsiwiki), Caroline Munro (Naomi), Walter Gotell (General Anatol Gogol), Geoffrey Keen (Sir Frederick Gray), Bernard Lee ("M"), Lois Maxwell (Miss Moneypenny), Desmond Llewelyn ("Q"), George Baker (Captain Benson), Michael Billington (Sergei Barsov), Olga Bisera (Felicca), Edward De Souza (Sheikh Hosein), Vernon Dobtcheff (Max Kalba), Valerie Leon (Hotel Receptionist), Sidney Tafler (*Liparus* Captain), Lenny Rabin (*Liparus* Crewman), Nadim Sawalha (Aziz Fekkesh), Sue Vanner (Log Cabin Girl), Eva Reuber-Staier (Rubelvitch), Robert Brown (Admiral Hargreaves), Marilyn Galsworthy (Stromberg's Assistant), Milton Reid (Sandor), Cyril Shaps (Dr. Bechmann), Milo

Sperber (Professor Markovitz), Albert Moses (Barman), Rafig Anwar (Cairo Club Waiter), Shane Rimmer (Commander Carter), Bryan Marshall (Commander Talbot), George Roubichek (Stromberg One Captain); Felicity York, Dawn Rodrigues, Anika Pavel, Jill Goodall (Arab Beauties); Bob Sherman, Doyle Richmond, Murray Salem, John Truscott, Peter Whitman, Ray Hassett, Vincent Marzello, Nicholas Campbell, Ray Evans, Anthony Forrest, Garrick Hagon, Ray Jewers, George Mallaby, Christopher Muncke, Anthony Pullen Shaw, Robert Sheedy, Don Staiton, Eric Stine, Stephen Temperley, Dean Warwick (USS *Wayne* Crewmen); Michael Howarth, Kim Fortune, Barry Andrews, Kevin McNally, Jeremy Bulloch, Sean Bury, John Sarbutt, David Auker, Dennis Blanch, Keith Buckley, Jonathan Bury, Nick Ellsworth, Tom Gerrard, Kazik Michalski, Keith Morris, John Salthouse (HMS *Ranger* Crewmen); Irvin Allen, Yasher Adem, Peter Ensor (Stromberg One Crewmen), Roy Alon (Russian Sub Crewman), Paul Bannon (Submariner), Jack Cooper (Cortina Gunman #1), George Leech (Cortina Gunman #2), Ralph Morse (Skier), Chris Webb (KGB Thug #1), Bob Simmons (KGB Thug #2), Victor Tourjansky (Man with Bottle), Jeremy Wilkin (Captain Forsyth), Michael G. Wilson (Man in Audience at Pyramid Theatre).

SYNOPSIS

One of Her Majesty's atomic submarines goes missing. One of Mother Russia's atomic submarines goes missing. The KGB puts their best agent, Major Anya Amasova (Barbara Bach), on the case, and Britain does the same with their agent James Bond (Roger Moore). But first Bond must elude and kill a group of Russian agents in a furious ski-chase. One of the men kills is Anya's lover. Anya vows to get revenge on the person responsible.

Both head to Egypt, where each hopes to obtain the plans for a submarine tracking system, which are on microfilm. They were stolen from Karl Stromberg (Curt Jurgens), one of the richest men in the world, who sends his henchmen Sandor (Milton Reid) and Jaws (Richard Kiel) to get them back.

Sandor tries to kill Bond, but Bond kills him instead. Jaws kills Bond's contact and disappears. Amasova has Bond attacked, but he fends off her thugs. They later meet again when both appear at the same club to bid on the microfilm; both know who the other is. But before either one can obtain the microfilm, Jaws kills the man holding it and takes it for Stromberg.

Anya and Bond trail Jaws and obtain the microfilm after a furious fight. Anya escapes with the microfilm when she knocks out Bond with a trick cigarette. They meet again when they discover their governments are working together. They travel to Sardinia to investigate Stromberg, but their journey is interrupted by Jaws, whom Bond kicks out a train window after another furious fight.

In Sardinia, "Q" delivers a specially equipped Lotus to Bond. and Anya and Bond pose as husband-and-wife marine biologists in order to infiltrate Stromberg's massive sea-station. They are met by the beautiful Naomi (Caroline Munro), who takes them to meet Stromberg. But Stromberg knows who they are, and orders Jaws to kill them as soon as they reach shore. After various skirmishes, Bond and Anya think they are in the clear when they are strafed by a helicopter piloted by Naomi, who winks at Bond

FILMS AND TELEVISION: *The Spy Who Loved Me* (1977)

The Japanese poster for *The Spy Who Loved Me* features Caroline.

Films and Television: *The Spy Who Loved Me* (1977)

The six actresses featured as Bond girls in *The Spy Who Loved Me*, clockwise from upper right: Caroline Munro, Dawn Rodrigues, Felicity York, Anika Pavel, Valerie Leon, and Sue Vanner.

when she flies past. She forces them off a dock and into the sea, but the Lotus converts into a mini-sub, from which Bond fires missiles that blow up the copter.

Anya discovers that Bond is the one who killed her lover, and vows to kill him when the mission is completed. They board a US Navy atomic submarine, and soon discover how the others disappeared: They were swallowed up by Stromberg's supertanker, the *Liparus*, and they become its next captives!

FILMS AND TELEVISION: *The Spy Who Loved Me* (1977)

Bond and Anya are discovered, and after they engage in a fight with his guards, Stromberg reveals his plan: He will fire nuclear missiles at New York and Moscow, and after the surface world has destroyed itself, he will be the master in a new world and era under the sea.

Stromberg has two of the captured submarines armed with the warheads and sets the plan into motion. He then exits the tanker and takes Anya with him to his sea-station. Bond frees the submarine crew member, many of whom die in an epic, battle with Stromberg's private army. Stromberg's computers are re-programmed so that the submarines fire their missiles at each other.

Bond must save Anya before the sea-station is blown up. He races there on a jet-ski. He kills Stromberg and has another fight with Jaws, who gets dropped in a shark tank — and kills the shark! Bond and Anya escape, and then Anya says the mission is completed. She points her gun at Bond. Does she keep her vow?

REVIEW AND NOTES

Contemporary review: David C. Chute wrote in *Movietone News* #55 (September 1977), "The sheer physical scale of *The Spy Who Loved Me* is so huge, and Moore such a puny personality, that he just about disappears.... [It's] big and safe, like every other big picture we see. The commercial genius of the early Bonds was that they were lavish and expensive without being stuffy; they juggled and danced with their hardware, and Connery held things together. In *The Spy Who Loved Me*, Bond becomes a laborious, respectable bore."

As Ian Fleming–James Bond fans are too well aware, the connection between the original novels and the films bearing the same name can often be called tenuous at best, and at times, non-existent. This *can* be a blessing, and nowhere is this more the case than the difference between the literary and celluloid versions of *The Spy Who Loved Me*. To quote Simon Winder, in his brilliant *The Man Who Saved Britain*:

> We can argue almost indefinitely about which Bond film is the worst — but in the end it is an argument that sullies us all. With the books, though, it is easy: *The Spy Who Loved Me* (1962) is dreadful. *The Man with the Golden Gun* (1965) is not very good; a sad work by a dying writer, but *The Spy Who Loved Me* is a potent weapon in the hands of those who claim that Fleming was in practice just a terrible novelist, written when Fleming was in reasonable health and no excuses could be made.... The chief offenses of this novel are two: that it has no ambition for Bond (he simply encounters and kills two small-time hoodlums in a Vermont hotel), and that it has the deranged ambition for Fleming ... of writing a novel as a first-person female narrative. It is a surreal performance, even crowding out the fact that the book must be seen as offensive to even the most brutalized and reactionary male reader ("the sweet tang of rape").

Well, obviously, the producers weren't having any of that, so in its place, we get yet another chapter in the continuing devolution of the Bond character and the Bond films themselves, with Bond as a daring light comedian and the films nothing more than a string of spectacular set pieces set in picturesque foreign lands. The villains, in particular, increasingly lost their stature, a critical element in the decline. While their plans still threatened the world as we know it, none of them, with the exception of Christopher Lee, looked or acted as if they had what it takes to pull it off. This malaise especially applies to the villains' henchmen. Whereas in previous films, most had been both strange and menacing (Red Grant, Rosa Klebb, and Oddjob, for example), now they trended towards a sort of funny-peculiar and as likely to be the butt of jokes as trying to kick or kill Bond's butt. The most ludicrous example of this, of course, is Nick-Nack from *Man with the Golden Gun*, but despite his menacing stature, Richard Kiel as "Jaws" is not far behind. His name alone signifies that; it's the type of joke which is not really that funny to begin with, and becomes less so with repetition — but at least trying to cash in on the success of an American blockbuster was limited to a character name, unlike the entire next movie, the *Star Wars*–inspired, *Moonraker*, which also featured Jaws. To be fair, it is obviously a showy, plum role within the film itself, and Kiel certainly makes the most of the opportunity; in truth, he is to this day one of the most popular supporting characters in the whole Bond film series. And actually, he is one of the few elements in the film that was directly inspired by Fleming: In the novel *The Spy Who Loved Me*, one of the small-time hoodlums is a charmer named "Horror," who has steel-capped teeth. But he is played as a character of straight menace, as opposed to his screen descendent (who was originally supposed to be played the same way).

A smaller, but just as showy a part, is Caroline's turn as the beautiful yet lethal Naomi, whose wink at Bond right before he blows her helicopter out of the sky may be her defining screen moment. She remains one of the most popular Bond Girls in the whole series. Caroline likes to think Naomi may not have gone up in a great ball of fire, as she revealed in an interview done as an extra for the *Flesh for the Beast* DVD: "Death scenes? Well, I suppose my most explosive would have to be in *The Spy Who Loved Me* ... but I might have had a parachute; I always think in the back of my mind I must have had a parachute, because she was too smart not to have been able to get out.... [Y]ou saw the explosion, but I think she hopped it before." The same cannot be said for Curt Jurgens, whose Stromberg is one of the foremost examples of the decline in the Bond villains' stature. A leisure-suited, would-be Captain Nemo, Jurgens is so laconic that one often wonders if he's going to nod off before he finishes his sentence. He has webbed fingers, but nothing is ever made of this fact, even when Naomi tells Bond that Stromberg does not like to shake hands. The producers also looked to a couple of other blockbusters as sources for humor, in both cases musical: In the film's beginning, when Amasova is in bed with her lover, his call to action comes on a music box that plays a snatch of "Lara's Theme" from *Dr. Zhivago*, and when she and Bond have to trek through the desert after their escape van breaks down, they do so to a few bars from *Lawrence of Arabia*.

Naomi is this film's "sacrificial lamb." Every Bond film has "at least one or two," as John Brosnan notes in *James Bond in the Cinema*: Quarrel in *Dr. No*, Kerim Bey in

FILMS AND TELEVISION: *The Spy Who Loved Me* (1977)

From Russia with Love, the Masterson sisters in *Goldfinger*, Paula in *Thunderball* and Aki in *You Only Live Twice*, to name just a few. More often than not, they are female, a point which only seems to reinforce the Bond films' attitudes towards women, and usually they are fellow agents, but I believe Naomi qualifies in this instance; not only is she, like the others, a likable character and one who is only doing her job. It also perhaps goes without saying that she would have been much more suited to the lead role than Barbara Bach, a woman of no fixed acting ability. This was especially apparent in their scenes together, as Bach had neither Caroline's beauty nor charm nor warmth, much less acting chops. If only their roles had been reversed, then fans would have had a lot more to remember than just Bond's silly Union Jack parachute and "The Wink." The bigger pity was the series' increasing reliance on the recycling of elements from earlier films. One can readily check off the influences: A super-villain plans to launch nuclear missiles against both American and Russian cities (*Thunderball* and *Diamonds Are Forever*). There's a ski chase (*On Her Majesty's Secret Service*), and a gadget-filled car (*Goldfinger*), and a sexy female pilot (*Goldfinger* again), and a big underwater battle (*Thunderball* again) and a beautiful Russian spy (*From Russia with Love*), and a fight on a train (*From Russia with Love* again, not to mention *Live and Let Die*). But the

Barbara Bach (left), Caroline and Roger Moore in *The Spy Who Loved Me*.

movie most plundered was *You Only Live Twice*. Instead of a super-sized spaceship swallowing up other spaceships, we now had a super-sized tanker swallowing up atomic submarines. There's a motorcycle chase, just like *You Only Live Twice*, and Marilyn Galsworthy's slide into Stromberg's shark tank recalls Helga's plunge into Blofeld's piranha pool. In both films, steel shutters the control rooms, and even the dialogue is practically the same: "The operations room is impregnable," as opposed to Blofeld's "Now we are impregnable."

Caroline was in two Bond movies, as was fellow Hammer alumnus Valerie Leon whose second turn was in Sean Connery's return to the Bond role in *Never Say Never Again* (1983). In *Spy*, Leon gets a nice little scene, although entirely too reminiscent of her function in the *Carry On* films, where she, as the hotel receptionist, appears at Bond's door in an eye-popping low-cut gown and announces, "I have a message for you," to which Bond replies, "I think you've just delivered it." Unfortunately for Caroline, her membership in the "Bond Girlx2" Club came at the expense of another role that of the evil Ursa in *Superman* (a part eventually taken by Sarah Douglas). At this time, she also turned down the chance to play opposite Faye Dunaway and Sir John Gielgud in *The Wicked Lady*, due to the fact that there was a nude love scene. That role was eventually played by Glynis Barber with the aid of a nude body double. "I didn't fancy the nudity," Caroline said in *Fangoria*. "Had it not been for that, I *would* have done *The Wicked Lady*. I didn't ask for a body double, because I thought that would have defeated the purpose — people would still have thought they were seeing *me* nude. It's not that I'm ashamed of my body. It's OK; I just don't want to show it all." Another thing she didn't show, in *The Spy Who Loved Me*, was her extreme discomfort in the scene when Naomi first encounters Bond and Anya. When she got into the speedboat, she sat on a bee which duly stung her bottom. Trouper that she is, she carried on, which accounts for her intense gaze during the scene.

The New Avengers (television series, 1976–77; 26 episodes) The Avengers Enterprises, IDTV Production, TF1, TV Productions

"Angels of Death" (Season 2, Episode 2; September 15, 1977)
Episode Crew: Producers: Brian Clemens, Albert Fennell; Associate Producer: Ron Fry; Director: Ernest Day; Writers: Brian Clemens, Terence Feely; Characters: Sydney Newman; Music: Laurie Johnson; Lighting Cameramen: Jack Atcheler, Ernie Steward; Film Editor: Alan Killick; Casting: Maggie Cartier; Production Design: Keith Wilson; Makeup: Alan Boyle, Alan Brownie; Hair Stylist: Mark Nelson; Post-Production Supervisor: Paul Clay; Unit Manager: David Munro; Assistant Director: Art Burgess; Assistant Art Director: Michael Ford; Construction Manager: Bill Waldron; Sound Recordists: Ken Barker, Paul Le Mare; Dubbing Editors: Mike Hopkins, Peter Lennard; Fight Arranger: Joe Dunne; Camera Oper-

FILMS AND TELEVISION: *The New Avengers* (1976–77)

ator: Malcolm Vinson; Wardrobe Supervisor: Maggie Lewin; Wardrobe for Joanna Lumley: Betty Jackson, Jilly Murphy; Continuity: Cheryl Leigh.

Episode Cast: Patrick Macnee (John Steed), Joanna Lumley (Purdey), Gareth Hunt (Mike Gambit), Dinsdale Landen (Coldstream), Terence Alexander (Manderson), Caroline Munro (Tammy), Michael Latimer (Reresby), Richard Gale (Pelbright), Lindsay Duncan (Jane), Pamela Stephenson (Wendy), Annette Lynton (Pam), Moira Foot (Cindy), Christopher Driscoll (Martin), Melissa Stribling (Sally Manderson), Anthony Bailey (Simon Carter), Hedger Wallace (Colonel Tomson), Jenny Goossens (Mrs. Pelbright).

SYNOPSIS

The Briantern Health Farm is anything but healthy! Steed, Purdey and Gambit uncover a plot to eliminate key personnel in vital areas of government and security, which involves a visit to Briantern and "special sessions" with Nurse Tammy and her Angels of Death, a bevy of buxom beauties.

REVIEW AND NOTES

The still popular *Avengers* television series began in 1961, and the original run of episodes lasted until 1969. In the beginning, the series chronicled the adventures of Dr. David Keel (Ian Hendry), seeking to avenge the murder of his fiancée, and John Steed (Patrick Macnee). When Hendry left the show, Macnee became the star and Steed the lead character. It was then the show settled into the format familiar to most viewers, that of Steed being paired with an action-ready female assistant. The series, which preceded James Bond (as a film series) by a year, featured some future Bond Girls: Honor Blackman, who was Steed's third partner Dr. Cathy Gale, left the series to portray Pussy Galore in *Goldfinger*; Steed's fourth and most famous partner, the legendary Emma Peel, was Diana Rigg, who played the doomed Tracey in *On Her Majesty's Secret Service*. That film featured Joanna Lumley, who would go on to play Purdey in this series, and this episode starred Caroline, who had just completed her turn in *The Spy Who Loved Me*. The series, shown all over the world, became known for its style and wit, eccentric characters, and far-out, heavily parodic, sometimes surreal stories, some of which guest-starred Hammer stalwarts Peter Cushing ("Return of the Cybernauts") and Christopher Lee ("The Interrogators" and "Never, Never Say Die").

Steed's fifth partner was Tara King, played by Linda Thorson. The popularity of the Tara King episodes in France led to a Macnee-Thorson reunion in a French champagne television ad, which in turn led to French financing interest in new episodes, which in turn led to *The New Avengers*. This time, the physical action was split between two assistants: one male, Mike Gambit (Gareth Hunt), and Purdey, essayed by Joanna Lumley, whose scenes had been cut from *Dr. Phibes*. But despite the urbane presence of Macnee and creative forces like Brian Clemens, Laurie Johnson, Robert Fuest (*Dr. Phibes* and *Dr. Phibes Rises Again*), and production designer Syd Cain (who performed the same duties for *On Her Majesty's Secret Service*, and had been art director for *Dr. No*, *From Russia with Love*, and supervising art director on *Live and Let Die*), the series

73

only lasted for 26 episodes. Fortunately, it lasted long enough to include Caroline in an episode.

In "Angels of Death," Caroline plays Tammy, the head nurse at a health farm of horrors, whose method of death-by-stress is caused by dancing with beautiful girls like Caroline all night and then being trapped like a rat in a maze. There are few better at the Hippy-Hippy Shake than Caroline, and she takes equal glee in manipulating the maze to frustrate the inhabitants. Her best moment, though, comes in a knock-down drag-out fight with Purdey, who emerges victorious because she's the star.

Starcrash (a.k.a. *The Adventures of Stella Star*; a.k.a. *Female Space Invaders*) — 1978, New World Pictures

Crew: Producers: Nat Wachsberger, Patrick Wachsberger; Director: Luigi Cozzi (as Lewis Coates); Screenplay: Luigi Cozzi (as Lewis Coates), Nat Wachsberger; Additional Dialogue: R. A. Dillon; Music Composer-Conductor-Arranger: John Barry; Photography: Paul Beeson, Roberto D'Ettorre Piazzoli (as Roberto D'Ettorre); Film Editor: Sergio Montanari; Production Designer: Aurelio Crugnola; Key Hair Stylist: Giancarlo De Leonardis; Production Supervisor: Luigi Nannerini; Assistant Director: Goffredo Unger; Set Designer: Maria-Teresa Barbasso; Sound Effects: Massimo Anzelotti; Dialogue Editor: Stephen Bushelman; Sound Re-Recording Mixers: Donald O. Mitchell, Tex Rudloff, Howard S. Wollman; Special Effects Directors: Germano Natali, Armando Valcauda; Special Effects: Matteo Verzini; Electronic Visual Effects Supervisor: Ron Hays; Model Maker: Paolo Zeccarra; Stunts: Ottaviano Dell'Acqua; Stunt Coordinator: Goffredo Unger; Assistant Camera: Fabrizio Vicari; Second Assistant Camera: Massimo Pau; Supervising Music Editor: Kenneth Hall; Dialogue Director: Joe Spinell; Dialogue Supervisor: Beatrice M. Thomas.

Cast: Caroline Munro (Stella Star), Marjoe Gortner (Akton), Christopher Plummer (The Emperor), David Hasselhoff (Simon), Robert Tessier (Thor), Joe Spinell (Count Zarth Arn), Nadia Cassini (Corelia, Queen of the Amazons), Judd Hamilton (Elle), Salvatore Baccaro (Neanderthal Man), Dirce Finari, Cindy Leadbetter (Amazon Women), Donald Hodson (Prisoner).

SYNOPSIS

From original pressbook:

The universe is in the grip of darkness, under the evil eye of Count Zarth Arn (Joe Spinell). Hidden deep within his damnable fortress, he seeks to destroy the good Emperor (Christopher Plummer) and his kingdom. Imperial battleships have already been lost or destroyed in the effort to explore the Count's haunted planet; therefore, the Emperor calls the best pilot in the galaxy, the saucy and irrepressible Stella Star (Caroline Munro), and her mysterious alien navigator, Akton (Marjoe Gortner), to find the Count's secret lair and destroy it. Stella and Akton are happy to oblige since they've been serving jail sentences for some smuggling shenanigans. Aided by one of the Emperor's loyal robots, Elle (Judd Hamilton), the motley threesome journeys to the haunted stars — dwelling space of the wicked Count.

FILMS AND TELEVISION: *Starcrash* (1978)

In a series of harrowing adventures, Stella and Elle run into war-mongering Amazons, are abandoned on a frozen planet by the treacherous police chief Thor (Robert Tessier), and rescued by Akton, who destroys the treacherous space cop. Later on, lovely Stella is kidnapped by some hulking prehistoric cavemen. Saved by a stranger firing laser beams from the eyes of his energy mask, Stella soon learns that he is the Emperor's lost son, Simon (David Hasselhoff). In yet another attack, Simon loses his shield mask, and the troglodytes close in for the kill. Akton the Alien ruins their primitive plans, scorching the cave and its prehistoric occupants with his sizzling laser sword.

Akton, with his mysterious powers, uncovers the control room that activates the Count's secret weapon, and as he and his comrades are about to destroy it the cruel Zarth Am intrudes. The Count leaves them in the hands of two killer robots while setting nuclear charges to destroy the planet. Noble Akton duels the robots to the death and suffers a mortal wound in the process; but his courage at least allows his friends to be rescued by the Emperor just before the planet explodes.

Having the Emperor in his web, the Count decides to launch a massive Zykoenian warhead (which he fiendishly dubs "The Doom Machine") directly at the Emperor's kingdom. Only one course of action remains: "The Floating City," a colossal craft intended for the future of his kingdom, is to serve as the Emperor's cosmic trump — *if* it can be slammed full-speed into the Count's deadly fortress. But *who* can be expected to pilot the monster ship on its death course? None other than fearless Stella herself! Taking a shuttlecraft to the cockpit of "The Floating City," she prepares herself for the most death-defying flight of her star-trekking life — STARCRASH!

Caroline gets ready for trouble in this publicity photograph from *Starcrash* (courtesy Paul C. Riggie).

REVIEW AND NOTES

In the wake of the success of *Famous Monsters of Filmland* magazine, the newsstands were flooded with imitations such as *World Famous Creatures*. History repeated itself in the wake of the success of *Star Wars*: The newsstands were flooded with a brand new wave of magazines, with blatantly derivative titles like *Star Warp, Star Encounters, Star Force, Star Battles, Super Star Heroes, Space Wars, Space Trek,* and *Space Monsters; Famous Monsters* publisher James Warren got into the act with *Creepy* and *Eerie* reprints repackaged as *Star Quest Comix, Galactic War Comix,* and *Empire Encounters* (as part of the *Warren Presents* series). And soon both small and large screens were awash with space junk, like *Battlestar Galactica, Laserblast, Buck Rogers in the 25th Century,* and *Flash Gordon.* One of the brightest-burning chunks of this cosmic debris was *Starcrash.*

Most of these space operas were content to mine *Star Wars,* but *Starcrash* cheerfully steals not just from *Star Wars* (Light Sabers, Hyper-Space effects, "Emperor" this and "Imperial" that, a cosmos packed with every last bit of stock from the local modelers' shop), but from a whole star system of classics such as *Invaders from Mars* (the intergalactic judge who sentences Stella to hard labor is a direct steal from the Martian Intelligence in that film), *Jason and the Argonauts* (a Talos-like metal giant — with nipples — and sword-wielding, skeleton-like robots), *2001—A Space Odyssey* (spaceships the size of every NFL stadium strung together), *Planet of the Apes* (beach scene with wreckage looming in the foreground), *Forbidden Planet* (Krell-like banks of machinery that pro-

Caroline and Judd Hamilton in *Starcrash*.

duce monsters of the id), and *Barbarella* (see below). Another possible influence, rarely if ever cited, was a 20-page comic story that appeared in the 1975 independent pro/am graphic 'zine *Star*Reach* No. 2, featuring the adventures of Stephanie Starr, a sexy outer space outlaw, more than competent in hand-to-hand combat or spacecraft-piloting, produced by Mike Friedrich and Dick Giordano (with a nifty cover by Neal Adams). Tim Moriarty reported in *Famous Monsters* No. 182: "Caroline is disappointed that *Starcrash* is not the film it could have been. Due to budget difficulties, some of the special effects were rushed or eliminated. Daily script rewrites damaged the story. Delays and confusion prolonged the shoot to a full three months. Her own voice was not heard on the soundtrack; she was never asked to dub it." Candy Clark, from *American Graffiti* and *Q*, was asked, and said yes. Caroline was none too pleased about this turn of events: "To take away your voice is like taking away half your performance," she lamented in *First Lady of Fantasy*. At first, she had been told that her own voice and British accent was perfectly acceptable and would be used:

> I worked for up to six months on that film ... [and] the promise was that we were going to fly out to California and I was going to dub the film, and I thought, "Wonderful," and I didn't hear and I didn't hear.... So finally we called them up and said "When is the dubbing?" and they said, "Oh, sorry, dubbing's already been done" ... "How could it have been done? I haven't done it; have you used the direct sound?" And they said, "No, sorry, didn't use the direct sound, we've actually dubbed it with someone over here," and I felt so hurt; I was completely devastated.

Most annoying is the interstellar overdrive of the by-now obligatory comedy-relief robot, Elle. Of course, the trend could be traced back much further than *Star Wars*, starting with Robby from the aforementioned *Forbidden Planet* and continued by B-9 from *Lost in Space*, but those characters were far more than mere comedic relief. Plus they spoke in well-modulated, robotic (yet distinctive) tones. But with the advent of C3PO, the genre became awash in robots with ridiculous accents silly dialogue. Elle gets the bulk of the avalanche of risible dialogue: "I haven't been programmed to walk on water"; "You can't keep a good robot down"; "I feel like a new machine." But poor dialogue was by no means limited to the robot. Christopher Plummer's discomfort is all too palpable, and entirely understandable with speeches like, "Well, it's done. It's happened. The stars are clear. The planets shine. We've won. Oh, some dark force, no doubt, will show its face once more. The wheel will always turn. But for now, it's calm. And for a little time, at least, we can rest." For an emperor, his "please either save me or kill me now" look is most inappropriate.

Caroline is entirely appropriate, in the lead role as a character who deserved to have several sequels to her name. Of course, Stella Star (wonderful name, that) has her share of dreadful lines like, "I can't leave you; you're the only human-like friend I've ever had." But she survives with dignity and grace intact, which can't be said for most of her co-stars. The *Barbarella* influence is obvious, but on the whole, Stella Star is actually a much more competent character, "the best star-pilot in the galaxy" and much more capable in action scenes, which are actually action scenes and not parodies of action scenes such as were contained in *Barbarella*. This is not to slag off *Barbarella*, just to point out the difference; *Barbarella* was a hip spoof of comic book and sci-fi clichés, whereas *Starcrash* is more like the comic books themselves. But the connection is certainly there, and just to make sure it connects, Stella, like Barbarella, faces off against a dark-haired alien queen, played by Nadia Cassini.

In her skimpy space bikini, Caroline also brings to mind another "-ella"—Vampirella. (Caroline had been offered the role of Vampirella when it was supposed to have been a Hammer production, but because it would have required nudity, she turned it down.) Caroline's a more-than-adequate action heroine, and she revels in the fact that, for once, she's not playing the victim or a simple damsel in distress or mere ornament. In fact, her enthusiasm got her a bit carried away, as she recounted in *Famous Monsters*: "One or two persons did get bashed about, I'm sorry to say. I bloodied somebody's nose and set his teeth wobbling a bit. He looked so surprised when it happened! I burst into tears." In the same issue, she talked about plans for a sequel to the movie; she and Judd Hamilton wrote a script with the working title *Star Patrol*, and it was reported that they would be employing a new type of special effects process that would "achieve the same quality as the blue screen process," but would be "quicker and less expensive." She added, "There are no stop-motion effects called for, but that doesn't mean there won't be any." The sequel never came to fruition.

Unfortunately, not all of Caroline's fellow cast members are up to the task as she is. Christopher Plummer, despite his silly costume and leaden dialogue, is still Christopher Plummer, and therefore adds a touch of class to the proceedings, whether he wants to or not, and Joe Spinell, who would later "cut a rug" with Caroline in *Maniac* and *The Last Horror Film*, gives an enjoyably hammy performance as the Ming–Darth Vader substitute, Count Zarth Arn. And Robert Tessier (*Doc Savage: The Man of Bronze*, *Hard Times*) is always welcome. But poodle-permed Marjoe Gortner and a young David Hasselhoff, looking like a deer caught in the headlights, are about as useful as a screen door in a submarine. Gortner was a former child evangelist who was later the subject of an Oscar-winning documentary (*Marjoe*) about how he was fleecing his audiences. He is best remembered today for getting to participate in Lynda Carter's only nude scene (in *Bobbie Jo and the Outlaw*). David Hasselhoff, with a huge pudding bowl of blow-dried hair, is basically playing the Princess Leia part, and he's not as tough as Princess Leia or Stella Star.

The sets, a sort of cross between *Barbarella* and *2001*, are great, and the music is by *the* John Barry, and although it's nowhere near as wonderful as his Bond scores, he too adds some gravitas. (The pressbook calls it "an uncompromising work of art.") The model work, of which there is plenty, would have been fine if the space vehicles had been left in long shots or medium shots, but once the camera zooms in for a close-up, it reveals that details have been achieved by using the left-over parts "trees" as accessories! But at least one of these kitchen-sink space buggies gets a good joke in: The first craft

FILMS AND TELEVISION: *Maniac* (1980)

Caroline's back in another lobby card from *Starcrash*, this one also featuring (from left) Judd Hamilton as Elle, Christopher Plummer, Marjoe Gortner and Robert Tessier.

we see is called the *Murray Leinster*. On the plus side of the special effects, *Starcrash* gets credit for using stop-motion animation. It's a bit herky-jerky but at least they made the effort, instead of using men in suits. But, good or bad, and despite the numerous problems in achieving the result, the result is there, and what shows up on screen is as free of pretension as its major inspiration is full of it. And to dismiss it merely as a "third-rate rip-off" of *Star Wars* does it a small disservice because, whatever the motivation was in its making, the term implies that *Star Wars* was that original to begin with, when, like *Starcrash*, it was nothing more or less than an entertaining sum of its influences.

Maniac—1980, Magnum Motion Pictures, Inc.

Crew: Executive Producers: Judd Hamilton, Joe Spinell; Producers: Andrew Garroni, William Lustig; Associate Producer: John Packard; Director: William Lustig; Screenplay: C.A. Rosenberg, Joe Spinell; Story: Joe Spinell; Music: Jay Chattaway; Photography: Robert Lindsay; Film Editor: Larry "Lorenzo" Marinelli; Makeup-Wardrobe: Candace Clements; Makeup Effects: Rob Bottin; Special Makeup and Effects: Tom Savini; Unit Production Manager: Andrew Garroni; First Assistant Director: Stephen Andrew; Second Assistant Directors: William Adams III, Nelia Bacmeister; Carpenters: Richard Behrens, Tom Costabile; Property Masters: Gary Martin, Nick Ward; Scenic Artist: Marla Schweppe; Assistant Sound Editor:

Films and Television: *Maniac* (1980)

Clint Elliot; Sound Effects: Sandy Rackow; Sound Mixer: Gary Rich; Sound Editor: Emo Sephy; Camera Operator: Robert Lindsay; Assistant Camera: James Canatta.

Cast: Joe Spinell (Frank Zito), Caroline Munro (Anna D'Antoni), Abigail "Gail Lawrence" Clayton (Rita), Kelly Piper (Nurse), Rita Montone (Hooker), Tom Savini (Disco Boy), Hyla Marrow (Disco Girl), James Brewster (Beach Boy), Linda Lee Walter (Beach Girl), Tracie Evans (Street Hooker), Sharon Mitchell (Second Nurse), Carol Henry (Deadbeat), Nelia Bacmeister (Carmen Zito), Louis Jawitz (Art Director), Denise Spagnuolo (Denise), Kim Hudson (Lobby Hooker), Terry Gagnon (Woman in Lobby), Joan Baldwin (First Model), Jeni Paz (Second Model), Janelle Winston (Waitress), Randy Jurgensen (First Cop), Jimmy Aurichio (Second Cop), Andrew Garroni (Jerry), William Lustig (Al the Hotel Manager).

Synopsis

A couple snuggles under a blanket at the beach. The beach boy goes to get firewood, and while he's gone, the beach girl's throat is cut. When the boy returns, he suffers the same gruesome fate.

Frank Zito (Joe Spinell) is a New York landlord whose tenants are severely neglected, as he is always too busy with his other line of work as a serial killer. Frank's mother was an abusive prostitute who was killed in a car accident, and now he keeps her memory alive by murdering pretty young women, scalping them, and putting the scalps on the collection of mannequins in his apartment.

Two hookers stand on a street corner; one of them propositions Frank. She's turned her last trick: Frank takes her to a motel room, strangles her, and scalps her.

Frank puts his gun in a violin case and follows a man and woman leaving a posh restaurant. They begin to have sex in their car, and their lovemaking reaches an ultra-violent climax when Frank blows their heads off. The next day, Frank spots photographer Anna D'Antoni (Caroline Munro) taking pictures in the park, and learns her name from a tag on her bag. That night, he follows a nurse into the subway, where he stabs her and scalps her. He then tracks down Anna, who goes out on a date with him.

At Anna's next shoot, she introduces Frank to her friend Rita. Frank steals Rita's necklace and, under the pretense of returning the "missing" object to her, kidnaps her, ties her up, stabs her and scalps her.

Frank picks up Anna in his car; she kisses him in gratitude for sending flowers to Rita's funeral. He asks her to stop by the graveyard with him so he can pay his respects to his mother, but while they are kneeling by her graveside, he quickly begins to lose his grip and Anna realizes he is the murderer. He chases her through the graveyard until she hits him with a shovel and escapes. In his delusional state, he returns to his mother's grave, where he imagines she rises up to strangle him.

Frank returns to his apartment, where the mannequins come to life as his victims and dismember him. Is it real, or another state of his shattered mind?

Review and Notes

"Disgusting ... in fact, really evil." "A lip-smacking relish for mutilated corpses ... alternates with gratuitous examples of sadism and lust." "Monstrous." "Loathsome."

One-sheet poster art for *Maniac.*

"Preoccupation with horror and gruesome detail." "Degrading." "The atmosphere of butchery pervades all." "Preparing Tete de Veau Vinaigrette from a live calf on TV could hardly be more explicit." "Depressing and degrading for anyone who loves the cinema."

Contemporary reviews for *Maniac*, right? Actually, these were all terms used at various points to describe *The Curse of Frankenstein*—from 1957. Similar words and phrases were used to describe *Maniac*: Gene Siskel said, "If *Maniac* doesn't deserve to be rated 'X' for violence, no film does," and the *Hollywood Sun*'s Chuck McCartney wrote, "*Maniac* makes you feel dirty after viewing it"—both of which, of course, became badges of honor proudly displayed on a version of the poster. This is certainly not to imply that *Maniac* is on a level with *The Curse of Frankenstein*, because it isn't; it's more to imply that reactions to certain films may simply be generational.

One could argue that the entire history of humankind has simply been a history of either large or small acts of murder, bloodshed and gore, starting with Cain and Abel. Our fascination with these acts and the motives behind them is just as old, and murder, bloodshed and gore have provided grist for entertainment for as long as there have been people to be entertained. Many "gorehounds" (fans of gory horror flicks) consider the terms "slasher" and "splatter" to be interchangeable, although aficionados will claim that each term has its own rules of engagement: Slasher films involve a deranged killer tracking down a set of victims and murdering them in acts of graphic violence, generally with a knife, while splatter films deliberately focus on deranged killers murdering victims with acts of graphic violence. This seems like splitting hairs— or scalps. *Maniac* contains heavy doses of both, which, one supposes, would make it a "splasher." It's mostly the former, in that the deranged killer dispatches most of his victims with a knife, but the shotgun-to-the-face and dismemberment scenes also qualify it for the latter. But it basically follows all the other conventions of the slasher film, including the already-tired device of the killer who may not be dead at the end after all, which ultimately wastes any potential frisson or realism created by Spinell's twisted portrayal.

One connection between Hitchcock's *Psycho* and *Maniac*, besides the theme and like titles, were their main inspiration: Ed Gein. Other films based on Gein's heinous crimes include Jeff Gillen and Alan Ormsby's *Deranged* (1974), *The Texas Chain Saw Massacre* (1974), *Silence of the Lambs* (1991), and *Ed Gein* (2001). *Ed Gein* and *Deranged* are the closest to the facts; according to Joe Bob Briggs in *Profoundly Disturbing* (Universe, 2003): "The least faithful, but one of the most entertaining, is William Lustig's *Maniac*, starring Joe Spinell as the fat, balding New York psycho who scalps women, then uses them to dress the family of mannequins he lives with in his claustrophobic apartment." Some of the murder methods also seem to have been taken from real-life killings in the Son of Sam case.

Maniac contains a compelling, tour-de-force performance from great character actor Spinell, who got his professional start in *The Godfather* and made his name with

Films and Television: *Maniac* (1980)

Caroline is set to snap in *Maniac*.

appearances in, among others, the first sequel to that movie, as well as the first two *Rocky* movies and *Taxi Driver*. It has been suggested that his Frank Zito character is the logical extension of Robert DeNiro's Travis Bickle, and there is more than a grain of truth to this assertion (Spinell even pays homage to and utilizes the famous "You talkin' to me?" quote). One can easily see Bickle venting his social and sexual frustration in the way Zito does, but then again, *Taxi Driver* was working with a much broader palette. The only point about society that *Maniac* makes is that life sucks for some people and they take it out on innocent people by killing them.

On the other hand, the character of Travis Bickle and his descent into psychosis engenders some audience sympathy, contrasting his own (however twisted) moral code with characters who seemingly have none. In Frank Zito's case, he is already past the point of no return when first encountered; we only have his word that he suffered at the hands of his mother, and he's so far gone from the first scene that these could very well be figments of his imagination, too. His few fleeting moments of seeming normalcy are what require a suspension of disbelief, although not as great as the one which requires us to believe that a character like Anna would ever have anything to do with a character like Frank.

Even though Caroline is the nominal female lead, she doesn't have many more lines than Spinell's victims. Anna certainly doesn't have any more brains than any of them; not once does she wonder how a strange man whose picture she just happened

FILMS AND TELEVISION: *Maniac* (1980)

Joe Spinell feeds Caroline a line in *Maniac*.

to take in the park just happens to show up at her door. But that's indicative of the overall misogynistic attitude towards women in the slasher and splatter genres; they aren't there to think, they're there to be victims, pure and simple (which, to be fair, is also true of *Psycho* and Herschell Gordon Lewis' *Blood Feast*, and is true of a goodly number of horror films, and not just the slasher and splatter subgenres). Caroline is more than competent in her role; it's just that it's not much of a role to begin with. Anna is not even seen as any sort of redemptive influence; she brings out whatever little bit of lucidity might be left in him, but her interest in him otherwise has no effect. Perhaps it never could, but if she serves no other purpose, then it still ultimately reduces her to just another potential victim. True, she whacks him with a shovel when he attacks her in the graveyard, and so it's taken for granted that she's the one who calls the cops, but she's not shown doing this. In fact, there's no resolution to her character. After she hits him with the shovel, she runs away, and that's the last we see of her, so she doesn't even exist so much as a character as a plot device.

After the film opened, Caroline, Joe Spinell and William Lustig were guests on the radio show *Sound Tracks*, hosted by Paul Wonder, on WVAI New York. Amusingly, after the host finished describing the movie as "high tech horror" and using "state of the art special effects," Spinell told him the brains were actually shrimp salad; Spinell also maintained that it wasn't a gore film, that it was a "suspense film that delivers in the murder scenes." Spinell dominates the interview, Lustig admits to having done every job in the film industry except direct, and Caroline admitted even then that she was terrified by the end result.

Chuck McCartney's quote about the film making one feel dirty is entirely appropriate; if the film does nothing else, it perfectly captures the sleazy squalor of New York in the late 1970s, and the presence of porn stars Sharon Mitchell and Abigail Clayton helps reinforce this notion. (Lustig had been a porno director.)

The Last Horror Film (a.k.a. *Fanatic*) — 1982, Shere Productions/Winters Hollywood Entertainment Holdings Corporation

Crew: Producers: Judd Hamilton, David Winters; Associate Producer (Castle Sequence): Sean Casey; Associate Producer (New York Sequence): Luke Walter; Director: David Winters; Screenplay: Judd Hamilton, Tom Klassen, David Winters; Music: Jesse Frederick, Jeff Koz; Photography: Thomas F. Danove; Film Editors: Chris Barnes, M. Edward Salier; Production Designer: Jeff Sharpe; Art Director: Brian Savegar; Costume Designer: Nancy Hardy; Makeup: Jane Barry, Dovey Rohl; Hair Stylist: Toni Caine; First Assistant Director: Devin Goldenberg; Second Assistant Director: Marty Heckleman; Second Unit Director: Marty Ollstein; Sound Re-Recording Mixers: David Dockendorf, Don MacDougall, John L. Mack; Sound Effects Editor: Anthony Ippolito; Supervising Sound Editor: Tim Lewiston; Boom Operator: Steve O'Brien; Sound Editor: Terry Poulton; Sound Recordist: Brad Sherman; Sound Mixer: David Stephenson; Sound Mixer (Second Unit): George Stephenson; Special Effects: Peter McKenzie; Special Effects Technicians: John Humphreys, Michael Jones, Jean Scott.

Cast: Caroline Munro (Jana Bates), Joe Spinell (Vinny Durand), Judd Hamilton (Alan Cunningham), Devin Goldenberg (Marty Bernstein), David Winters (Stanley Kline), Susanne Benton (Susan Archer), Filomena "Mary Spinell" Spagnuolo (Vinny's Mother), Glenn Jacobson (Bret Bates), J'Len Winters (Girl in Jacuzzi/Beach Girl Teaser), Sharon Hughes (Stripper), Sean Casey (Jonathan), Don Talley (Cowboy), John Kelly (Man in Theater); Simone Overman, Malgosia Casey, Patty Salier (Women in Theater); George Valismis, Chip Hamilton, Peter D'Arcy (New York Men); Robert Paget, Katia Malmio, Dennis Beasnard, Richard Marner, Jenny Lipmann, Holly De Jong (Screening Room Jury), Tony McCann (Blowtorch Man), Jane Wellman (Burn Effect Girl), Valerie Devereaux (Fan); Joanne Hicks, William Whittington (Miss Bates' Secretaries), John Claude (Delivery Boy), Noreen Kantala, Corina Burkli (Girls in Lobby), Lavana Hakim, Marika Laususer (Beach Girls); George Alschul, Ronald Dessautels (Bouncers); Marie Jose Welsch (Topless Girl on Pier), Marty Ollstein (Doorman); June Chadwick, Robin Leach, John Austin (Reporters), Jane Rawlins (Old Lady), Mark Hutchinson (Young Boy), David Jones (Rock Star); Melissa Carr, Judy Duckett (Girls by Pool); John Hamilton, Luke Walker (Bodyguards), Tammy Hamilton (Michelle Wagner), Marty Heckleman, Thomas F. Danove (Policemen), Henri Marchal (Announcer); Isabelle Adjani, Karen Black, Cathy Lee Crosby, Kris Kristofferson, Marcello Mastroianni (Themselves).

SYNOPSIS

A beautiful nude girl slips into a Jacuzzi, and a gloved hand slips a hot wire into the hot tub, electrocuting her. But it's only a movie....

Films and Television: *The Last Horror Film* (1982)

Vinny Durand (Joe Spinell) is a mentally unbalanced mama's boy and cabbie. Obsessed with beautiful horror film actress Jana Bates (Caroline Munro, he dreams of making a film with her and travels to the Cannes Film Festival to meet her. Jana is married to producer Bret Bates (Glenn Jacobson), but makes no secret of her romantic relationship with Alan Cunningham (Judd Hamilton).

Jana receives flowers with a note that says she has made her last horror film; her husband receives a bottle of champagne with the same note. Jana goes to see him about it, but finds him mutilated. By the time the police arrive, the body has disappeared! And somebody is getting it all on film....

More people receive the notes. Agent Marty Bernstein gets an additional note, supposedly from Bret Bates. Marty goes to a deserted theater to meet him, and is hacked to pieces. Vinny goes to see a horror movie, but is sickened by the violence. When he sees the director, he swears to get even. Later, when the director and his girlfriend are playing love games at a secluded spot, the director is stabbed and his girlfriend is shot in the back of the head. The filming continues....

Jana is taking a bath when Vinny comes in through the bathroom window with a bottle of champagne and begins babbling about his movie idea. When Jana screams at him to get out, he first begins to cry and then breaks the bottle, threatening Jana. She runs away, dressed only in a towel, but the crowd thinks it is a publicity stunt and begins to clap! Vinny becomes caught up in the applause, and his delusions take over as Jana gets away.

Alan takes Jana to a friend's remote castle. Vinny follows them, but is chased away by security. Jana and Alan go to an awards ceremony, but Vinny, disguised as a gendarme, kidnaps Jana. He takes her to another castle, ties her up, and films the climax of his movie — but he's not the only filmmaker in the castle. Bret Bates is alive and unwell — but how? Vinny runs away when Bates grabs Jana, but when Jana breaks away from his grasp, Vinny returns and makes sure the job is done for real this time when he cuts Bret's head off with a chainsaw. But it's only a movie ... or is it?

Review and Notes

The Last Horror Film reunites Caroline with Joe Spinell, but it's not a replay of *Maniac*. It's not as brutal or relentless, and there are some fun moments and the added attraction of the setting of the 1981 Cannes Film Festival, with a funny twist in the tale. Spinell as Vinny Durand is likewise not as brutal or relentless; he's still a stalker and a killer, but he's not so much a pure force of evil as he is delusional and determined. In fact, Vinny's like an extreme version of the delusional fanboy in the *Dragnet* episode "Burglary: DR-31": Stanley Stover (Tim Donnelly), the archetypal media-damaged, lonely, mother's-boy–geek, dresses in a homemade superhero costume and steals stuff from studios. Vinny has delusions of grandeur (he has dreams in which he's both the powerful, mocking director and his usual downtrodden self; he also has delusions of making a movie with Jana Bates, and he will stop at nothing to make that vision a reality.

FILMS AND TELEVISION: *The Last Horror Film* (1982)

Caroline gets much more screen time and a much meatier role than in *Maniac*. As internationally renowned scream queen Jana Bates, she makes the most of it. Jana has come to Cannes to promote her latest film (titled *Scream*, long before that actual movie), and is also in the running for Best Actress (in competition with Meryl Streep, Jane Fonda, Julie Christie, and Faye Dunaway!). She is appropriately shocked and stunned when her husband's head falls off into the sink in front of her and appropriately frustrated when nobody will believe her. She manages to retain her composure when reciting silly dialogue ("I've seen enough fake blood to know the real thing when I see it!" and "So as long as I can pretend not to believe my own eyes, and forget about it, we can live happily ever after, is that what you want?"), and when fending off Spinell after he's broken in on her taking a bath, which leads to her best scene in the film, running through the hotel lobby and the streets of Cannes in a bath towel. The reactions of the punters in the lobby were quite authentic, as revealed by Caroline in the April 1982 *Starlog*: "I ran soaking wet with a towel wrapped around me through the lobby of the Hotel Martinez — the most exclusive and expensive hotel in Cannes — screaming at the top of my voice past all these jewel-bedecked people. We wanted to get their natural reactions, and obviously they thought I was *potty*. It was a strange thing to do." And quite possibly, not planned out in advance: "As we were shooting at the festival, it often happened that we shot spontaneously. Whatever happened happened. Come hell or high water, we went ahead. There was a great deal of improvisation. It became more interesting to make changes as we were actually filming. With Joe Spinell, anything is possible" (*Famous Monsters* No. 182). And in a case of life imitating art, the movie actually did win an award: the 1982 Catalonian International Film Festival's Clavell de Plata award for best cinematography. The following year, it was nominated for the Saturn Award for Best International Film, and Joe's mom was nominated for Best Supporting Actress by the Academy of Science Fiction, Fantasy and Horror Films.

Caroline doesn't have a monopoly on the silly dialogue; it's quite democratically spread around to all the other characters, like when Vinny's mom tells him, "You don't eat right! More protein and you wouldn't have all these crazy ideas." Or Judd Hamilton, with his suspicion of Bret Bates: "He's probably up in the room with a bottle of champagne and a silly ass grin on his face." Even lowly security guards get in on the act; in fact, they get one of the film's best exchanges: "This place gives me the creeps." "You get the creeps taking a piss."

The movie was shot guerrilla-style, without permits. The idea for the film was conceived when Judd Hamilton and business associate–director David Winters were planning on attending the Festival to generate interest in the *Starcrash* sequel: "Why not kill two bats with one stake and make a movie while they were there?" It only took them three days to write a working script. "It was like nothing else on Earth," Caroline recalled in the *Fangoria* interview:

> It was totally chaotic, but very exciting, because we never knew what we were going to get. We only had one go at every scene, so we had to get it right the first time. A lot of the shooting was at night, because many of the premieres were held then. For example, we went

to the opening of *Heaven's Gate*. Judd and I stepped out of our limousine in front of the real press and had our pictures taken. Our cameramen were set up in the crowd and we went up the stairs behind Kris Kristofferson and director Michael Cimino into the theater, where we watched for five minutes and then had to sneak out to change our costumes and rush to another location. I just hope they didn't see us leave, because that would have been so rude.

This also helps to explain the presence of (and thanks given to) Kristofferson, Karen Black, and the other celebrities who make "cameos" in a film they still might not be aware that they appeared in! Another instance of the storyline being changed through real-life circumstances was when Jana and Alan go to a castle to get away from Vinny; what they were actually doing was getting away from a hotel bill that Spinell had run up. They literally packed their bags and ducked out in the middle of the night and flew to Geneva, Switzerland, where the castle was located. Although originally budgeted at $500,000, the film ended up costing over $2,000,000.

Tami Hamalian runs the fan club for Caroline, and was a vital link in our communication; she is also Judd Hamilton's daughter, and appeared in *The Last Horror Film* as Michelle Wagner, Caroline's double, under her given name, Tammy Hamilton: "Yes, I played her double — a very fun experience for a 15-year-old. I do remember sitting in a coffin during a late-night shoot and falling asleep in it — [it's a] shame no one outside the film happened upon me! But alas, the crowd I was with didn't think it odd at all!"

The most interesting (and sometimes confusing) aspect of the movie is its film-within-a-film-within-a-film-within-a-film concept. Every character is involved somehow with film; film is the dominant aspect of their lives in one way or another: Caroline plays Jana, who is a film star in a city with a film festival where she is to compete for a film award and is making a film at the same time. Vinny is obsessed with film, and wants to make a film, and films Jana from afar, but his actions are being filmed as well. And then there's the twist ending, which reveals that the preceding 90 minutes or so have all been a movie, that Vinny has actually made his movie, which is showing to his mom (his real-life mom, in his real-life apartment), with whom he shares a joint! This life-as-film idea is put across much more successfully (and perhaps inadvertently) than the movie's other main conceit, which is fairly heavy-handed in its attempt to show that "real life" is far worse than anything horror films can conceive, with radio and television reports of violence, including the Reagan assassination attempt. But it's the blurring of where "film" starts and "film" ends that keeps the viewer guessing and ultimately lifts it above the run-of-the-mill slasher flick, and keeps it from being as unrelentingly grim as *Maniac*.

Slaughter High (a.k.a. *April Fool's Day*) — 1986, Spectacular Trading International/Vestron Pictures

Crew: Producers: Stephen Minasian, Dick Randall; Screenwriters-Directors: George Dugdale, Mark Ezra, Peter Mackenzie Litten; Music: Harry Manfredini; Photography: Alan Pud-

FILMS AND TELEVISION: *Slaughter High* (1986)

ney; Film Editor: Jim Connock; Production Design: Geoff Sharpe; Makeup: Craig Berkeley, Alison Hall; Production Manager: Laurence Rooke; Assistant Director: Chick Norris; Design Assistant: Aram Allen; Property Master: Terry Allen; Sound Mixer: Dick Hunt; Boom Operator: Dave Pierce; Dubbing Mixer: Ted Ryan; Prosthetics: John Humphreys; Special Effects Designer: Peter Mackenzie Litten; Special Effects Rigger: Robert Turner; Opticals: Rex Neville; Mechanical Designer: Richard Pirkis; Camera Operator: Michael Connor; Wardrobe: Lee Scott; Seamstress: Isabelle Blaire.

Cast: Caroline Munro (Carol Manning), Simon Scuddamore (Marty Rantzen), Carmine Iannaccone (Skip Pollack), Donna Yeager (Stella), Gary Martin (Joe), Billy Hartman (Frank), Michael Saffran (Ted Harrison), John Segal (Carl Putney), Kelly Baker (Nancy), Sally Cross (Susan), Josephine Scandi (Shirley), Marc Smith (Coach), Dick Randall (Manny), Jon Clark (Digby), Mark Ezra (Jester).

SYNOPSIS

Class nerd Marty Rantzen (Simon Scuddamore) thinks he has made the grade when class sexpot Carol (Caroline Munro) takes him into the girls' locker room for some sex education, but it turns out to be a cruel April Fool's Day joke, and now naked nerd Marty is humiliated in front of his classmates. Their jokes turn deadly when they cause his chemistry experiment to explode, which dumps nitric acid onto his face, scarring him physically and mentally. Marty is sent to the asylum.

Ten years later, Carol and her classmates decide to hold a reunion at their old school, which has been closed down because of government cuts in education. As they party, a storm comes up and forces them inside. While wandering the deserted halls, two of them encounter the old janitor, who is now the caretaker. After they give him a beer, he encounters Marty, dressed as a jester, who takes care of the old man by hanging him on a coat hook. And then the party really gets started....

A beer is spiked with nitric acid, and a stomach explodes. Shirley (Josephine Scandi) goes to wash the blood off, but the bathwater turns to nitric acid, which washes her right down to the bone. Another tries to escape in a car when he finds out he has a backseat driver—with a knife.

Looking for any way to escape, Skip (Carmine Iannaccone), Frank (Billy Hartman) and Joe (Gary Martin) find a lawn tractor. When Joe stays behind to fix it, his wife Stella (Donna Yeager) tells Frank that their child is really his, and talks him into bed. Joe is cut to pieces under the mower, and Frank and Stella reach a shocking climax when they are electrocuted in bed.

Skip is strung up, but manages to escape. Marty chases Nancy into a cesspool. Marty goes after Carol with a baseball bat, but then decides he could make the point better with a javelin. Hidden behind some stage scenery, Carol hears footsteps on the other side of it. She swings a hatchet around and plants it squarely in the eye of—Skip!

When Marty attacks Carol again and falls to the gym floor below, she thinks he is dead and throws the javelin down beside him. He isn't, but she soon is, as he uses

FILMS AND TELEVISION: *Slaughter High* (1986)

The Mexican lobby card for a British film in which everyone is pretending to be an American, *Slaughter High*.

the javelin to finish what she started in the girls' locker room. Marty begins to hear voices — the voices of his victims who have now returned!

Then Marty wakes up in the asylum, and that's when the real screaming starts...

REVIEW AND NOTES

If *Revenge of the Nerds* had been a slasher movie, it would have been *Slaughter High*. Originally titled *1 April Fool's Day*, the title was changed when co-producer Stephen Minasian sold the rights to the title to Paramount, who promptly used it for Fred Walton's *April Fool's Day*. As is the case with many movies of this ilk, the plot, or what there is of it, merely exists as a framework to string together gore effects, and the "theme" of the unofficial holiday is never exploited to its fullest, either in the execution of the executions or in the persona of the killer. Late in the movie, the characters start talking about how it's almost noon, and it should be time for Marty to stop, but besides the fact that it hadn't been a plot point before that time, it was confusing to audiences not based in the UK, New Zealand, Cyprus and South Africa, where traditional April Fool's pranks are supposed to stop at noon. (Those who make them after that time are taunted with "April Fool's Day's past and gone, you're the fool for making one.") Perhaps that's because it was made in the UK, which perhaps accounts for the film's strange

FILMS AND TELEVISION: *Cinderella, or the Shoe Must Go On* (1986)

rhythms: It's a British film with mostly British actors trying to convince us that it's taking place in America. Or perhaps they're not trying to convince us at all — it's actually supposed to be a parody of American slasher films, which would explain a lot of things, but even in this regard it comes up a little short; the same as an American film with American actors attempting British accents and trying to speak convincingly about studying for their O-Levels would. It rather falls between two chairs, then; not serious and tense enough to be remembered as a thriller, and not intentionally funny enough to be remembered as a spoof. This isn't to say that it doesn't offer up a dollop or two of good dumb fun.

Much derision has been directed at the fact that all the players are well past high school age, but this is a great movie tradition — certainly none of them look as inappropriate as a teen as, say, Steve McQueen did in *The Blob*. And at least they don't try to pull it off for the whole movie. As in her previous slasher, *The Last Horror Film*, Caroline plays an actress, but this has no bearing whatsoever on the plot. She probably chose the profession based on the way she was able to hoodwink Marty, and sure, Marty should know that something was amiss when a miss like Carol Manning offers to pump him up in the girl's locker room. He's such a dork that it's hard to work up any sympathy for him; his only saving grace is that his classmates are such complete bastards and bitches. Carol is not a complete bitch; she's the only one of the group that shows even the slightest hint of regret for what happened to Marty. But all this gets her is the number one chart position in his slit parade.

The rest of the cast is quite hopeless. Kelly Baker, who plays Nancy, appeared with Caroline in (yet another) slasher film, *Don't Open Till Christmas*, Kelly's only other film role. And so it went with most of the rest of the cast, many of whom would only make one or two other films; only Marc Smith, Gary Martin and Billy Hartman had substantial careers outside the halls of Slaughter High. Simon Scuddamore took his own life shortly after the film was completed.

Also in 1986, Caroline shot a pilot for a British astrology series called *Zodiac*, directed by Mike Mansfield, who had previously directed her in the Adam Ant video "Goody Two Shoes" (see next section); the pilot was rejected. The next year, she was slated to appear in the big-budget *Doctor Who: The Movie*, helmed by the *Slaughter High* team of Dugdale, Litten, and Ezra, but that did not get made. Topping off a trifecta of disappointments, Dugdale and Litten (the creators of Max Headroom) created a female version of the character for Caroline called Roxscene, but that too was consigned to the Great Dustbin of Unrealized Projects.

Cinderella, or the Shoe Must Go On—1986, Central Television

Crew: Associate Producer: Nigel Crowle; Producer/Director: Jon Scoffield; Writers: Barry Cryer, Dick Vosburgh; Designer: Richard Plumb; Choreography: Nigel Lythgoe; Music Director: Laurie Holloway; Music: Laurie Holloway, Keith Strachan; Willie Rushton (Narrator)

FILMS AND TELEVISION: *Cinderella, or the Shoe Must Go On* (1986)

Cast: Danny La Rue (Stepmother), Roy Kinnear (Baron Hardup), Cheryl Baker (Cinderella), Jimmy Cricket (Buttons), Michael Howe (Prince Charming), Brian Conley (Dandini), Basil Brush (Himself), Bob Carolgees (Himself), Spit the Dog (Himself), Faith Brown (Fairy Godmother), Brian Murphy (Amnesia), Roy Hudd (Magnesia), John Wells (Denis Thatcher), Steve Nallon (Maggie Thatcher), Ross Davidson (Himself), Mike Reid (Major D'Omo), Judith Chalmers (Herself), Roy Walker, Les Dennis (Brokers Men), Shaw Taylor (Himself), Jim Bowen (Game Show Host), Caroline Munro (Game Show Hostess); Roy Gayle, Tony Griffiths, Tony Parry, Stewart Avon Arnold (Mice); Luke Batchelor, Karen De Beaufort, Kim Gavin, Sandra Easby, Jerry Manley, Karen Landau, Paul Shearstone, Claire Alexander, Gess Whitfield, Carol Hoffman, John Willet, Dina Michel (Dancers).

SYNOPSIS

From the UK's *TV Times*: "A star-studded version of *Cinderella, or the Shoe Must Go On*—a traditional pantomime for the ever-changing world. Although small departures have been made for modern science, the performers earnestly hope that any child viewing the story for the first time will be as enchanted as their mums and dads were just a few Christmases ago."

REVIEW AND NOTES

After serving as a game-show hostess for three years on the *3–2–1* series, Caroline sought to escape identification with that role by appearing in *Cinderella: The Shoe Must Go On* as ... a game-show hostess. *Shoe* was originally broadcast on Christmas Day, 1986, and is a pantomime, which is not to be confused with mimes of the more familiar sort. British pantomime, traditionally performed at Christmas, is quite a different beast than silent, pasty-faced ghouls; it is a lavish song-and-dance show featuring elements of comedy, topical subjects, winks and nods, and, of course, cross-dressing. Caroline has also performed in live pantomime (the traditional method of performance, in a theater); during her tenure at *3–2–1*, in 1985, she essayed the role of Fairy Twinklestar (stop snickering, you lot) in *Jack and the Beanstalk* at England's Theatre Royal Lincoln: "I wanted to test myself," she said in her *Fangoria* interview. "It turned out to be the most physically and emotionally terrifying work I've ever done. I had to go out on a stage night after night—sometimes three shows a day—and lay bare my soul." She faced an even more demanding schedule when she took another trip to Geneva, in October 1987, to appear on stage again in the "industrial show," *The New Travels of Marco Polo*, which was not so much a play as a live infomercial. The 30-minute show was produced on behalf of Japan's NEC Electronics, for promotion of a new line of products at a computer convention, at a clip of eight shows a day for eight straight days.

El Aullido del Diablo (a.k.a. *Howl of the Devil*, a.k.a. *Curse of the Devil*)—1987, Freemont-Nasch International

Crew: Producers: Paul Naschy, Augusto Boue, German Monzo; Director: Paul Naschy; Screenplay: Paul Naschy, Salvador Sainz; Music: Fernando Garcia Morcillo; Photography: Julio Burgos; Film Editor: Jose Antonio Rojo; Art Director: Tony Pueo; Makeup: Fernando Florido; Assistant Production Manager: Emilio A. Pina; Special Effects: Francisco Garcia San Jose.

Cast: Paul Naschy (Hector Doriani/Alex Doriani/Frankenstein's Monster/Mr. Hyde/The Phantom of the Opera/The Werewolf/The Devil/Quasimodo/Psycho Killer/Chainsaw Killer), Caroline Munro (Carmen), Howard Vernon (Eric), Fernando Hilbeck (Father Damian), Mariano Vidal Molina (Guardia Civil #1), Isabel Prinz (Lorena), Serge Mill (Adrian), Chris Huerta (Zacarias), Emilio A. Pina (Guardia Civil #2), Malena Gracia, Chema Gomez, Joseph Garco, Roberta Kuhn, Carmen Plate, Pascual Marco, Tamara Greys, Mabel Ordonez, Nuria Lucas.

SYNOPSIS

A wanton woman of the night sits at the wheel of her car, counting up her hard-earned booty. Just as she lights a cigarette, her protein-enriched throat is cut!

Hector Doriani (Paul Naschy) is a cut-rate actor who is bitter that he never receives the recognition afforded to his much more famous actor brother and twin, Alex, who is now dead, supposedly by his own hand. Hector's promiscuous wife has overdosed on heroin, leaving their young son Adrian (Serge Mill) in the care of Hector, who likes to dress up as twisted historical figures and play harrowing sex games with prostitutes who are transported to his decadent mansion by his faithful chauffeur Eric (Howard Vernon). He dresses as Rasputin for his next encounter. As the call girl leaves the mansion, she is called to the hereafter with a knife in her sperm-filled belly!

Hector will not let Adrian have any contact with other children, so he takes refuge in a fantasy world where his only friends are monsters from the movies. Hector lusts after the beautiful chief cook and bottle washer, Carmen (Caroline Munro), who resists his advances but stays in his employ because she needs the money to care for her sick parents.

When a female camper goes outside her tent, her throat is cut! To add insult to death, she is despoiled and dismembered in the morgue!

Eric contacts the spirit of Alex through black magic. Carmen rebuffs the local priest Father Damian, with whom she once had an affair. More killings ensue, and Carmen dreams of horrifying danger followed by terrifying events. Adrian is visited by a werewolf in the woods while the fat, greasy wino that Father Damian uses to spy on Carmen sneaks into Hector's shed and grabs a sickle with murderous intent, only to have an axe planted in his fat back.

A woman comes to Hector looking for her sister who is one of the murdered madams. She succumbs to Hector's debauched desires, and when she leaves the maniac mansion, she succumbs to a knife in the back of her forgiving head.

FILMS AND TELEVISION: *El Aullido del Diablo* (1987)

The Phantom of the Opera visits Adrian, while a desecrated damsel who has survived Hector's perverted pleasures has come back for more of his degenerate dirty deeds. When Eric draws her a bath, she is stabbed to death! Father Damian tries to rape Carmen, but she escapes back to the mansion, where she finally gives in to Hector's desires. Just as they reach simultaneous orgasm, they are simultaneously stabbed by a masked marauder, who takes off his mask and he reveals himself to be Adrian.

Father Damian comes to the mansion looking for Carmen, but all he finds is death at the hands of a gruesome monster that Adrian calls "Papa." The misshapen fiend continues his bloody work by ripping Eric's eyes out of his head. The monster shows Adrian all of his victims, and then shows him that he is not Adrian's father at all, but the father of all evil: he's the devil in disguise. But is Adrian something more than just the Devil's messenger?

REVIEW AND NOTES

It's not just hard to find reviews of this film, it's just hard to find the film, period — it was never released in American theaters (or Spanish ones, for that matter; see below) or home video, whereas the Universal monster rallies *House of Frankenstein* and *House of Dracula* boasted all-star casts and a lineup of their most famous monsters, *Howl* features all the monsters and more, every one of them played by Naschy. It's a loving (and gory) tribute to those Universal monsters that he loved so much. Naschy not only plays all of the monsters, but twin brothers, and as one of those brothers also masquerades as Rasputin, the Marquis de Sade, and Fu Manchu during his various twisted sex games, so there is very little time that Naschy is either not on screen or out of makeup. He invests each part with detail and gusto; just because the Werewolf or Frankenstein's Monster or Mr. Hyde are only on screen for a few minutes each, does not mean that the makeups are hastily done or the characterizations rushed. The same goes for the sex-game masquerades; no simple leather mask or bondage pants for nasty Naschy, no, he goes all-out and not only wears clothes associated with the various characters, but complete makeup (which he apparently takes time to remove before actually bedding the women). His character is not pleasant — he's egomaniacal, brutal, abusive, perverted, sadistic, and misogynistic, given to choice lines of dialogue like "Bitches! You use them and throw them away!" As previously mentioned, the film is gory, and can technically be called a slasher or splatter film, but unlike most entries in that tired genre, the movie surrounding the gore scenes is done with style, existing as a tour-de-force for Naschy rather than simply a showcase for gruesome effects. It exists as a family affair, too: Naschy's brother, Vidal Molina, plays one of the nosy gendarmes, and Serge Mill is actually Naschy's son, Sergio Molina.

There's precious little time for Caroline to strut her stuff, either physically or as an actress. As she said in an interview in *Gorezone* #6, "I hope people will see more range as an actress than they've seen from me before. I had to extend myself more in the role. I had some initial reservations, but everything felt right when we were making it. There was nothing about my scenes that offended me. Of course, I don't know how the finished film will turn out, but for my part, I'm really pleased I did it." She elaborated a bit on her role as Carmen the maid in the May 1988 *Starlog*: "It was a chance to do something different. The clothes I wore were very plain; I wouldn't be seen *dead* in them, walking about as myself. But when I put them on, with flat shoes, a little apron, and my hair pinned back, it seemed absolutely right. I was comfortable, because I felt like the character. In fact, the Spanish women on the set and said I looked authentic. Perhaps, when people see me in *Howl of the Devil*, they'll think, 'My goodness, what an old *bag*.'" Surely *nobody* thought that; Caroline could have worn the proverbial potato sack and her natural beauty would have shown through. Her performance is earthy, determined and sensual, and since she has committed one of the ultimate sins by sleeping with a priest, in this most Catholic of countries, she pays the ultimate price. Caroline performed the part in her own voice in English, per Naschy's instructions, but was later dubbed into Spanish by another actress. This was offset by the perk that Caroline got by being allowed to re-write her own lines of dialogue: "I'm hopeless at writing," she said in *Gorezone #6*, "but the script left something to be desired because it was translated too literally from Spanish to English. Many of the lines were archaic and ungrammatical. So I rewrote my dialogue to make it more conversational. I offered to help rewrite the rest of the dialogue as well, but Paul didn't want to confuse the other actors!" The reason that Naschy wanted her to do her lines in English was because he was going to dub all the other lines into English to try and make a serious effort at cracking the American market. But the film was plagued by post-production obstacles and, as a result, never premiered theatrically, eventually making its first showing on Spanish television, which explains its scarcity.

Faceless—1987; ATC 3000, Ibero Films Internacional S.A., Les Films de la Rochelle, Rene Chateau Productions

Crew: Producer: Rene Chateau; Director: Jesus Franco; Screenplay: Rene Chateau ("Fred Castle"), Dominique Eudes, Jesus Franco, Michel Lebrun, Jean Mazarin, Pierre Ripert; Music: Romano Musumarra; Photography: Jean-Jacques Bouhon, Maurice Fellous; Film Editor: Christine Pansu; Assistant Film Editors: Anne Wasels, Sandrine Flaud; Production Design: Bernard Ciberot; Set Decoration: Yann Arlaud; Assistant Director: Frederic Bal; First Assistant Director: Elisabeth Parniere; Second Assistant Director: Geraldine Petrovic; Second Unit Director: Lina Romay; Sound: Jean-Louis Ducarme; Post-Synchronization: Fred Mays; Special Effects: Jacques Gastineau; First Assistant Camera: Francois Hernandez; Production Manager: Nicole Boisserie; Chief Makeup Artist: Eric Pierre; Makeup Artist: Soraya Boulay; Hair Stylist: Martial Corneville; Costumes: Daniele Bersiaud.

Cast: Helmut Berger (Dr. Frank Flamand), Brigitte Lahaie (Nathalie), Telly Savalas (Terry Hallen), Christopher Mitchum (Sam Morgan), Stephane Audran (Mrs. Sherman), Caroline

Munro (Barbara Hallen), Christiane Jean (Ingrid Flamand), Anton Diffring (Dr. Karl-Heinz Moser), Tilda Thamar (Mrs. Francois), Howard Vernon (Dr. Orloff), Florence Guerin (Herself), Gerard Zalcberg (Gordon), Henri Poirier (Inspector Legros), Laure Sabardin (The Receptionist), Amelie Chevalier (Melissa), Marcel Philippott (Maxence), Tony Awak (Doudou), Mony Dalmes (The Baroness), Doris Thomas (The Singer), Daniel Beretta (L'Homme du bois de Boulogne), Antonina Laurent (Karen), Isabelle Cnokaert (Gina), Nicky Gorska (Woman in Parking Garage), Jean Tolzac (Desk Clerk), Jacques Couderc (Man in the Morgue), Pascale Vital (The Barmaid), Lina Romay (Mrs. Orloff), Alain Barbier (Rachid), Thierry Fouques (Secretary), Daniel Grimm (Wallace).

Synopsis

Dr. Frank Flamand (Helmut Berger), his sister Ingrid (Christiane Jean), and his other lover, Nathalie (Brigitte Lahaie), are about to get in their car when they are confronted by a scarred woman on whom Flamand's technique has not worked. She throws a vial of acid at Flamand — but it misses him and destroys Ingrid's face. He becomes obsessed with trying to restore it, by whatever means possible.

Beautiful fashion model Barbara Hallen (Caroline Munro) is at a shoot, and she takes a pause to refresh with some cocaine. Little does she know her connection is Nathalie, who kidnaps her. Barbara is put in a padded cell at the doctor's clinic; she is now one of many gorgeous girls whom the doctor has stolen for his unholy experiments. When one of the women tries to strangle Nathalie, Flamand's half-witted, depraved henchman Gordon chops off her arms.

The wheelchair-bound Mrs. Sherman, a patient at Flamand's clinic, threatens to expose him. Barbara's father Terry (Telly Savalas) hires detective Sam Morgan to find her. Meanwhile, Flamand consults with the awful Dr. Orloff (Howard Vernon), who cannot perform the operation Flamand wants for Ingrid, but knows who can: former Nazi death-camp doctor Moser (Anton Diffring).

Gordon rapes Barbara, and as punishment, Nathalie forces him to submit to Ingrid's unholy desires. Mrs. Sherman threatens to call the police, so Nathalie kills her by plunging a hypodermic needle into her eye. Since Gordon has damaged Barbara's face, Flamand and Nathalie must find a new subject. They get a call girl, and they each have their way with her before they pay her by letting Moser strip her — of her face! Gordon decapitates the corpse with a chainsaw and makes love to it.

The face graft does not take, so Flamand and Nathalie find a starlet who doesn't know she is about to play her last role. Nathalie finds a male prostitute to satisfy Ingrid's lust. She meets him masked, but he takes the mask from her face and Nathalie takes his life with a pair of scissors through his throat.

Morgan tracks down Flamand, who tries to throw him off the trail. Flamand's receptionist discovers his hidden secret, but when she hides from Gordon in a cabinet, he locks her in it and kills her with a power drill.

Morgan returns to the clinic that night, kills Gordon and finds Barbara! Nathalie locks them in the cell, and Flamand has it bricked up. While Flamand, Nathalie, Moser and Ingrid toast a successful operation, Terry Allen receives Morgan's desperate message for help. Will he make it in time to save his dying daughter and the daring detective?

REVIEW AND NOTES

Faceless is Jess Franco's slick, glossy updating of his own 1962 movie *The Awful Dr. Orloff* (*Gritos en la Noche*), which itself was a carbon copy of Georges Franju's *Eyes Without a Face* (*Les Yeux sans Visage*, 1960). Howard Vernon even returns in *Faceless* to reprise his role of Orloff, although only for one scene, so it's not considered as an official entry in the Orloff series. (There were four other Orloff films, all done by Franco: *The Secrets of Dr. Orloff* [1964], *The Orgies of Dr. Orloff* [1969], *The Sinister Eyes of Dr. Orloff* [1973], and *The Sinister Dr. Orloff* (1984). Vernon also appeared as Orloff for another director, Pierre Chevalier, in *Dr. Orloff's Invisible Monster* [1971; a.k.a. *The Invisible Dead* and *Orloff and the Invisible Man*]. Franco used the character, but not Vernon, in *Doctor Mabuse* [1971].) Earlier in 1987, Vernon co-starred with Caroline in Paul Naschy's *Howl of the Devil*. *Rue Morgue*, in their October 2008 issue, cited *Faceless* as one of their "50 Essential Gore Films" (*Maniac* also made the list):

> In prolific Spanish director Jess Franco's best film, a wealthy plastic surgeon kidnaps pretty young women to use for skin grafts on his sister's face, which was disfigured in an acid attack by a disgruntled former patient. When he kidnaps a famous model, her father sends a private detective to find her. Franco's umpteenth sleazy riff on Georges Franju's *Eyes Without a Face* (1960) includes a stellar B-List cast, wince-inducing ocular trauma, surgical gore and power-tool violence.

Caroline begins the movie in her usual glamorous fashion, but becomes progressively more disheveled as the frames advance, having to endure a brutal attack by Flamand's sadistic, necrophiliac henchman Gordon and continuing drug injections: "I wanted to look as extreme as I could get," she said in *Fangoria*. "In fact, I encouraged them to make me look *worse*. It actually helped me as an actress. The worse I looked and felt, the better my performance. When I was crying, my tears were real; I didn't need any glycerin, because I felt truly *degraded*. It had to be that way, it was so important to see the change in Barbara — to show the glamourous, confident, attractive woman at the beginning, and the poor, sad, pathetic creature at the end. Otherwise, the film wouldn't work." Unlike most of her European films, in which she was dubbed, Caroline's own voice is heard in *Faceless*, and she even attempts an American accent: "It's better than the American accent I did in *Slaughter High*, because I've had more experience at it. But it's still quite soft ... I suppose it's more of a mid–Atlantic accent. I just hope people won't assume I've been dubbed by an American actress again." Although the events are set in motion by her disappearance, and the role offered Caroline a chance to stretch her boundaries as an actress (which she certainly does), she had to do it in a relatively short amount of screen time and even shorter boundaries, as she spends most of the movie in her cell.

The rest of the cast is willing, and some are more able than others. Helmut Berger, nominated for a Golden Globe Award in 1969 for his performance in *The Damned*, makes a suitably sleazy Dr. Flamand, who has an incestuous relationship with the sister whose face he wants to restore, as well as engaging in all manner of sexual games with his lover Nathalie and the girls whose faces will later be forcibly removed. Nathalie seems even worse than Flamand, taking great pleasure not only in her perversity but her ability to inflict pain and death; a truly kinky performance by French hardcore porn queen Brigitte Lahaie in a rare non-porn role. Anton Diffring (*The Man Who Could Cheat Death, Where Eagles Dare*, so many others) is wonderful and, despite his actions, makes the most coherent statements in the film, about the lengths that people will go to preserve their beauty—although it is rather worrisome that a Nazi is the movie's voice of reason. Christopher Mitchum is indeed the son of the legendary Robert Mitchum, and if you squint hard you might think you're seeing Bob the younger, in one of the many detective roles he essayed. It's nice to see Howard Vernon do one last turn in his signature role, but as his appearance is little more than a cameo (as is Lina Romay's) he has little chance to make an impression. Caroline says that Gerard Zalcberg, as the moronic, perverted Gordon, was quite the opposite of his role: "He was a sweet man, a very big, tall man, as I remember ... and he was actually very gentle, but I believe Jess had said to him before we went to do the take, he said, 'You make it look as real as possible' ... So at the end of the scene, which I think actually worked quite well, he was crying, the actor was crying, he said, 'I'm so sorry, I'm so sorry, but I had to make....' And I said, 'We're fine'; it was quite emotional, really, and Jess was smiling away, and he said, 'That looked good, Caroline, that was good.'"

For some odd reason, even though the entire film has been dubbed into English the last line is left in the original French. So if the viewer doesn't understand the language, it makes the situation for Caroline and Christopher seem that much more hopeless (and they looked in pretty bad shape as it was). But if they do, it offers a glimmer of hope; Telly Savalas says "Get me out to Paris immediately." Caroline says of the ending: "It's a *very* ambiguous ending! At least, I think it is; Chris and I liked to think we got rescued, and in our heads, somehow we do.... But, no, there wasn't an ending, that was left to the viewer's imagination.... It's however one wants it to be, really."

Maigret—1988, TV Movie; Columbia Pictures Television

Crew: Executive Producers: Robert M. Cooper, Patrick Dromgoole, Johnny Goodman; Supervising Producers: Patrick Dromgoole, Johnny Goodman; Consulting Producer: Harold Tichenor; Producer-Screenplay: Arthur Weingarten; Director: Paul Lynch; Music: Alan Lisk; Photography: Bob Edwards; Film Editor: Lyndon Matthews; Assistant Film Editor: Helen Garrard; Casting: Davis Zimmerman; Production Designer: Caroline Smith; Art Director: Steve Groves; Costume Design: Graham Williams; Makeup Supervisor: Barbara Southcott; Assistant Makeup Artist: Pamela Haddock.

Cast: Richard Harris (Jules Maigret), Barbara Shelley (Louise Maigret), Patrick O'Neal (Kevin Portman), Victoria Tennant (Victoria Portman), Ian Ogilvy (Daniel Portman), Dominique Barnes (Tara Portman), Eric Deacon (Tony Portman), Caroline Munro (Carolyn Page), Richard Durden (Julian Braden), Andrew McCulloch (Sergeant Lucas), Annette Andre (Judith Hollenbeck), Don Henderson (Barge Captain), Mark Audley (Ekers), Eve Ferret (Mrs. Tippet), Lachele Carl (Sgt. Leila Normand), Milo Sperber (Durbin), Vernon Dobtcheff (Gannett), John Abineri (Renault), Adrian Cairns (Dr. Parton).

Synopsis (from the UK's *TV Times*): "A return to the small screen for the famous Parisian detective character, Jules Maigret, created by Georges Simenon. Inspector Maigret takes a special interest when an old colleague, no longer in the service, is murdered on a train and the body is hurled into the Seine. The action moves from Paris to a luxury liner at sea."

REVIEW AND NOTES

Richard Harris, in an interview in the *TV Times*, noted that he prepared for the role by reading every Maigret book he could find, as well as reading the biography of Georges Simenon, Maigret's creator.

Demons 6: De Profundis (a.k.a. *The Black Cat; Dead Eyes*) — 1989, 21st Century Film Corporation, World Pictures

Crew: Producer: Lucio Lucidi; Director: Luigi Cozzi (as Lewis Coates); Story and Screenplay: Luigi Cozzi, Daria Nicolodi; Suggested by "The Black Cat" by Edgar Allan Poe and *Suspiria De Profundis* by Thomas De Quincey; Music Composer-Conductor: Vince Tempera; Photography: Pasquale Rachini; Film Editor: Piero Bozza; Art Director: Marina Pinzuti (Anzolini); Costume Designer: Donatella Cazzola; Makeup Supervisor–Special Makeup Effects Artist: Franco Casagni; Special Makeup Effects Artist: Rosario Prestopino; Hair Stylist: Piero Cucchi; Production Manager: Piero Amati; Production Supervisor: Giovanni Mongini; Post-Production Supervisor: Lillo Capoano; First Assistant Director: Stefano Oddi.

Cast: Florence Guerin (Anna Ravenna), Urbano Barberini (Marc Ravenna), Caroline Munro (Nora McJudge), Brett Halsey (Leonard Levin), Luisa Maneri (Sara), Giada Cozzi (Sybil), Maurizio Fardo (Dan), Michele Soavi (Carl the Film Director), Karina Huff, Alessandra Acciai, Michele Marsina, Jasmine Maimone, Antonio Marsina.

SYNOPSIS

A baby floats through outer space. On Earth, a masked man cuts a young man's throat and attacks his girlfriend. But it's only a movie called *The Black Cat*, starring Anna Ravenna (Florence Guerin), who is married to the director, Marc (Urbano Barberini), and Nora McJudge (Caroline Munro), who is married to the writer, Dan (Maurizio Fardo).

Anna and Marc go home, where their babysitter Sara is watching their infant son.

Sara asks Anna if her cousin William, a fan, can visit them; Anna says yes. When Anna puts the baby to sleep, a spectral voice rings out: "Death is drawing near!"

Marc and Dan have an idea for a new movie based on Levana, Queen of the Witches. Both promise the lead part to their wives. That night, when Anna looks in a mirror, Levana breaks through it and tells Anna they'll die before they show her face on screen. But it's only a nightmare ... or is it?

Asleep again, Levana calls to Anna. Anna sees a little girl, who calls herself Sybil. Anna's refrigerator explodes, and up through the fridge comes blood. But it's only a nightmare ... or is it?

Marc and Dan sell their idea to a producer named Levin. The next day, Anna goes home to find a man repairing the refrigerator. She also finds William in the baby's room. Later, Sara tells her no one has been there all day! It's only a nightmare ... or is it?

Marc and Dan try to hire an occult expert as an advisor for their movie. When they tell her it's about Levana, she tells them they must not use the name or it will summon her. Later, when she tries to locate them and warn them again, her stomach explodes.

Dan is attacked. Sybil tells Anna to touch the television, and the television explodes in a welter of intestines! A knife appears, and Sybil tells Anna she must choose whether or not to become Levana. Anna seizes the knife and goes to the baby's room. As she raises the knife, Marc bursts in and she stabs him. Then he pulls the knife out and stabs *her*! The baby is gone! Dan's car crashes through the wall! Dan has been stabbed in the back! Marc and Nora are having an affair! Anna goes to shoot Levin, who is already dead, but tells her of the affair and that Nora has the baby! She kills him again, and then kills his secretary!

Nora gives Anna her baby, and follows her when she leaves. She picks up the refrigerator repairman and meets with Levana, who tells her she has failed. Levana blows up the car and makes Nora cut her own throat.

After Anna gets the baby home, the house is wrecked by cosmic blasts of energy bolts. Sara, who is really Levana, kills Anna with an energy blast, but Anna, who can now control time, turns back the clock so that Marc can run Levana through with a stake. But it's only a nightmare, and everything is back to normal ... or is it?

REVIEW AND NOTES

If you think the synopsis is confusing, just wait until you see the movie. The behind-the-scenes story is almost as interesting as the movie itself. Let's begin the confusion by explaining the reasoning behind the title and numbering. At first glance, it would appear to be the sixth installment of Lamberto Bava's *Demons* film series, but it's not. The explanation actually starts with Dario Argento's *Suspiria* (1977) and its sequel, *Inferno* (1980), the first two films of Argento's "Three Mothers" trilogy, concerning three ancient witches in three different modern cities. Bava directed *Demons* (1985) and *Demons 2* (1986). Then he assisted, uncredited, in the scripting of a movie called *The Church*, directed by Michele Soavi, which then became known as *Demons*

3. Soavi then directed *The Sect*, which Bava had nothing to do with, but it was released in some quarters as *Demons 4*. Then Bava remade his father Mario's *Black Sunday*, which for some reason was also released as *Demons 5*. Then Luigi Cozzi got into the act with *Demons 6*, which has nothing to do with either the first two or any of the other films (or Poe's "The Black Cat," for that matter). It *does* have something to do with *Suspiria* and *Inferno*, trying to pass itself off as the concluding installment of the "Three Mothers" trilogy (even going so far as to namecheck both *Suspiria* and Argento), which Argento would complete himself in 2007 with *The Mother of Tears*. In short, *Demons 6* is another muddled disasterpiece from the Ed Wood of Italy.

The Ed Wood analogy is not employed simply because both made "bad" movies. True, both made films that have, shall we say, a unique worldview, but it goes a bit deeper than that; both had constant troubles financing their films and would often shut down for extended periods while they were securing more suckers ... er, investors; both had trouble paying their actors (much more on that aspect in a moment); and maybe most importantly, both of them loved movies, although that love did not necessarily translate into a talent for making them. Cozzi was content to be an avid follower of trends rather than a creator of them. His films are always derivative, sometimes amusingly so, sometimes infuriatingly so, and incorporate so many different sources to derive from that they take on bizarre, surreal atmospheres — surreal not in the sense of a self-conscious attempt to create such a milieu, a world of its own, but the disorienting effect of throwing too many disparate elements together. For instance, a supposed story about an ancient witch taking over a modern-day actress opens, for some reason, with a steal from *2001: A Space Odyssey*—a fetus enveloped in womb of light—and the ending includes cosmic tourist shots of the Moon (none of the characters interact with it in any way) interspersed with all the other scenes. Is Lavana from the moon? Does the moon give Anna her sudden super-power to be able to control time? Is a werewolf going to show up? It's just like the scene of stampeding buffalo in *Glen or Glenda?* There's a "creepy" graveyard tableau (looking something like an assemblage of Aurora-like monster model accessories, which it could very well have been), whence the voice of Lavana speaks out to worm its way into Anna's brain; so at least it ties into the story somehow. But again, none of the characters interact with it in any way. Then again, that's part of what we love about Wood and Cozzi, and wouldn't want it any other way.

According to an article in *Fangoria* #102 (which was published more than a year after the finish of the film), "Ripped Off in Rome," she had yet to receive a penny of her contracted salary: "Quite frankly, I'm *furious*. I've been very, very badly used.... I don't think I'll *ever* get the money." And, oh, what a tangled web was woven. The ordeal was made even worse by the death of her father, who had expended a great deal of time advising her on the legal aspects of the situation. Cozzi originally contacted Caroline on April 13, 1989, and she received the script about three weeks later. Although she expressed doubts about aspects of the script, she quickly agreed to it because the character of Nora McJudge appealed to her: "*That* is really why I jumped at it. I wanted to see if I could bring it off. Nora is *not* a nice piece of work at all." Cozzi struck a deal with agent Dennis Selinger, but soon after, Selinger fell ill and had to have an operation, which put him out of action for several months and left his assistant, Rebecca Blond, in charge. Thinking that her contractual house was in order, Caroline flew to Rome on May 20, 1989, to begin filming, even though she had not actually received the contract. Blond informed Caroline that her salary check had not arrived but told her not to worry (Blond had been assured that the money was in *a* bank. Since Caroline's per diem was being paid in cash, she saw no reason to think anything was wrong.

But the situation quickly turned sour: After only two days of filming, she was given three weeks off. Her contract expired during this period; she came back to work for two more days before the film closed down. Cozzi alleged that he had money problems due to Menahem Golan. "Luigi told me he wanted me to return to Italy in two weeks, to finish off my scenes and do several new ones." But she refused to return until she was paid. After assisting Argento once more, as second unit director on Argento's contribution to *Two Evil Eyes*, Cozzi contacted Caroline and asked her to return to Rome in September to complete the film. "Luigi assured me that everything was fine. He promised me I would get paid and I believed him. Rebecca said she was sure that the money was there and that I should go ahead and finish the film. I was to receive my entire salary on my last day of shooting. This time, I had no doubt everything was fine." It was not.

Months of legal wrangling followed. Injunctions that turned out to be mere memos, avoidance, half-truths, creative accounting methods, and seeming outright lies compounded the matter. Amazingly, she expressed no ill will towards the man seemingly responsible for the affair, Luigi Cozzi, forever willing to give him the benefit of the doubt: "I like the man, and think he has some very clever ideas. I still don't know the truth of what went on behind the scenes, so I can't point the finger of guilt at anybody. But I do feel very disillusioned. What happened to me should be a lesson to all actors, big and small, going off to do a foreign film. Be prepared. Even though you have a contract, don't step on the plane until the money is in your bank." To this day, she told me, she has still never been paid.

And knowing those circumstances certainly does distract one a bit when watching the film, so one must try to separate the life from the art—although the term "art" is used very loosely in this case. The role itself is a good one for Caroline, being so atypical of her usual casting: a nasty, lying calculating bitch in league with the forces of evil. She's especially good in the confrontation scene with Anna—taking a luxurious bath and then in sexy lingerie painting her fingernails, cold and spiteful and collected in the face of Anna's emotional upheaval. "Hello, Anna. You've come for your baby. You can have him. Go ahead; take him, no one's stopping you. Go home, Anna; Lavana's about to visit you in person." When Anna takes the baby and leaves, Nora, quite pleased with herself, draws a long, deep breath, as if inhaling the very evil that hangs heavy in the dark and stormy night. To Caroline's credit, she didn't let the adversity of the situation affect her performance; although not formally trained, she is every inch the professional.

Armchair Detective—1990, Central Independent Television

Crew: Producer: Diane Campbell; Director: David Dunn; Writer: Dick Sharples; Designer: Norman Smith; Production Assistant: Val Nieberle; Production Secretary: Jo Beard; First Assistant Director: George Gerwitz; Second Assistant Director: Nigel Keen; Wardrobe: Anna Taylor; Make Up: Dee Hickin; Prop Buyer: Joe Vaughan.

Cast: Matthew Kelly (Matthew Kelsey), Max Wall (Mervyn Musprat), Jean Alexander (Agnes Rumbold), Richard Gibson (Lance Rumbold), Ken Morley (Arnold Braithwaite), Caroline Munro (Carmen Sanchez), Robert Warner (Vicar), Stephen Barber, Robin Kyle (Gravediggers), Reginald Rogers (Head Funeral Director), Don Daily, John Scott King, Dave Sawford (Pall Bearers).

SYNOPSIS

Mystery

REVIEW AND NOTES

Paul Gooding describes this outing as "a light-hearted Agatha Christie/Poirot-type murder mystery.... Actually, it's kind of like those *Ellery Queen* episodes from the 1970s where he asked the viewer if they had worked out who the killer was before the final reveal."

Sweating Bullets (a.k.a. *Tropical Heat*; television series, 1991–93; 75 episodes) IO International, Safri Tel

"Stranger in Paradise" (Episode #45; November 9, 1992)

Episode Crew: Executive Producer: David Goldstein; Associate Producers: Diana Dru Botsford, Myron Lee Nash, George Vukojevic; Producer: Harel Goldstein; Line Producer: Nanna Nepgen; Co-Producer: Bill Venter; Director: Allan Eastman; Creator: Sam Egan; Teleplay: R. Scott Gemmill; Boom Operator: Felipe Arago; Sound Re-Recording Mixer: Sherry Klein.

Episode Cast: Rob Stewart (Nick Slaughter), Carolyn Dunn (Sylvie Girard), Ian Tracey (Spider Garvin), Caroline Munro (Alicia Simmons), Pedro Armendariz Jr. (Lieutenant Carillo), Mia Kirshner (Sandy), Aviva Marks (Vera), Jonathan Sagall (Jimmy).

SYNOPSIS

Ex–RCMP and ex–DEA agent Nick Slaughter (Rob Stewart) relocates to sunny Key Mariah, Florida, and begins a detective agency with travel agent Sylvie Gerard (Carolyn Dunn). Naughtiness in picturesque locations ensues.

FILMS AND TELEVISION: *To Die For* (1994)

REVIEW AND NOTES

When a show is a third-rate rip-off of *Baywatch* and *Miami Vice*, you know you're in trouble, especially when it has a lead character named Nick Slaughter — with a ponytail. A real guy named Nick Slaughter would not have a ponytail. Caroline's episode is not available on DVD, because people were even less interested in first season episodes on DVD than they were when it was originally aired, which put the kibosh on any further episodes seeing the light of day. Perhaps it was because of dialogue like, "I'm not interested in loose ends — I want the whole rope!"

To Die For (a.k.a. *Heaven's a Drag*) — 1994, British Screen Productions, London Lighthouse, TDF

Crew: Director: Peter Mackenzie Litten; Screenplay: Johnny Byrne; Story: Peter Mackenzie Litten, Paul McEvoy; Music: Roger Bolton; Photography: John Ward; Film Editor: Jeffrey Arsenault; Makeup: Helen Lennox, Darren Philips, Victoria Wright; Sound Recordist: Julian Dawton; Stunts: Doug Coleman; Stunt Performer: Danny Lima; Assistant Camera: James Brian Nopper; Production Coordinator: Bettina Gracias.

Cast: Thomas Arklie (Simon), Ian Williams (Mark), Tony Slattery (Terry), Dillie Keane (Siobhan), Jean Boht (Mrs. Downs), Caroline Munro (Mrs. Pignon), Gordon Alexander (Drop Dead Gorgeous), Nicholas Harrison (Siobhan's First Lover), Ian McKellen (Quilt Documentary Narrator), Paul Cottingham (First Poxy Shirt Lifter), Lloyd Williams (Bodybuilder), Robert Sturtz (Chris), Benjamin Sterz (Man in Gym), Brian Carter (Leather Man), Mark Hutchinson (Hospital Visitor), Janet Allen (Ward Sister), Nigel Fairs (Mark Lookalike), Robert Whiton (Man in Cruise Bar), James Greaves (Man in Lavatory), Brian Ross (Nick); Tony London, Richard Cope, Dick Bradnum (Yobs), Ken Kennedy (Mister Willoughby), Andrew Kennedy (Steve), Alan Lowe (Young Man in Club), Will Pollett (Young Mark); Wayne Amiel, Helio, Henrique de Silva (Go-Go Dancers), John Cannon (Jesse Biscuit), David Ingram (Archangel), Gary Martin (Additional Voices), Phill Curr (Skinhead); Mark Ardell, Andy Spur, Carl Robinson, Tony MacDonald, Paul Kevin, Zeus, Danny Boy, Dark Angel, The Bronze (Angels).

SYNOPSIS

Simon and Mark, they were lovers, Lordy, oh how they did love. Mark swore to be true to Simon, true as the stars above; he was his man, he wouldn't do him wrong.

Mark, he would sit in the front room, quietly stitching his quilt, while Simon took other lovers, and never felt any guilt. Mark was his man, but he was doing him wrong.

Mark died and Simon was lonely, but he said it was time to move on. But things began to go haywire, you see, Mark wasn't really gone. Simon was his man, and still doing him wrong.

Mark can only be seen now by Simon, never will leave him alone. Simon he's getting frustrated, and tells Mark just to leave him alone; says he never loved him, Lord knows that was wrong.

Mark's life is shattered all over, Simon has hurt him again; tells him much that he loves him, and that will never end, though Simon always done him wrong.

Simon finds dad didn't hate him, loved him with all of his heart; when Simon found just how wrong he'd been the news tore him apart; Mark wasn't the only man he was doing wrong.

Simon, he gets what he wished for, when he gets home Mark is gone; knows he's been selfish and stupid, and he cries the whole night long; Simon works on the quilt, until the morning dawn.

Mark, he appears back to Simon, and then time itself seems to cease; Mark can now leave with the angels, and can finally rest in peace; their love will last as long as time goes on.

REVIEW AND NOTES

Variety's Emmanuel Levy wrote, "*To Die For*, a remarkably forthright film about life in the age of AIDS, features engaging characters, lively dialogue, snappy humor, and, above all, affecting emotion. According to *The New York Times'* Stephen Holden, "[It's] a film so determined to find emotional uplift in the AIDS crisis that it seesaws wildly between witty drawing-room comedy and tear-drenched pathos.... [T]he movie also finds time to offer politically pointed vignettes on homophobia and gay-bashing. With all its inconsistencies of tone, [it] is still clumsily endearing for the way it wears its heart on its sleeve."

This movie really does deserve to be seen; thought-provoking, at times heart-breaking and at times, yes, terribly funny. (Mark: "I might as well be dead, for all you care." Simon: "But you are dead!" "Oh, trust you to nitpick.") And when it's over, besides all of the other food for thought it offers, you're thinking, wow, this was done by one of the guys who directed and wrote *Slaughter High*? The only really disappointing thing about it, for fans of Caroline, is that she's only in it for about two minutes, if that; she plays a lonely widow who spends most of those two minutes sizing up Simon's bum. But it was nice of Litten to remember her for a part, and at least she doesn't get slaughtered. The other alumnus on hand from that film is Gary Martin. Dillie Keane does an absolutely hilarious and heartwarming turn as Mark and Simon's ditzy upstairs neighbor, and Tony Slattery is nearly as funny as her hyper–politically correct boyfriend. The original title *To Die For* was changed to *Heaven's a Drag* for the release in the States, to avoid being confused with the Nicole Kidman film *To Die For*.

Flesh for the Beast— 2003, Fever Dreams, Media Blasters

Crew: Executive Producer: John Sirabella; Producer–Special Effects Coordinator: Carl Morano; Line Producer: Csaba Bereczky; Director-Story-Screenplay: Terry M. West; Music:

FILMS AND TELEVISION: *Flesh for the Beast* (2003)

Buckethead; Photography–Second Unit Director: Richard Siegel; Film Editor–Sound Mixer: Andrew Sterling; Production Designer: Steward Noack; Special Effects Makeup Artists: Pete Gerner, Brian Spears; First Assistant Director: Terrence L. Moore; Second Assistant Director: Jenny Cadenillas; Set Dresser: Ruby Larocca.

Cast: Jane Scarlett (Erin Cooper), Sergio Jones (John Stoker), Clark Beasley Jr. (Ted Sturgeon), Caroline Munro (Carla the Gypsy), Jim Coop (Jack Ketchum), David "Victor Flynn" Runco (Joseph Monks), Aaron Clayton (Douglas Clegg), Michael Sinterniklaas (Martin Shelley), Caroline Hoermann (Pauline), Ruby Larocca (Cassandra), Barbara Joyce (Irene), Kevin G. Shinnick (Joey/Zombie), Isadora Edison (Shower Silhouette), Aldo Sambrell (Alfred Fischer); Keith Leopard, Kelly Troy Howard, Zoe Moonshine, Michael Roszhart, Jonathan Lees (Zombies).

SYNOPSIS

John Stoker (Sergio Jones) invites a group of paranormal investigators to "cleanse" his house of evil. The house had been owned by Alfred Fischer (Aldo Sambrell), who dealt in drugs, prostitutes and the occult. Erin Cooper (Jane Scarlett) looks at a portrait of Fischer and three women and faints.

Group leader Ted Sturgeon (Clark Beasley Jr.) is suspicious of Stoker, but begins the investigation in a heavily foreboding atmosphere. When he touches the portrait, he begins to shake, and the room takes on an eerie glow. He tries to bolt from the room, but the door slams, and blood seeps out from under the door.

Shelley (Michael Sinterniklaas) is in one of the rooms stealing jewelry when he turns and sees zombies. But when he makes the sign of the cross with his fingers, they disappear.

Ketchum (Jim Coop) is investigating another room, and it takes on the eerie glow, revealing a young, pretty girl who calls herself Pauline. She strips and asks him if he'd like to fulfill his domination fantasies, so he takes her forcefully. She then takes him by turning into a beast and eating his flesh.

Erin has a vision of Fischer and Carla the Gypsy (Caroline Munro). Carla sells Fischer a scarab amulet with which he hopes to consolidate his occult power, and gives him a warning, after which he cuts Carla's throat. Erin faints.

Clegg goes into another room, filled with toys and that eerie glow. There's another pretty young girl there, Cassandra (Ruby Larocca). She strips and climbs on top of him, but their torrid sex breaks one of Cassandra's toys, so she squeezes another and he literally pukes his guts out!

Stoker demands that Erin reveal the whereabouts of the amulet, and knocks her out. While she is unconscious, "Erin" appears to Monks. She strips and has sex with him, but then humiliates him. When he slaps her, she disembowels him. When Erin awakes, Stoker tells her he needs Fischer's amulet to control the succubae, and knocks her out again.

Shelley enters a room that is filled with the eerie glow. A pretty young girl who calls herself Irene strips and climbs on top of him, and after he comes she becomes a beast, tears out his guts and begins to gorge herself.

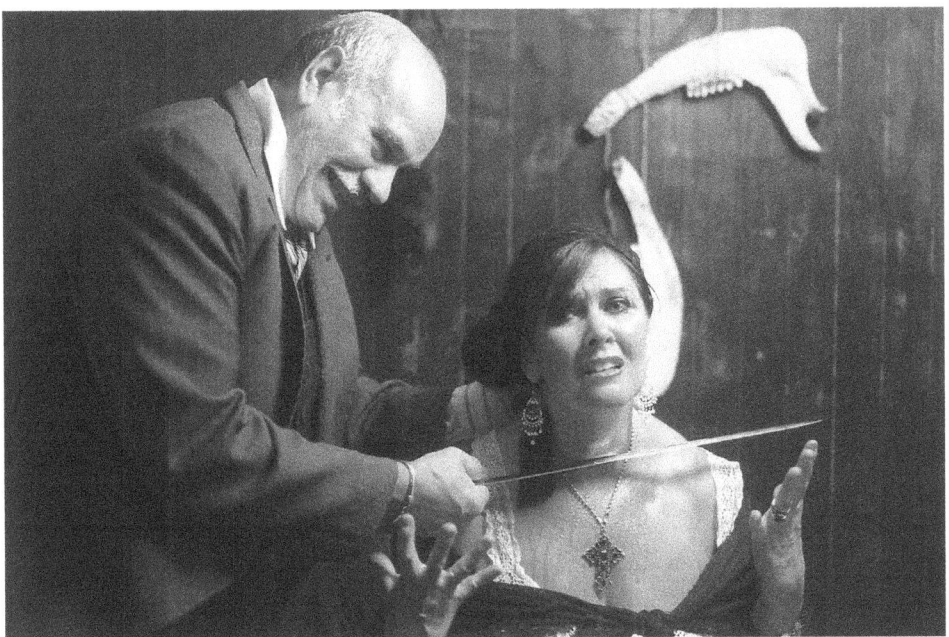

Aldo Sambrell cuts Caroline to the quick in *Flesh for the Beast*.

Stoker finally discovers the fate of Sturgeon, who has been crucified. Sturgeon's body explodes, showering Stoker in blood. Then Stoker breaks on through to the other side of the painting and finds the amulet inside a skull.

Erin comes across the succubae feasting on Shelley, and they chase her down the hall into a corner. When she screams at them, her pupils dilate to hideous dimensions, and Irene says, "Welcome home!" Erin strips and changes into a red dress. Stoker calls on the succubae to eat her, but she is one of them. They attack him instead and Erin drives the amulet into his skull. The amulet has been returned to its proper resting place, and the zombies drag Stoker's corpse away to *its* proper resting place, behind the painting. With Stoker dead, the other succubae wonder who will procure their meals for them, but Erin tells them that there are enough greedy and lustful men to keep them supplied for a long time. Then Erin disappears, and returns to her proper resting place — now there is a fourth woman in the painting.

REVIEW AND NOTES

According to *The Hollywood Reporter*, "Although cheap-looking and amateurishly acted, *Flesh for the Beast*, which features a music score by eccentric guitarist Buckethead, doesn't invite huge critical derision, if only for the palpable enthusiasm of both the cast and filmmaker for their gory shenanigans." A *Village Voice* critic opined, "It's all gleefully over the top, but neither particularly campy nor scary. For those who like a little T & A with their blood and gore however, *Flesh for the Beast* serves up ample portions of each." *New York Post*'s V.A. Musetto carped, "The script is obvious and clichéd and the action is more disgusting than frightening." According to Ken Fox of *TV Guide*, "Derivative, indifferently acted, artlessly photographed, and awash in nudity and rudimentary gore effects, this direct-to-DVD mars the producing debut of longtime horror and exploitation distributors Media Blasters."

Flesh for the Beast is another direct-to-DVD delicacy brought to us by the man responsible for such Misty Mundae epics as *Play-Mate of the Apes* and *Lord of the G-Strings*, Terry West. As such, the eternal question is always: is it soft-core porn that includes horror, or is it horror that includes soft-core porn? To which the eternal answer would be: yes.

Caroline is around for only one scene, which she shares with Aldo Sambrell, whom she had previously appeared with in *The Golden Voyage of Sinbad* twenty-nine years before. She was offered the part after some members of the production crew produced the *"Beauty Behind* Faceless*"* interview extra for the 2004 DVD release of *Faceless*. Sambrell was a joy as a character actor, and with his range he appeared in everything from Sinbad to Spaghetti Westerns (*The Good, the Bad, and the Ugly*, *For a Few Dollars More*, *Fistful of Dollars*) to Blaxploitation (*Shaft in Africa*) to the A-list production *Dr. Zhivago* to TV shows like *The Rat Patrol*. Caroline's character's name is a reference to her role as Carla the gypsy girl in *Captain Kronos*, but instead of playing it as befitting her natural personality, she goes all out and seems to be channeling Maria Ouspenskaya. All of the male characters are named after famous horror authors — Stoker, Shelley, Theodore Sturgeon, Jack Ketchum, Joseph Monks, and Douglas Clegg. Aldo Sambrell's character name could refer to any one of three famous Germans by the name of Alfred Fischer: One was an architect, one was a judge, and one was an S.S. officer. But due to the brutal nature of the character, one could probably surmise that it's the third man.

The film would seem to be a tribute to the *Giallo* films and the sex-and-gore films of Jess Franco, only the actors are inexperienced and the direction not as stylish. Of course, everybody has to start somewhere, and, yes, there's an agreeable type of "Hey, gang, let's all put on a horror show" atmosphere, but at what point does the whole enterprise begin to cave in on itself? Not this film per se, but the horror film in general? Whereas the earlier efforts were derived from literature or legend or other sources, now horror films reference other horror films to an increasingly alarming degree. It's the same with many aspects of popular culture: The Rolling Stones' "Sympathy for the Devil" was inspired, lyrically, by a cult called "The Process" and Mikhail Bulgakov's novel *The Master and Margarita*; Oasis just rewrites "Street Fighting Man" as "Lyla." Jack Kirby was inspired by Howard Pyle and mythology; modern comic artists are inspired by the guys who were inspired by the guys who were inspired by Kirby. Of course, this isn't an unheard-of practice; many incisive and significant pieces of pop culture draw upon others for some of their most important moments, expanding the ideas in different directions, but at what point does it stop being ironic or clever and become simply derivative?

At least it can be said that, out of the depths of its murky plot, *Flesh for the Beast* seems to try to subvert the standard tropes of the genre a bit in that practically all of the victims are male (Caroline is the only woman who gets killed). And while it can hardly be called a feminist film, it does put all the power in the hands of the women — certainly there will never be a shortage of lustful, greedy and dishonest men. But is this, too, an illusion, simply a case of one male-driven stereotype being replaced by another, a clichéd aspect of femininity as seen through the eyes of a man; the archetype of predatory womankind as his ruination? Does the fact that the film was conceived by a male who specializes in exploitation answer that question? Of course, it can be claimed that it's all done consciously and ironically, but irony seems to be in short supply here, unless it's the kind of irony that's simply another way of not having to mean what you say.

But perhaps this is to take it all too seriously. Perhaps we should view it in the grindhouse spirit of the drive-in, the former natural habitat of low-budget exploitation in the days before they went straight to DVD. And so, in that spirit, and because, as much as any other film reviewed in the book, *Flesh for the Beast* absolutely cries out to be reviewed in such a manner, it will be reviewed not just in the spirit of the Great American drive-in, but in the style of the Keeper of the Drive-In Flame, the great Joe Bob Briggs: "Eight breasts. Seven dead bodies. Heads roll. Guts roll. Approximately 87 & ½ gallons of blood, every ounce of which is absolutely necessary to the story. A 96 on the vomit-meter. Great special effects when their eyes look like they been down in the root cellar for six months and then all of a sudden you shine a flashlight on 'em. No motor vehicle chases. No Kung Fu, but Crucifixion Fu, Amulet Fu, Zombie Fu, Toy Fu, Gun Fu, Sex Fu, and Intestinal Fu, if you know what I mean and I think you do. Only two stars, but 'Bobb' still says check it out."

The DVD contains quite a few extras, one of which is an interview segment with Caroline and Aldo Sambrell, both of whom are immensely entertaining: "I'm Caroline Munro, and the film is *Flesh for the Beast*, and I play which was an old man's part, wasn't it, Aldo ... but now it's been changed to a gypsy, who can sort of see what's about to happen ... not everything that's going to happen ... so that's the premise I thought was good, it's a supernatural thriller-y kind of thing ... with lots of blood, for those of you who like blood; I don't know about anything else, I don't know if there's sex, I'm not sure ... is there, Carl? Oh, he's gone quiet now!"

Domestic Strangers — 2005, USA

Crew: Producer-Director-Screenplay: Jeffrey Arsenault; Line Producer: Yunah Hong; Film Editor: Victor Mignatti; Property Master: Deidre L. Fleischer.

Cast: Anthony Albanese (Danny), Patrick Askin (Ken), Harriet Atkins (Danny's Mum), Quentin Crisp (Mr. Davis), Kevin Cristaldi (Alex), Michael J. Cummings (Los Angeles Roommate), Alan Edwards (Jeremy), Veronica Manning (Ada), Caroline Munro (Counselor), Hud-

FILMS AND TELEVISION: *The Absence of Light* (2006)

sen River (Sassy Roommate), Davide A. Slocum (Danny's Boyfriend), David Squire (Broke Roommate), Gordon Synn (Brandon), Christine Taylor (Linda), Marcus Teo (Corey).

SYNOPSIS

Drama.

NOTES

Caroline plays an expressive psychiatrist in this meller about those nutty kids and their crazy problems. It reunited her with Jeffrey Arsenault, who produced, wrote and directed *Night Owl* twelve years earlier.

The Absence of Light— 2006, New Illusions Pictures

Crew: Producer-Director-Screenplay-Photography-Film Editor-Sound Designer-Steady Cam Operator-Visual Effects Supervisor-GCI Animation-Digital Compositing-Lighting-Opening & End Titles Animation & Design: Patrick Desmond; Music-Assistant Editor-CGI Animation-Digital Compositing-Postproduction Audio-Opening & End Titles Animation & Design: Andy Halter; Music: Andy Halter, Richard Conant, Todd Skeie; Casting: Rebekah Gardner, Michael Bradley, Fritz Chess, Linda Orick; Film Graphic Design Artist–Lighting: Gary Dile; Lighting: Rebekah Gardner, Eric Thornsberry; Lighting-Special Effects Supervisor-Special Makeup Effect Artist-Set Designer-Head Electrician-Prop Design-Head Gaffer: Jerry C. Gatewood.

Cast: Richard Conant (Puritan), Eric Thornsberry (Sultan), Caroline Munro (Abbey Church), Michael Berryman (The Seer), Tom Savini (The Higher Power), David Hess (Whiplash), Rick Scarry (Senator Criswell), Tony Todd (The Alchemist), Tom Sullivan (Dr. Corrigan), Kevin Van Hentenryk (Jenkins), Robyn Griggs (Fiona), Rebekah Gardner (Jezebel), Mark Cullison (Fetish), Keith Kline (Fiona's Assistant), Linda Orick (Velvet), Fritz Chess (Arcane), Beth Westgerdes (April), Jerry C. Gatewood (Clayton Marduke), Mark Hlavin (The Surgeon), Robert Flanagan (The Grand Inquisitor), Nicole Hall (Sex Video Girl), Andy Halter (The Slug), Michael Bradley (Reynolds), Emilie Carson (Sultan's Fiancé), Steve Palmer (Steven Black), Sean Ashbrook (Seth), Sherry Fisher (TV News Reporter), Dax Davis (The Spyder), Gary Dile (Dr. Garrett Lee), Danielle Liebsch-Hilton (Mrs. Criswell), Lori Stahl (Criswell Houseguest #1), Angela Kuhnes (Criswell Houseguest #2/Vampire Girl), Joanna Hamilton, Elizabeth Cironi (Vampire Girls), Holleigh Romeno, Tabitha Foster (Criswell Limo Girls), Derek Anderson (Plague Biker), Jeff Rinehart (Nate Hasselnhopf), Joe Gatewood (Cutler), Todd Skeie (Implanted Plague Member), Adam Furay (Jezebel Torture Victim), Kimberly R. Noble-Hite (Josephine), Karen Gatewood (Criswell's Secretary), Boru (TV Commercial Dog), Patrick Desmond (TV Commercial Director); Scott Carter, Christopher Craig, Steve Craig, Justin Ferst, Levi Fraley, Jeremy Kennedy, Anthony Shoemaker (Plague Members), David Nelson (Dr. Buchanan).

SYNOPSIS

Two shadowy organizations vie for control of the political system and other avenues of power: The Plague, under the control of ex–government operative "Whiplash" (David

FILMS AND TELEVISION: *The Absence of Light* (2006)

Caroline, Michael Berryman and Tom Savini are featured in this one-sheet poster for *Absence of Light*, designed by Gary Dile (courtesy Gary Dile).

FILMS AND TELEVISION: *The Absence of Light* (2006)

Lobby card featuring Caroline and Tom Savini used to promote *Absence of Light* in foreign markets (courtesy Gary Dile).

Hess), and Section 8, run by "Higher Power" (Tom Savini). Blackmail, murder-for-hire, and covert operations are their business, and business is good.

The first order of business is the elimination of one of Senator Criswell's (Rick Scarry) sex partners, who has a video of their encounter. Section 8 assigns its top hit man, Puritan, and his new partner Sultan to the job of tracking her down and eliminating her with extreme prejudice.

The Plague and Section 8 then engage in a deadly game of cat-and-mouse, and a race against time. Will Section 8 get the Senator re-elected, or will The Plague get him first?

REVIEW AND NOTES

Film Threat: "One of the most ambitious independent movies I've seen in a long time." *The Last New Jersey Drive-In on the Left*: "A cool indie action/conspiracy thriller." *Killer Film*: "Fast-paced, intelligent, and endlessly inventive horror thriller."

It's an ambitious effort, to say the least, as it was filmed mostly on location — at horror fan conventions! I remember seeing the movie for the first time and thinking,

FILMS AND TELEVISION: *The Absence of Light* (2006)

Poster featuring Caroline as the ruthless Abbey Church in *Absence of Light* (courtesy Gary Dile).

"Wow, that scene looks like it was taking place in the parking lot of Monster Bash"— and indeed it was. When I asked Bash head honcho Ron Adams if it had been, he replied, "Oh, yes, that's why he thanked all of those conventions at the end, because he shot all the guest stars' scenes at them. Instead of having the stars come to him, he went to the stars." The movie certainly has star power, much more than one can normally expect from a low-budget independent film: Michael Berryman (*The Hills Have Eyes, Doc Savage: The Man of Bronze*), David Hess (*Last House on the Left, Swamp Thing*), Tony Todd (*Candyman, Minotaur*), Kevin Van Hentenryk (*Basket Case* series), Tom Savini (*Maniac, From Dusk Till Dawn*), and Caroline, who plays the ruthless Abbey Church. As Gary Dile, who plays Dr. Lee, and was also the film's primary graphic artist, told me in an email, Caroline's character Abbey Church is named after an actual road in the Columbus, Ohio, suburb of Dublin, the Abbey Church Road.

All of Caroline's scenes were shot at different conventions; look closely and you'll see that each takes place in a different room. Her first scenes were shot at Monster Bash, literally an hour before she got on the plane to go back to England. Additional scenes were shot at the Frightvision and Wonderfest conventions, and not all in the same year. The story and filming began in 2000, after director Patrick Desmond became acquainted with Tom Savini, who was instrumental in helping to secure the rest of the cast. Desmond, a lifelong fan of *House of Frankenstein*, told me that he was inspired to create his own "monster rally," although not in terms of monsters, but horror stars. When Caroline was shown an early trailer, she wanted to be involved. She didn't see the script until the night before her first part was shot but, true pro that she is, she had it memorized for the time-compressed shoot the next day. The filming was not completed until 2007.

Gary graciously provided many more behind-the scenes glimpses into the making of *Absence of Light*. Since everyone involved had "regular" jobs, shooting was only done when the crew was available. The parking lot where David Hess's car is parked is the parking lot of the stadium of the New York Giants; you can see the Giants' logo in the background. Both he and Pat Desmond told me that scenes were filmed, by necessity, in various hotel rooms and hallways dressed to look like office suites, but this isn't incongruous; given the nature of all the corporate tomfoolery, it's only natural that a lot of action takes place in this type of locale, itself ever changing. The main camera on the film was called "The Baby," and until he learned the crew's code, he was startled and disturbed to hear so many cries of "Who's watching 'The Baby'?" Rick Scarry, who has appeared on 100 TV shows, including *L.A. Law* and *Married with Children*, is Patrick Desmond's uncle, and his character's name was inspired by prognosticator Criswell, who appeared in a few Ed Wood films. Gary calls Caroline "the consummate professional actress"; he didn't join the cast until about two years into filming, at which time some of her scenes had already been filmed. He remembers the first time he met her: He had just worked an overnight shift at a TV station and then driven 90 miles to Cleveland, and upon arrival, the rest of the crew were nowhere to be found. Caroline was the first person associated with the film that he saw, and she immediately set his mind at ease and helped him locate Patrick and the rest of the gang. She has remembered him and treated him with the same amount of genuine kindness and respect ever since.

Some horror fans may be disappointed when they first see the movie; with all of the horror star power, one would naturally assume that it will be a real, er, monster

FILMS AND TELEVISION: *The Absence of Light* (2006)

Absence of Light graphic artist Gary Dile poses with Caroline and Tami Hamalian; Caroline is holding a ten-pound cement skull made by Tom Savini and autographed by the entire cast. It now sits in Gary's office (courtesy Gary Dile).

bash, but it's really more of a thriller, with science-fictional and horror overtones — a sort of "Secret Agents Meet the Monsters," somewhat like our beloved Mexican monster movies where, say, El Santo and a Bond clone will face off against a mad scientist who creates monsters in an aquarium or something. But they won't be disappointed by any of the stars' performances; Caroline is having a fine old time playing a corporate battle-hardened bitch, and the wonderful Michael Berryman is mondo creepy in his quasi-mystical cameo as "The Seer." Tony Todd turns in a titanic performance in his short scene, and David Hess is a rock (not to be confused with David "The Rock" Nelson, who also has a cameo and comes to a nasty end).

Admittedly, the storyline could be a bit more linear, and at times, the guest stars' experience sometimes throws the less-experienced actors' limitations into too bright a light, but it's a much more thought-out concept than most independent films which are cheap excuses to show tits and zombies. The DVD contains a raft of extra features, one of which is a short but sweet interview with Caroline:

> It was just a delightful experience. Patrick approached me with his associates, and he said, "I'd like for you to be involved with the film..." and I said, "I'm interested" ... and so he

FILMS AND TELEVISION: *Turpin* (2009) / *Eldorado* (2011)

showed me some footage, and I thought it was just amazing.... It was just five or ten minutes' footage, and I said, "Yes, I want to be involved," and he said, "Great! Can we start in half an hour?" The part I play ... she's a really nasty piece of work, named Abbey Church, and it's a very apt name, because she's not a very churchy lady at all.... She was basically an assassin, although she didn't dirty her hands.... So, thank you, Patrick, I hope to do another one.... Don't forget me when you get big!

Turpin (short)—2009, Hemstone Productions

Crew: Producers-Screenplay: Les Hemstock, Chris Stone; Director–Film Editor: Chris Stone.

Cast: Les Hemstock (Dick Turpin), Richard Jack (Tom King), Caroline Munro (Lady Victoria), Emily Hall (Harriet Brazier), Jeremy Bulloch (Sir Guy), Mark Johnston (Captain Ainsworth), Ray Johnson (Judge Rookwood), Katie Reddin-Clancy (Lady Charlotte Delancey), Trudi Ross (Bar Wench), Napoleon Ryan (Francis Delancey).

SYNOPSIS

This short depicts the amazing origin of Dick Turpin, the most wanted highwayman in 18th Century England.

REVIEW AND NOTES

Dick Turpin is part of a long-standing British tradition of romanticizing criminals (not that we Americans don't or haven't done it, but they've just been at it longer than us). *Turpin* is a well-made, action-packed little costume drama, and it's nice to see Caroline in a piece with quality production values, that is a nice change of pace from the knife-wielding psychos and buckets of blood that characterize much of her later output. Jeremy Bulloch, who plays Caroline's husband Sir Guy, had already appeared with her in *The Spy Who Loved Me* (as a member of the British submarine crew), and became a member of the *Doctor Who* universe in the "Time Warrior" story arc before finding his greatest fame as Boba Fett in the original *Star Wars* trilogy. He chalked up his second Bond appearance with *Octopussy* (1983).

Eldorado—2011, House of Fear

Crew: Executive Producer: Keith Howell; Producer-Director-Screenplay: Richard Driscoll; Music: Buster Bloodvessel, Howie Casey, Tim Renwick; Photography: Francois Coppey; Film Editor: Robert James; Casting: Darren Moore, Jayne White; Production Designer-Art Director: Lee Fenton-Wilkerson; Costume Design: Gemma Bedeau; Makeup: Aimee Florence, Emma Mash; Special Makeup Effects Artist: Sean Kenrick; Makeup Department Head: Emslie Mills; Production Manager: Laura Cakebread; First Assistant Director: Will Nash.

Cast: Darryl Hannah (The Stranger), Peter O'Toole (Narrator), David Carradine (The Spirit Guide), Jeff Fahey (Doc Martin), Michael Madsen (Ted), Patrick Bergin (Roy), Brigitte Nielsen (Angel), Steve Guttenberg (Martin), Rebecca Linley (Jessica Albino Jones), Rik Mayall (Chef Mario), Darren Morgan (Stanley Rosenblum), Sylvester McCoy (General Zwick), Bill Moseley (Lemmas), Robin Askwith (Mick the Shoe), Robert Llewellyn (Meat), Caroline Munro (Lilly), Oliver Tobias (Dick Wheeler), Richard "Steven Crane" Driscoll (Oliver Rosenblum), Vass Anderson (The Mayor), Dave Sommer (Man-Mountain), Alexis Caley (Lesley Dean), Steve Munroe (Eduardo), Daniel Steven Lopez (Deputy Atkins), Jason Collins (Backstage Manager), Mick Barber (Tommy), Michael Lanchbury (Mini-Mountain), Anthony Neale (Assistant Stage Manager), Marius Smuts (Bill), James Michael Rankin (A Face in the Crowd), Tom Savini, Buster Bloodvessel.

SYNOPSIS

From advance publicity:

After wrongly being sent to a Neo-Nazi fundraiser, Blues Brothers tribute band "The Jews Brothers," Stan and Ollie, get offered a gig in Eldorado to make amends for a gig gone sour.

At the very same time, Jessica, a beautiful but despondent wife, is on the run with a million dollars from her cheating husband's night club. All roads lead to Eldorado, these lives intersect, and at this point it means trouble. While these small lives revolve around each other, a bigger power is controlling the action to make their visit to this town one that they will never forget.

It's Eldorado's 200th anniversary, the townsfolk are hungry to celebrate, which does prove unfortunate to the tourists who come to visit and find that they are the dish of the day.

A parody of films including *The Blues Brothers*, *Sweeney Todd*, and *Little Shop of Horrors*, Eldorado is more than just bad table manners and a little light music; it becomes a way of life.

NOTES

Production of this film has been completed, and it was set for release in both the USA and the UK in November of 2010, but was not released until 2012.

Stellar Quasar and the Scrolls of Dadelia—2012, Midnight Marquee Productions

Crew: Producer: Gary J. Svehla; Executive Producers: George Stover, Nicholas Anez; Co–Executive Producers: Joseph Higgins, Paul Krueger, John Tydings; Director-Writer: A. Susan Svehla; Photographer–Film Editor: Jeff Herberger; Production Assistants: Albert Finlay, Paul Krueger, Charlie Wittig; Set Designer: Kelly Shaw, Jason Presson; Costume Designer: Susan Melissa Miller; Costume Department: Juliana Cochran, Lucinda Cochran; Makeup

FILMS AND TELEVISION: *Stellar Quasar and the Scrolls of Dadelia* (2012)

Department: Suzanne Busch, Susan Melissa Miller; Assistants to A. Susan Svehla: Laura Stotler, Tristan Watts, Cindy Blanchard.

Cast: Nichole Chimere Davis (Stellar Quasar), Zachary Steffey (First Officer Heinlein), Jessica Felice (Pilot Clarke), Leo Dymowski (Comtech Sprocket), Barry Murphy (Engineer Sapper), George Stover (Android Ike), Buddy Svehla (Astrobuddy), Ellecina Eck (Airella), Matthew Harding (Drago Potter), Marat Buberman (First Officer Ellison), Michael N. Smith (Com Officer), Jung Lee (Pilot Nieshlar Baily), Lianna Oliver (Navigator Austen), Jason Patrick Presson (Harrison Cooper), Shawn Anthony (Zolton), Steve Rifkin (Com Officer Lightdor), Karla Sauter (Captain Dryden), Mitch Klein (Navigator Pherb), Wayne Shipley (Overseer Esuriant), Tom Proveaux (Right Reverend Fazon), Paul Harne (Pilot Thomas Adonis), Garron Butler (Jartar Lucason), Bill Littman (High Bishop Mendicious Manget), Tyrus Rice (Techhead 1), Mike Lord (Techhead 2), Dominique Spencer (Doogle Madison), Al Finlay (Paparazzi 1), Bernie Noeller (Paparazzi 2), Mary Eck (Paparazzi 3), Tony Apollo (Marma Dimonia), William Steffey (Gareth Verne), Savanna Leigh (Butler), Suzanne Busch (Dancing Girl), Alfred Guy (Fred); Annabelle Browne, Michael Glenn Brill, Elizabeth Chapman, Ponch Fenwick, Beth Goodwin, Sarah Goodwin, Izabelle Greer, Ben Hosek, Emma Jackson, Lucinda Jackson, Cordy Justice, Jenna Justice, B.J. Mitchell, J. Leanne Mitchell, Anastasia Nitsios, Josh Pritchett, Andy Wagner, Betty Wiley, C.J. Frosch, Erin Gray, Tom Tom Martin, Mische Ren, Roma Mafia, Jessica Schimpf, Christopher Inlow, Curtis Prather, Julianna Cochran; Special Guest Appearances: Amanay (Caroline Munro), Sayang (Veronica Carlson).

SYNOPSIS

The story involves a quest for the scrolls that hold the answer to the universe.

REVIEW AND NOTES

At the time of this writing, post-production work was being completed on the film.

Documentary and Guest Appearances, Archival Footage and Other Works

This section contains information about television shows, films, documentaries, and promotional films which feature Caroline as herself or in archival footage. It also features information about Caroline's recording career and appearances in music videos and television commercials, as well as a listing of genre magazines that contain features on, interviews with, or covers of Caroline. Every attempt has been made to provide as much information as possible, but there are still certain appearances which eluded me. These are: *The Main Attraction*, *Give Us a Clue*, *The Live at Five Show*, *The Mike Douglas Show*, and *The Joe Franklin Show*.

Film and Television

A Whole Scene Going (television series, 1966; 24 episodes)
British Broadcasting Corporation (BBC)

Episode #1; January 5, 1966

Episode Crew: Producer: Elizabeth Cowley; Directors: John Crome, Tom Savage; Film Editor: Dave King; Production Design: Ken Jones; Titles: Barry Fantoni, Derek Nice.

Episode Cast: Barry Fantoni, Wendy Varnals (Presenters); *Guests*: Lulu, Spike Milligan, Caroline Munro, and The Who.

Synopsis

The first episode of a short-lived British telly series focusing on teen scene, it featured tips on fashion, interviews with and performances by celebrities and musical guests.

Review and Notes

An attempt to cash in on the success of shows like *Top of the Pops* and *Ready, Steady, Go*, this show lasted six months and featured a whole raft of top-flight talent such as The Who, Manfred Mann, The Dave Clark Five, Peter & Gordon, Dave Berry,

The Spencer Davis Group, Herman's Hermits, The Small Faces, The Animals, Ravi Shankar, Dave Dee Dozy Beaky Mick and Tich, and the omnipresent Cilla Black. In this first episode, a 16-year-old (and apparently very nervous) Caroline is introduced as "The Face of 1966." She has no lines, and simply sits on a stool while host Wendy Varnals describes her thusly: "We think it's a great face, but a continuation of 1965, with a definite touch of the Shrimptons about it ... virtually no makeup, except around the eyes, emphasis here on the lower lashes. Her hair is its own brown-y color, and worn in the style of the 1900s, and if you look like her, to the experts, you'll have the face of 1966!" Caroline is still on the stool for a Who performance of "Out in the Street," to which she sways and smiles.

The Des O'Connor Show—1963–1973, Associated Television (ATV) Network Production

Episodes June 26, 1971; July 10, 1971; August 7, 1971; Episode June 26, 1971: *Episode Crew*: Executive Producer: Mort Lachman; Producer: Alan Tarrant; Director: John Scoffield; Writers: Tony Hawes, Barry Cryer, Ronnie Cass, Stan Dreben, Lila Garret, David Pollock, Elias Davis; Production Design: Brian Bartholomew; Musical Director: Jack Parnell; Choral Director: Mike Sammes; Choreographer: Paddy Stone. *Episode Cast*: Des O'Connor (Host), The Jack Parnell Orchestra, The Mike Sammes Singers (Music); Jack Douglas, Caroline Munro, Connie Stevens, Dom DeLuise, The Dolly Birds Plus Two (Guests)

Episode July 10, 1971: *Episode Crew*: Executive Producer: Mort Lachman; Producer: Alan Tarrant; Director: Jon Scoffield; Writers: Gig Henry, Bill Larkin, Charles Lee, Michael Magee, Paul Wayne; Production Design: Brian Bartholomew; Musical Director: Jack Parnell; Choral Director: Mike Sammes; Choreographer: Paddy Stone. *Episode Cast*: Des O'Connor (Host), The Jack Parnell Orchestra, The Mike Sammes Singers (Music); Jack Benny, Harry Corbett, Barry Cryer, Jack Douglas, Winnie Holman, Caroline Munro, Winifred Sabine, Connie Stevens, The New Faces (Guests); Other Series Cast: Patrick Newell, Dom DeLuise, Charlie Callas.

Episode August 7, 1971: *Episode Crew*: Executive Producer: Mort Lachman; Producer: Alan Tarrant; Director: Jon Scoffield; Production Design: Brian Bartholomew; Musical Director: Jack Parnell; Choral Director: Mike Sammes; Choreographer: Paddy Stone. *Episode Cast*: Des O'Connor (Host), The Jack Parnell Orchestra, The Mike Sammes Singers, The Paddy Stone Dancers (Music); Phyllis Diller, Joe Baker, Caroline Munro, Connie Stevens (Guests)

SYNOPSIS

Variety show.

OTHER WORKS: Film & TV—*The 7th Annual Sci-Fi Film Awards* (1980)

REVIEW AND NOTES

The much-loved British comedian equals American Bob Barker for television longevity, and has been a fixture on the small screen since 1963; he also made regular appearances on the British music charts, recording 36 albums, with four top-ten singles, including the #1 smash, "I Pretend." *The Des O'Connor Show*, in various formats, ran from 1963 to 1973; originally broadcast in black and white, when the show switched to color, it became more popular internationally, and nine episodes were picked up by NBC as a summer replacement series. It was retitled to fit under the *Kraft Music Hall* umbrella. Other Hammer heroines to appear with Des included Veronica Carlson and Maddy Smith, as well as Hammer hulk Milton Reid, "The British Tor Johnson."

The Seventh Annual Science Fiction Film Awards— 1980, Fantasy Productions

Crew: Co-Producer: Judd Hamilton; Director: William Rainbolt.
Cast: Caroline Munro, Mark Hamill (Hosts); *Guests and Presenters*: Kenny Baker (R2D2); Maud Adams, William Peter Blatty, Roger Corman, Buster Crabbe, Scatman Crothers, Sheila B. Devotion, Electric Light Orchestra, Peter Fonda, Erin Gray, George Hamilton, Tippi Hedren, Arte Johnson, Sam J. Jones, Irvin Kershner, Richard Kiel, John Phillip Law, Stephanie Mills, John Saxon, A.E. Van Vogt.

SYNOPSIS

The presentation of the year's Saturn Awards as voted for by the Academy of Science Fiction, Fantasy and Horror Films.

REVIEW AND NOTES

Caroline reminisced about her involvement with the show in the April 1982 *Fangoria* interview: "It all came about very quickly. I had originally been asked to be a presenter, but two days beforehand, Judd let me know I'd be co-hosting, which terrified me. They arranged a lunch for me to meet Mark Hamill, and all the press was there. He was such a nice person, and his wife was so sweet. It was very strange for me because Mark said, 'It's so nice to meet you after seeing you in films,' and I felt the same way about *him*. To meet him under those circumstances was very unusual, but we got on really well." She also got along with the celebrity presenters, some of whom she hadn't seen in years, such as John Phillip Law. She filmed her segment with Roger Moore beforehand at a hotel in London. Others she encountered for the first time included Peter Fonda, George Hamilton, and John Saxon. Halfway through a rehearsal the morning of the taping, Caroline fell ill with a high fever and nearly fell from the stage from dizziness, but she soldiered on. Despite her less-than-ideal physical condition, she admits to having loved every minute of doing the show. "I was also very worried about my voice, because it was very croaky and I really did sound like Kermit the Frog. I didn't quite know what to expect from the audience, but I think they were with us." This was the last of the three awards ceremonies to be televised.

The Making of a Horror Film—1984, Spectacular Trading International

Cast: Derek Ford, Valerie M. Ford, Peter Mackenzie Litten, Belinda Mayne, Stephen Minasian, Caroline Munro, Edmund Purdom, Dick Randall, Alan Selwyn, Gerry Sundquist, Linzi Drew (Model).

SYNOPSIS

A documentary–promotional feature for the movie *Don't Open Till Christmas*.

REVIEW AND NOTES

One of the nuttier "documentaries" to make its way down the pike, this is just as entertaining, if not more so, than the film itself, and taken even less seriously. It supposedly chronicles an "average" day in the life of Dick Randall, who would go on to produce *Slaughter High*, and had already been responsible for such grindhouse classics as *My Seven Little Bares*, *The Wild, Wild World of Jayne Mansfield*, *The Real Bruce Lee* and *Crocodile*. Some people are still wondering if the whole thing is a joke.

Don't Open Till Christmas—1984, Spectacular Trading International, 21st Century Film Corporation

Crew: Producers: Stephen Minasian, Dick Randall; Director: Edmund Purdom; Screenplay: Derek Ford; Story–Writer of Additional Scenes–Director: Al McGoohan; Music: Des Dolan; Photography: Alan Pudney; Film Editor: Ray Selfe; Makeup: Giuseppe Ferranti; Special Effects: Peter Mackenzie Litten; Still Photographer: John Fonseca.
Cast: Edmund Purdom (Inspector Ian Harris), Alan Lake (Giles), Belinda Mayne (Kate Briosky), Mark Jones (Sergeant Powell), Gerry Sundquist (Cliff Boyd), Kelly Baker (Sherry Graham/"Experience" Girl), Kevin Lloyd (Gerry), Wendy Danvers (Housekeeper), Pat Astley (Sharon), Laurence Harrington (Kate's Father), Ken Halliwell (Restaurant Commissionaire), Ray Marioni (Maitre D'hôtel), Wilfred Corlett ("Experience" Santa Claus), Ricky Kennedy (Theater Santa Claus), Sid Wragg (Dungeon Santa Claus), Max Roman (Store Santa Claus), George Pierce (Market Santa Claus), Ashley Dransfield (Drunken Santa Claus), Derek Ford, Adrian Black (Circus Santa Clauses), John Aston (Car Santa Claus), Maria Eldridge (Girl in

Car), Des Dolan (Detective Constable), Derek Hunt (Police Constable), Pauline Meadows (Dungeon Secretary), Caroline Munro (Herself).

SYNOPSIS

A bad Santa and a woman climb into a low-rider for a little Christmas cheer, but their holiday is ruined when Santa gets a knife in his breadbasket. The woman screams in horror and receives the exact same gift!

Kate Briosky (Belinda Mayne) helps her father get into his Santa costume, while her boyfriend Cliff Boyd (Gerry Sundquist) makes jokes. But nobody's laughing, and Kate is screaming in horror, when Daddy Santa gets a sword through his mouth.

Inspector Harris (Edmund Purdom) and Sgt. Powell (Mark Jones) of Scotland Yard are stumped by the serious seasonal slew of savage Santa slayings. Meanwhile, a Santa selling sizzling chestnuts soon finds the only other thing roasting on an open fire is his face! Harris receives a present marked "Do Not Open Till Christmas." A man named Giles (Alan Lake) calls Sgt. Powell, tells him that he's a reporter, and asks him if he'd like the glory of solving the case himself.

The last shot a drunken Santa imbibes is one through the lips and over the gums, out the back of his head it comes! "Experience" peep-show girl Sherry starts to dance for a shy Santa, whose last "experience" is a knife in the back. After more people are killed, Scotland Yard decides to deploy decoys. At the circus, two of them hunt the killer, but death finds them first.

Sherry scorns police protection, and is soon at the mercy of the killer, who chains her in a room. He leaves to chase another drunken Santa into a theater, where the famous Caroline Munro is performing her newest hit, "Warrior of Love." The only thing that rises faster than that song in the charts is the stage platform containing the body of the drunken Santa, whose vision has been slightly impaired with a machete across the eyes. Caroline screams in horror.

Giles breaks into Kate's house; he is not only the killer, but Harris' brother! As she screams in horror, Giles decks the halls with Kate's bloody belly. He is tracked down by Powell, who is absolutely shocked when he is electrocuted by Giles.

Why does Giles hate Christmas? What deep dark secret from his past haunts his tortured psyche? Will Sherry escape, or die screaming in horror? And what sort of present is in store for Inspector Harris when he finally tears the wrapping off of the gift marked "Do Not Open Till Christmas"?

REVIEW AND NOTES

Part of the great tradition of holiday-themed or special-occasion slasher films, *Don't Open Till Christmas* takes great joy in finding as many ways as possible to fold, spindle and mutilate seedy characters in Santa suits. A little boy finds his dad, dressed as Santa, schtooping someone other than his mum at a Christmas party, a perfect occasion for the already obviously-disturbed little bugger to try out his Christmas present:

a shiny new Swiss Army Knife. So for some odd reason, he grows up hating Christmas, and when he breaks out of the booby hatch, he starts killing anybody dressed as Santa Claus. Now, you'd think that after two or three murders of guys dressed like Santa, people would stop going out dressed as Santa, but this apparently doesn't jingle any bells. There's a good girl-bad girl thing going, but the bad girl (the stripper) is actually the good girl, while the good girl is actually a spoiled brat who has inherited all of her father's money, yet still feels the need to slum it with her boyfriend, busking in the tube station *with a flute*, and gives all the indications of tossing the spiv over for father-substitute Harris until his deranged brother disembowels her. No sympathy there, then.

Caroline is only on screen for a few minutes, but she is at least peripherally connected to the plot this time, and at least gets to interact, as it were, with one of the dead Santa brigade. She performs a saucy rock-disco number, "Warrior of Love" (she wrote the lyrics), shakes her booty with abandon, and quite adequately reinforces her Scream Queen credentials with her reaction to the sliced Santa surprise.

3-2-1 (television series, 1978–87; 138 episodes) Yorkshire Television (YTV)

Caroline and Ted Rogers hosted the following 56 episodes:

"Arabian Nights"—Episode #61, January 29, 1983: *Episode Cast*: Sonny Hayes & Company.
"Sherlock Holmes"—Episode #64, February 19, 1983
"Legion's Lost Patrol"—Episode #68, March 19, 1983: *Episode Cast*: Dilys Watling.
"Easter Parade"—Episode #70, April 2, 1983: *Episode Cast*: Julie Dawn Cole.
"Shakespeare"—Episode #73, April 23, 1983
"Music Hall III"—Episode #75, December 3, 1983
"Down South"—Episode #76, December 10, 1983
"It's All Greek to Me"—Episode #77, December 17, 1983: *Episode Cast*: Toni Palmer.
"Dick Whittington"—Episode #78, December 24, 1983: *Episode Cast*: Kenneth Connor, Alan Curtis, Billy Dainty, Dana, Chris Emmett, Mike Newman, Charlie Williams.
"Come into the Garden, Eve"—Episode #79, December 31, 1983
"Swinging Sixties"—Episode #80, January 7, 1984
"It's Magic"—Episode #81, January 14, 1984
"Roaring Twenties"—Episode #82, January 21, 1984
"Drake's Progress"—Episode 83, January 28, 1984
"Raffles"—Episode #84, February 4, 1984: *Episode Cast*: Robert Dorning, Stacy Dorning, Chris Emmett, John Inman, Robin Parkinson, Honor Shepherd, Dr. Geoff Tomlinson.

OTHER WORKS: Film & TV—*3-2-1* (1978–87)

"Nightclub"—Episode #85, February 11, 1984
"My Word Is My Bond"—Episode #86, February 18, 1984
"Country Style"—Episode #87, February 25, 1984
"Newcomers"—Episode #88, March 3, 1984
"Aesop's Fables"—Episode #89, March 10, 1984
"Venice"—Episode #90, March 17, 1984
"Victorian Music Hall"—Episode #91, September 1, 1984
"Mayhem at the Manor"—Episode #92, September 8, 1984: *Episode Cast*: Karen Berry, Felix Bowness, Bonita Bryg, Leslie Crowther, Chris Emmett, Helen Jenkins, Sandy Lawrence, Mike Newman, Bill Pertwee, Dilys Watling.
"Showcase I"—Episode #93, September 15, 1984
"The Gallery"—Episode #94, September 22, 1984
"Circus"—Episode #95, September 29, 1984
"Showcase II"—Episode #98, October 20, 1984
"Further Fables"—Episode #99, October 27, 1984: *Episode Cast*: Karen Berry, Duggie Brown, Bonita Bryg, Anna Dawson, Chris Emmett, Helen Jenkins, Sandy Lawrence, Mike Newman, Jeff Stevenson, Frank Thornton.
"Country & Western"—Episode #100, November 3, 1984
"Swingtime"—Episode #101, November 10, 1984
"Escape from Stalag 17"—Episode #102, November 17, 1984: *Episode Cast*: Christopher Beeny (Tiger), Sydney Bromley (Chalky White), Chris Emmett (Commandant), Michael Knowles (Major Rupert Fawcett-Gently), Ed Bishop, Brian Coburn, Mike Newman.
"Bulldog Drummond"—Episode #103, November 24, 1984: *Episode Cast*: Tim Barrett, Alan Curtis, Chris Emmett, Barbara Hicks, John Inman, Mike Newman
"Let's Rock"—Episode #104, December 1, 1984
"Variety"—Episode #105, December 8, 1984
"Showcase III"—Episode #106, December 15, 1984
"Pantomania"—Episode #107, December 22, 1984: *Episode Cast*: Felix Bowness, Bernie Clifton, Bill Dainty, Susan Dando, Chris Emmett, Arthur English, Fred Feast, Anita Harris, Roy Hudd, John Inman, Davy Kaye, Mike Newman, Larry Noble, Norman Vaughn, June Whitfield, Barbara Windsor, Bernie Winters.
"Country and Western II"—Episode #109, September 7, 1985
"Saturday Night Out"—Episode #110, September 14, 1985
"Music Hall IV"—Episode #112, September 28, 1985
"Forties"—Episode #113, October 5, 1985
"City Life"—Episode #114, October 12, 1985
"International Cabaret"—Episode #116, October 26, 1985
"The Magic of Merlin"—Episode #119, November 16, 1985: *Episode Cast*: Jon Pertwee (Dracula), Jeremy Conner, Kenneth Conner (Merlin), Chris Emmett, Aimi MacDonald (Marilyn Monroe).

"In the Mood"—Episode #122, December 7, 1985
"London"—Episode #123, December 14, 1985
"Sinbad the Sailor"—Episode #124, December 21, 1985: *Episode Cast*: Norman Collier, Lynsey DePaul, Chris Emmett, Arthur English, John Inman, Nigel Lythgoe, Anthony Schaeffer, Victor Spinetti.
"Sea Cruise"—Episode #126, September 6, 1986
"Roaring Twenties II"—Episode #128, September 20, 1986: *Episode Cast*: Faith Brown.
"Show Stoppers"—Episode #129, September 27, 1986: *Episode Cast*: Faith Brown.
"Magic"—Episode #130, October 4, 1986
"Boogie and Jive"—Episode #131, October 11, 1986
"Pictures"—Episode #133, October 25, 1986
"Sixties"—Episode #134, November 1, 1986
"Winners"—Episode #135, November 8, 1986: *Episode Cast*: Gina Mayer (Hostess).
"Pop on the Box"—Episode #136, November 15, 1986
"Christmas at Toad Hall"—Episode # 137 (Special), December 21, 1986: *Episode Cast*: Felix Bowness (Chief Stoat), Kenneth Connor (Mole), Anna Dawson, Chris Emmett, Lance Percival (Chief Weasel), Bill Pertwee (Badger), Tony Selby (Toad), John Boultor (Rat), The Brian Rogers Connection, Lynda Lee Lewis.

Synopsis

The Christmas Special, which was Caroline's last appearance, had contestants representing three famous children's hospitals all trying to win something special.

Review and Notes

Hugely popular with viewers (and producers, because it was inexpensive to make), the show began the year the Sex Pistols disintegrated, and was five years into its run when Caroline came on board. The opportunity was bittersweet; although it provided steady work and offered her the chance to appear with many of Britain's top entertainers; it came as her 13-year marriage to Judd Hamilton was coming to an end, so it was as much a safety net as anything: "I foundered for about three years... I was on my own, and went through a bad state in my mind," she confessed in *Fangoria*. But soon this was not enough, and coupled with increasingly less to do on the show, she decided to quit: "I didn't know if there would be any other work for me, but chose not to do another season." It was around this time that she shot a pilot for the proposed astrology series *Zodiac*, but the series never materialized.

Jon Pertwee (*The House That Dripped Blood*) is featured as Dracula in the episode "The Magic of Merlin" (November 16, 1985). The "Sinbad the Sailor" episode (December 21, 1985) featured Victor Spinetti from The Beatles' *Help!*, where he was outrageously funny as a mad scientist who wants to, dare I say it, rule the world. Paul Gooding comments: "The thing about *3–2–1* was that it was positively reviled by the critics. It was a light entertainment — very light on the entertainment! The funniest thing about it was the cryptic questions which, even when explained, never made sense; I mean *never*!"

Cue Gary (television series, 1987–88; 8 episodes)
UK Television Series

"The Film Star" (Episode # 7; July 23, 1988)
Episode Crew: Executive Producer: Tony Wolfe; Producer: Brian Wesley; Director: Dennis Liddington; Music: Garry Judd; Production Design: Tony Ferris.
Episode Cast: Gary Wilmot, Windsor Davies, Keith Barron, Stanley Lebor, George Lane Cooper, Martin Beaumont, Nikki Boughton, and Caroline Munro.
Synopsis (from the UK's *TV Times*): "Gary's chance to be a film star, but does he kiss the girl? How would Rajah Patel play the part, who is the Sgt. Major kidding, and is the prince a possible contender?"

REVIEW AND NOTES

According to Paul Gooding, "Windsor Davies found fame in the British comedy *It Ain't Half Hot Mum*, written by Jimmy Perry and David Croft, the men behind the popular British sitcom *Dad's Army*." Gary Wilmot, the sketch show's star, had a successful career as a television and theater actor, though this particular series was short-lived.

Headliners (UK Television Series) Thames Television

Episode January 24, 1989
Episode Crew: Producer/Director: Brian Klein; Program Consultant: Roy Bottomley.
Episode Cast: Derek Jameson (Host), Nigel Dempster, Philippa Kennedy (Themselves), Caroline Munro, Henry Cooper, Gloria Hunniford, Alastair Stewart (Themselves; Guests).

SYNOPSIS

A television quiz show hosted by Jameson, with Nigel Dempster and Philippa Kennedy as regulars. Caroline and Henry Cooper were on Nigels' team.

REVIEW AND NOTES

According to Paul Gooding, Dempster and Jameson worked for tabloid newspapers before somehow finding themselves part of this game show, along with fellow journalist Philippa Kennedy.

This Is Your Life (television series, 1969–2003; 719 episodes) Thames Television International

"Peter Cushing" (Episode #514, February 21, 1990)
   Episode Crew: Creator-Writer: Ralph Edwards.
   Episode Cast: Peter Cushing, Ursula Andress, Freddie Jones, Christopher Lee, John Mills, Caroline Munro, David Prowse, David Rintoul, Peter Ustinov, Ernie Wise (Themselves).

Synopsis
Celebrities are feted by family, associates, and long-time (sometimes nearly forgotten) friends.

Review and Notes
The hugely successful series, which spanned four decades, was both a warm-hearted tribute to the stars it honored and an affirmation of that stardom. And none was more touching than this celebration of "Saint Peter," as Forry always called him. With death only a few years away, and still grieving for his beloved Helen, Cushing is so visibly touched by the presence of Caroline, not to mention the honor itself, that it is virtually impossible to watch without weeping uncontrollably ... and unashamedly.

World of Hammer (1990, 13 episodes) Best of British Films Productions

Episode #4 — "Vamp"
   Crew: Executive Producer: John Thompson; Producer-Director: Robert Sidaway; Creators-Writers: Robert Sidaway, Ashley Sidaway; Composer (Main Title): Brian Bennett; Film Editor: Ashley Sidaway; Production Manager: Evan M. Jones; Sound: Paul Hamilton; Production Secretary: Joanne Atkins; Production Assistant: Caroline Beecham; Film Archivists: Mike Dragesic, John Herron, Steve Rickerby, Steve Leroux; Online Editing: Mike Peatfield; Assistant Editors: Amanda Jenks, Alyssa Osment; For Hammer: Graham Skeggs, Karen Woods, Wendy Smith.
   Cast: Oliver Reed (Narrator), Ingrid Pitt, Peter Cushing, Christopher Lee, Yutte Stensgaard, Freda Jackson, Andree Melly, Valerie Gaunt, John Van Eyssen, Barbara Shelley, Suzan Farmer, Francis Matthews, Clifford Evans, Wanda Ventham, Caroline Munro, Pippa Steele, Jon Finch, Madeline Smith, Kate O'Mara, Mike Raven, Ralph Bates, Damien Thomas, Katya Wyeth, Mary Collinson, Madeleine Collinson (archive footage).

OTHER WORKS: Film & TV—*Night Owl* (1993)

SYNOPSIS AND REVIEW

Produced in 13 installments of 25 minutes each, this was not so much a documentary as a "Best of Hammer" compilation show, featuring lengthy clips from the films and the welcome, velvety tones of Oliver Reed to pull them all together. As advertised by the title, this episode spotlights the incomparable female vampires of Hammer, with clips from *The Brides of Dracula, Dracula Has Risen from the Grave, The Kiss of the Vampire*, and the Karnstein trilogy. There are no interviews, and there is no revelatory information, but it is a nicely produced clips show that, for once, the viewer doesn't feel clipped by.

Night Owl (a.k.a. *Nite Owl*)—1993, Franco Productions

Crew: Producer-Director-Screenplay-Film Editor: Jeffrey Arsenault; Associate Producer: Harriet Atkins; Co-Producer-Assistant Editor: June Lang; Music: Rubio Hernandez, Mark Styles; Photography: Pierre Clavel, Howard Krupa, Neil Shapiro; Makeup: (Mary Ann) Skiba; Sound Editors: Chip Helman, Rob Taz, Maureen Tilyou; Assistant to Director: Matteo Masiello; Production Manager: Martin Presberg.

Cast: John Leguizamo (Angel), Lisa Napoli (Frances), David Roya (Dario), Caroline Munro (Herself), Ali Thomas (Anne), James Raftery (Jake), Holly Woodlawn (Barfly), Yul Vazquez (Tomas), Karen Wexler (Zohra), Screamin' Rachel (Herself), Skiba (Woman in Alley), Charles Verde (Charlie), Michael Musto (Club M.C.), Andrew Marks (Voice of Newscaster), Don Wallace (Voice of Dr. York), Suzen Murakoshi (Woman at Bar), Mark Carbonaro, Joe Clarke, Kristen Connors, Alan Edwards, Evan Eisenberg, Meredith Jacobson, Claudia Kaye, Jerome Kuehl, Tom Merchant, Bert Robinson, T. Scott Lilly, Asher Segal, Alyce Wittenstein.

SYNOPSIS

Jake (James Raftery) lives in an abandoned building in New York City, along with his cat. Jake works in a pizza shop. Jake definitely prefers "extra sauce," as he has been a vampire since World War II; in the present day he gains his sustenance from taking a bite out of the Big Apple's nightlife!

Jake hooks up with a girl in a club and takes her back to his apartment, where he has sex with her, then kills her. When she does not return home that night, it arouses the suspicions of her brother, Angel (John Leguizamo).

Jake falls in love with a poet, Anne (Ali Thomas), and they have sex after carving a pumpkin.

Out of love for Anne, Jake refrains from vampirizing others, which causes him grave illness and he becomes desperate, even resorting to drinking his own blood. When Anne visits him, he can contain himself no longer — he has sex with her, and then kills her. Jake feels shame, and his friends Dario and Frances feel concern.

Angel finally corners Jake in an alley, where he taunts him twice, bites his nipples and sodomizes him with a beer bottle; Jake retaliates by putting the bite on Angel and leaves him covered in papers in the alley. Frances watches an interview with famous actress Caroline Munro on television, then goes to see Jake, who throws her out, but first gives her his cat. Jake then kills Dario. When Frances gets the call, she prepares to leave the pizza shop ... but who's that waiting in the corner, with blood on his lips?

REVIEW AND NOTES

Caroline's "role" in this movie is rather puzzling, as in, exactly why is it here? She plays herself in a five-minute interview where she discusses her parts in movies like *Dracula A.D. 1972* and *Captain Kronos*—an interview that has absolutely no relation to the rest of the film except that one of the characters watches it on TV. Even more puzzling is that the interview is not archival footage, but was shot specifically for *Night Owl* ... good call, too, as it's infinitely more interesting and watchable than the film proper, especially the "performance" of large-breasted chanteuse "Screamin' Rachel," who does not actually scream, but instead "sings" a brand of dance-pop for which generic would be a charitable description.

The film proper is grim and gritty, shot in black-and-white; it looks as if most of the money was spent on Caroline's cameo. The grainy B & W perfectly captures the seedy atmosphere; unfortunately, the story and characters aren't compelling. Oh, Caroline is always compelling, but she's disconnected from the proceedings. What are left are characters who engender little, if any, sympathy, even the victims. Jake is one of the more classless vampires to grace the screen (Can you see Christopher Lee puking?), Angel has many issues besides his sister's disappearance, and the rest of the cast are as seedy as the surroundings. If you don't care about the characters, then you don't care what happens to them, then you wonder why you've just spent 90 minutes watching this movie when you could have been eating pizza or having sex (without turning your partner into a vampire).

The Vampire Interviews—1994, Heidelberg Films, Rhino Home Video

Crew: Executive Producers: Richard Foos, Amy Schorr; Producer-Director: Ted Newsom; Associate Producer: Bill Kelley; Film Editors: Ray Baden, Keith Fernandes, Tom Reichlin; Makeup: Lydia V. Duffy; Assistant Director: Jonny M. Duffy; Assistant Director (New York): Bruce G. Hallenbeck; Assistant Directors (London): Chrissie Hynes, John Stoker; Sound: Harvey Edwards, David Lakin; Camera Operators: Ron Hamill, Robert Hayes, Andrew Watt; Lighting Technician: Janis Erwin; Production Liaison: Mark Kalmus; Business Affairs: Craig Kamins.

Cast: Roy Ward Baker, Nick Bougas, Veronica Carlson, Michael Carreras, Joe Dante, Freddie Francis, Donald F. Glut, Christopher Lee, Colleen M., Joan Marlowe, Ferdy Mayne,

OTHER WORKS: Film & TV—*Flesh and Blood* (1994)

Douglas McFerran, Caroline Munro, Christopher Neame, Amanda Osborne, Robert Osborne, Robert Quarry, Robert Sloane, Jimmy Sangster, Bozena V. (Themselves); John Carradine, Peter Cushing, Bela Lugosi (Themselves in Archive Footage).

SYNOPSIS

The original origins and legends of the vampire are compared and contrasted with the screen versions and variations.

REVIEW AND NOTES

The Vampire Interviews is an informative, entertaining, and sometimes just weird documentary. It starts with the history of vampires, noting that the legends had existed long before Bram Stoker's novel *Dracula*, and then elaborates on the many myths about vampires that most believe to be part of that history, but have become accepted part of lore via the movies. It then segues into various film clips and trailers and even some occasional behind-the-scenes footage. Two of the movies discussed are *Captain Kronos* and *Dracula A.D. 1972*; Caroline says of the latter, "The actual words that were used, that they do use, supposedly, in these various ceremonies ... it was slightly frightening, because they built this wonderful church inside the studio; and all the doors were closed, because it's a sound studio, so you have to have all the doors securely closed. And it had big black curtains at the top, and I'm sure when Christopher Neame started chanting ... this chant, these curtains—and I know all the crew saw it, too—started to move! It really did start to move, so we really ... we really I think were in the mood of the film ... no explanation, no doors were opened, nobody knows to this day why it happened, but it was pretty ... Woooo!" They also show the clip of her falling victim to Dracula: "And at that moment, I was being bitten by Dracula—and *I* believed it!" There are some other very amusing moments, like the great Robert Quarry's candid revelations about the seedy origins of the Count Yorga movies, Joe Dante's blunt (yet essentially correct) observation that once a film or genre is successful, there will be hundreds of Italian imitations, and Freddie Francis on his unasked-for status as a horror director: "I don't see many horror films ... please don't tell anybody!" The last interviewees are real people who drink blood (apparently doing this and listening to heavy metal makes you a vampire), and there is footage of them cutting each others' wrists and drinking each others' blood.

Flesh and Blood: The Hammer Heritage of Horror—1994, Heidelberg Films, Bosustow Media Group

Crew: Producers: Tee Bosustow, Ted Newsom; Associate Producers: Joe Dante, Bill Kelley, Richard Nathan, Roy Skeggs; Associate Producer–Stills: Michael Baron; Director-Writer: Ted

Newsom; Composer (Archive Music): James Bernard; Film Editors: Tee Bosustow, Alexander Gittinger, Noriko Miyakawa, Sean Okin; Assistant Director (Los Angeles): Kevin M. Glover; Assistant Director (New York): Bruce G. Hallenbeck; Assistant Director (Canterbury): Jane (Hughes) Herd; Assistant Director (Manchester): Stephen Laws; Assistant Director (London): John Stoker; Assistant Directors: Donald F. Glut, Chrissie Hines, Harry Nadler; Sound Recordists: Harvey Edwards, Matthew Harrison, David Lakin, Robert Meeker; Lighting Technicians: Tee Bosustow, Janis Erwin; Camera Operators: Ron Hamill, Robert Lloyd, Anthony Penatta, Andy Watt; Main Title Animation: Gary Heilman; Off-Line Editorial Assistants: Michael Costanza, Tom Reichlin; Title Music Conductor: Phillip (Phil) Kimbrough; Conductors (Archive Music): Philip Martell, Neil Richardson; Music Producer (Archive Music): Eric Tomlinson; Acknowledgments: Lance Alspaugh, David Booth, Lori Broda, Joyce Broughton, Colin Cowie, Sue Cowie, David Del Valle, James Fitzpatrick, Sophie James, Russ Lister, William Lustig, Mark Miller, John Robins, Max Rosenberg, Roy Skeggs, Steve Swires, Robert (Bob) Tinnell, Mark Verheiden, Richelle Wilder, Ron Wilson.

Cast: Peter Cushing, Sir Christopher Lee (Narrators), Roy Ward Baker, James Bernard, Martine Beswicke, Veronica Carlson, Michael Carreras, Hazel Court, Joe Dante, Freddie Francis, Val Guest, Ray Harryhausen, Anthony Hinds, Andrew Keir, Francis Matthews, Ferdy Mayne, Caroline Munro, Christopher Neame, Ingrid Pitt, Jimmy Sangster, Yutte Stensgaard (Archive Footage), Raquel Welch.

Synopsis and Review

This documentary is affectionate, honest, well-researched and well-presented. There are neat little revelations (Val Guest says that the monster in *The Quatermass Xperiment* was literally a piece of tripe) and rare behind-the-scenes footage. The most coverage is devoted to the Frankenstein and Dracula series, although everything is pretty well covered with the exceptions of the "Cornwall Classics" *The Reptile* and *The Plague of the Zombies*. Caroline gets quite a bit of screen time; most of her comments have to do with *Dracula A.D. 1972*, including her statement "That was the first time, I think, in my short career, at that time that I realized I actually did want to act, this was really it, because I believed in what I was doing." On her "tall, dark, and gruesome" leading man Christopher Lee: "You don't have to act much, 'cause he's very frightening when he has all his gear on, with the white face and the contact lenses and he's very tall ... I'm not small, and he is very tall." She explained her turning down a role that eventually went to her "best mate," Martine Beswicke: "There was some talk about me playing Sister Hyde, which a very fine actress went on to play; there was quite a bit of nudity, and I wasn't that keen on that." She also told the story of how she came to Hammer: "I'd been doing a poster for an English campaign called Lamb's Navy Rum, and apparently [Sir James Carreras] used to see ... this big poster every day, and supposedly he said, 'Find that girl and bring her in!' And I was put under contract for a year, which was wonderful...."

On her character Carla's love scene with Horst Janson in *Captain Kronos, Vampire Hunter*: "They wanted it to appear nude, so we came to sort of a compromise ... insofar as my hair was a lot longer in those days ... and so that covered my upper chest [*laughter*]

... and I think I actually used some sort of gaffer tape or something to stick it down; so I felt quite secure in that sense, and then a pair of flesh-colored knickers, briefs, and I was all right; I was all set, so it was like being on the beach, really...."

Hammer's decline is noted as well, and special attention is paid to the irony that contributed to that downfall: Hammer became famous for its use of color, breasts and blood, but ultimately, as these elements became commonplace, Hammer became more imitator than imitated, and the company could not compete without losing its identity. Sir Christopher and "Saint Peter" provide the narration; the frailty in Cushing's voice, recorded not long before he passed away, is heartbreaking. It is somewhat disappointing that Lee sticks to his somewhat disingenuous story concerning the reason he did the last few Dracula films, making it seem that his only concern was that so many people will be "out of work" if he didn't do the films. The reality was that Lee was more or less forced to do them because all of the other film projects he had signed up for had fallen through.

The Horror of Hammer—1994, All Day Entertainment, Hammer Films movie trailer compilation

Audio Commentary: Ted Newsom, Gary H. Smith, Stuart Galbraith IV; Audio Commentary Producer: David Kalat.

SYNOPSIS

The compilation features trailers and archive footage from *The Curse of Frankenstein, The Revenge of Frankenstein, The Evil of Frankenstein, Frankenstein Created Woman, Frankenstein Must Be Destroyed, Horror of Frankenstein, Frankenstein and the Monster from Hell, The Abominable Snowman of the Himalayas, The Hound of the Baskervilles, The Creeping Unknown, Enemy from Space, 5 Million Years to Earth, X the Unknown, These Are the Damned, One Million Years B.C., When Dinosaurs Ruled the Earth, Creatures the World Forgot, The Old Dark House, Nightmare, The Devil's Own, The Devil's Bride, To the Devil a Daughter, The Plague of the Zombies, The Curse of the Werewolf, The Mummy, The Curse of the Mummy's Tomb, The Mummy's Shroud, Blood from the Mummy's Tomb, Rasputin the Mad Monk, The Reptile, The Stranglers of Bombay, The Man Who Could Cheat Death, The Gorgon, Night Creatures, The Phantom of the Opera, House of Fright (The Two Faces of Doctor Jekyll), Doctor Jekyll and Sister Hyde, Horror of Dracula, The Brides of Dracula, Dracula Has Risen from the Grave, Taste the Blood of Dracula, The Scars of Dracula, Dracula A.D. 1972, Count Dracula and His Vampire Bride (The Satanic Rites of Dracula), The Kiss of the Vampire; Captain Kronos, Vampire Hunter; The Vampire Lovers, Lust for a Vampire, Twins of Evil, Vampire Circus, Countess Dracula*. Bonus and alternate trailers: *When Dinosaurs Ruled the Earth, The Brides of Dracula, Dracula A.D. 1972, Countess Dracula*; original show reels: *Beauties and Beasts, Prince of Terror*.

REVIEW AND NOTES

A comprehensive collection of trailers, more or less grouped by subject. The biggest surprise comes in the selection of bonus trailers, where we get a trailer for *Dracula A.D. 1972* with a voiceover from the great Orson Welles. It also contains two little-seen "show reels" (promotional films): *Beauties and Beasts* concerns the making of *When Dinosaurs Ruled the Earth* and Hammer's endless searches for the "most beautiful girls in the world" to populate their films, this one ending with the selection of Victoria Vetri. *Prince of Terror* is a promo piece for *Dracula A.D. 1972*, with excerpts from Christopher Lee's scene with Caroline.

Thriller Zone—1995, Victory Multimedia, Karl James Associates

A Gary Gray-Joseph Wanamaker Production. A Film by Glenn Takajian, Michael Alimo, Lawrence Simeone.

Producer: Joseph Wanamaker; Executive Producer: Gary Gray

"The Final Hour" Director: Lawrence Simeone; *Cast:* William Forsythe (Marcus Deerfield), Carol Kottenbrook; "The Last Hand": Rowan Sutherland, Harry Yelmon, Alan Schwartz, Lee Ryans, John Gowan; "Fanatical Extreme": Caroline Munro (Jana Bates), Joe Spinell (Vinny Durand), Robin Leach (Second Reporter).

SYNOPSES

"The Last Hand": Suffering from heart trouble, old Morty, a company's director of sales and marketing, is to be replaced by the owner's son David. Morty shoots and kills David in a deserted parking garage. Imagine Morty's surprise when the young urban professional shows up at the weekly poker game anyway! As David stares at Morty, Morty's Jack of Diamonds begins to bleed, and when Morty opens a beer, it turns into a revolver, with which Morty proceeds to blow away his poker buddies. But it's just an illusion, and the game continues. At midnight, David turns into a zombie and deals the last hand. Morty gets five aces of Spades and keels over ... but this, too, is an illusion. The whole episode has been an illusion. Back in time (and back in the garage), David gives Morty his heart pill, but the old ingrate Morty still wants to kill him. He struggles with David, gun in his hand, and suddenly the sound of a shot rings through the dank garage. But which man falls to the floor?

"The Final Hour": Space ... the final frontier. This is the voyage of Marcus Deerfield. The star date is 2213. The nuclear holocaust is history, and ex–space commander Deerfield, a convicted murderer, is imprisoned aboard Justice Shuttle 7. His mercy request granted, he awaits his appeal before the ultimate power of the high court.

"Fanatical Extreme": See *The Last Horror Film*, p. xxx.

REVIEW AND NOTES

Thriller Zone is so bad, it cannot be described, yet it must; but as Superintendent Waverly says in *Dr. Phibes*, "Words fail me." It is only available on a long out-of-print VHS tape, and commands very high prices that are in exact inverse proportion to its aesthetic worth. There are hardly any technical credits, as if the parties responsible were embarrassed to attach their names to the project, and it's very easy to see why. Actually, there is a long list of credits at the end ... from another movie. Caroline, Joe Spinell and Robin Leach are featured in the "Fanatical Extreme" segment, and if it sounds like *The Last Horror Film*, that's because it is—not just the cast, but the segment itself, which is culled from *The Last Horror Film*. Presumably, "The Last Hand" and "The Final Hour" were made for this, but who knows? The producers obviously weren't telling. They couldn't even spell: Caroline is listed in the credits as Carol Munro, and Joe Spinell is credited as Joe Spinnel. Even more egregiously, the only production credits they omit are the producers and director of *The Last Horror Film*. But at least by appropriating *The Last Horror Film*, they have some sort of semblance to competent filmmaking, and genuine stars with genuine presence, which is a lot more than can be said for the other two segments. "The Last Hand" tries for an Amicus or EC feel, but it's about twenty thousand leagues under EC. "The Final Hour" is about 59 minutes and 59 seconds too long.

Heroes of Comedy (television documentary series, 1995–2003; 30 episodes) Thames Television International

"Frankie Howerd" (Episode #1, January 1, 1995)

Crew: Producer/Writer: John Fisher; Associate Producer: Tessa Le Bars; Director: Ian McLean; Makeup: Wendy Brown, Elizabeth Yianni-Georgiou; Production Manager: Jenny Moir.

Cast: Clive Anderson, Cilla Black, Nicky Campbell, Barry Cryer, Craig Ferguson, Ned Sherrin, Madeline Smith, Eric Sykes (Themselves); Frankie Howerd, Denis Healey, Katie Johnson, Brian Johnston, David Kernan, Eartha Kitt, Royce Mills, Warren Mitchell, Caroline Munro, Hugh Paddick, Alan Rebbeck, Vera Roper, Joan Sims (archive footage).

SYNOPSIS

A tribute to the life and career of Frankie Howerd.

REVIEW AND NOTES

Caroline is among the guests remembering Howerd in the first episode of this short-lived series, which each week covered the career of a different British comedian; succeeding episodes included pieces on Terry-Thomas, The Goons, Spike Milligan and

OTHER WORKS: Film & TV—*100 Years of Horror* (1996)

Benny Hill. Howerd a staple of the "Crumpet" films *Carry On Doctor*, *Carry On Up the Jungle* (as Inigo Tinkle) and *Up Pompeii*, had passed away a few years earlier.

---

100 Years of Horror—1996, Passport International Entertainment, video documentary series (five short films)

"100 Years of Horror: Blood-Drinking Beings"

Crew: Executive Producer: Dante J. Pugliese; Producer-Director-Writer: Ted Newsom; Film Editors: Trudi Jo Marie Keck, Brian Q. Kelly; Assistant Directors: Kevin M. Glover, John Stoker, Gordon Smith, Bruce Hallenbeck; Camera Operators: Tee Bosustow, Paul Bloch, Jill Harper, Graham Mauder, Gus Novak, Bob Lloyd; Animation Designer: Dante J. Pugliese; Computer Animation: Doyle Smith; Production Controller: Jeanette Pugliese; Acknowledgments: Eric Hoffman, Brett McCormick, Heidelberg Films, SabuCat (Jeff Joseph), Bill Kelley, Steve Swires, Roger Hurlbur, Tom Weaver.

Cast: Christopher Lee (Host-Narrator), Roy Ward Baker, Carroll Borland, Veronica Carlson, John Carradine, Michael Carreras, Roger Corman, Robert Cornthwaite, Peter Cushing, Nina Foch, Freddie Francis, Hugh M. Hefner, Bela Lugosi Jr., Ferdy Mayne, Dick Miller, Caroline Munro, Fred Olen Ray, Jimmy Sangster, Brinke Stevens, D.P. Smith (Themselves).

SYNOPSIS

Variations on the vampire theme are examined in a jocular vein in this installment of the series.

REVIEW AND NOTES

Parts of some of the interviews with Caroline in this series had already been used in *Flesh and Blood*.

"100 Years of Horror: Dracula and His Disciples"

Crew: Executive Producer: Dante J. Pugliese; Producer-Director-Writer: Ted Newsom; Film Editors: Trudi Jo Marie Keck, Brian Q. Kelly; Assistant Director: Kevin M. Glover; Camera Operator: Tee Bosustow; Animation Designer: Dante J. Pugliese; Acknowledgments: Bill Kelley, Steve Swires, Tom Weaver.

Cast: Christopher Lee (Host-Narrator), Roy Ward Baker, Carroll Borland, Veronica Carlson, John Carradine, Michael Carreras, Roger Corman, Robert Cornthwaite, Peter Cushing, Nina Foch, Freddie Francis, Hugh M. Hefner, Francis Lederer, Bela Lugosi Jr., Ferdy Mayne, Dick Miller, Caroline Munro, Fred Olen Ray, Jimmy Sangster, Brinke Stevens (Themselves).

SYNOPSIS

The various screen incarnations of Dracula are examined, as well as vampires who were derivatives of Dracula.

OTHER WORKS: Film & TV—*100 Years of Horror* (1996)

REVIEW AND NOTES

The historical image of vampires as putrescent children of the grave was eclipsed by the stage and Hollywood's well-dressed, smooth-mannered foreigner, an image that was to become iconic due to the impact of Bela Lugosi, the gold standard for Dracula until Christopher Lee entered the picture. After his greatest success, Lugosi spent the rest of his life either playing the count (once more on film, many times on the stage) or vampires that were Dracula in all but name. This installment looks at all of these portrayals, as well as the overlooked gems *The Return of Dracula* (basically *Shadow of a Doubt* with dear old Uncle Charlie as a vampire) and the Hammer series. Caroline is on hand to reminisce about where it really all started for her, as one of Dracula's comeliest victims.

"100 Years of Horror: Dr. Jekyll and Mr. Hyde"

Crew: Producer-Director-Writer: Ted Newsom; Acknowledgment: Tom Weaver.

Cast: Christopher Lee (Host-Narrator), John Agar, Roy Ward Baker, Martine Beswicke, Michael Carreras, Donald F. Glut, Sara Karloff, Caroline Munro, Fred Olen Ray, Gloria Talbott (Themselves).

SYNOPSIS

Jekyll and Hyde are together again in this exploration of their cinematic dualing selves and other films that were inspired by the theme.

REVIEW AND NOTES

Another very entertaining installment, devoted to that most famous split personality, Jekyll and Hyde. Some of the examples used as variations on the theme seem to stretch a bit in making the analogy; for instance, *The Mad Monster* is really more of a werewolf movie, albeit a scientifically created werewolf. Christopher Lee is very entertaining in this episode, reminiscing about starring in the obscure Amicus classic *I, Monster*. It's not a variation on Jekyll and Hyde; it *is* Jekyll and Hyde, except for one very important difference (besides the title and a change in the ending): The lead character's name was changed to Dr. Marlowe, with his beastly alter ego now christened Mr. Blake.

Caroline doesn't have much to do with the saga of Jekyll and Hyde except that she turned down one of the most interesting takes on the story, *Doctor Jekyll and Sister Hyde*: She tells the anecdote in the same footage we saw *Flesh and Blood*. She elaborated a bit in an interview in *Little Shoppe of Horrors* #22; she mentions definitely being considered for the role, and interviewer Mark Redfield notes that it went to Martine Beswicke. Caroline responds, "My best mate! And she was fabulous! They looked perfect together, she and Ralph Bates. If I was casting it, I wouldn't choose me; not at all."

"100 Years of Horror: Maniacs"

Crew: Executive Producer: Dante J. Pugliese; Producer-Director-Writer: Ted Newsom; Film Editors: John D. Johnson, Trudi Jo Marie Keck, Brian Q. Kelly; Assistant Director:

Kevin M. Glover; Camera Operator: Tee Bosustow; Animation Designer: Dante J. Pugliese; Acknowledgments: Bill Kelley, Steve Swires, Tom Weaver.

Cast: Christopher Lee (Host-Narrator); William Alland, John Carpenter, Roger Corman, Hazel Court, Joe Dante, Richard Denning, Freddie Francis, Donald F. Glut, Hugh M. Hefner, Herschell Gordon Lewis, Mark Thomas McGee, Caroline Munro, Lori Nelson, Fred Olen Ray, Jimmy Sangster, Harlene Stein (Themselves).

SYNOPSIS

As the disc packaging says, "Ax-murderers, chainsaw-wielding madmen, serial killers, cannibals — they're all here — and more!"

REVIEW AND NOTES

The history of madmen in the movies is a long and winding road, with many few stops before Norman Bates. Talking about her film *Maniac*, Caroline says, "[It] did well in the States, it made a lot of money in the States ... but it was very graphic, and I didn't realize when we were shooting it as to how graphic it was going to be in its violence; it was very violent against women, a little bit too explicit ... Good special effects, I mean, Tom Savini, he's a bit of a wiz, I believe, at special effects ... Good acting ... terrific, I mean, it had Joe Spinell and some very fine actors ... [A]pparently, the women's groups in Los Angeles actually banned it, they were so against it...."

"100 Years of Horror: Scream Queens"

Crew: Executive Producer: Dante J. Pugliese; Producer-Director-Writer: Ted Newsom; Film Editors: Trudi Jo Marie Keck, Brian Q. Kelly; Assistant Director: Kevin M. Glover; Camera Operator: Tee Bosustow; Animation Designer: Dante J. Pugliese; Acknowledgments: Bill Kelley, Steve Swires, Tom Weaver.

Cast: Christopher Lee (Host-Narrator), Carroll Borland, Roger Corman, Hazel Court, Richard Denning, Beverly Garland, Hugh M. Hefner, Peggy Moran, Caroline Munro, Lori Nelson, Linnea Quigley, Fred Olen Ray, Brinke Stevens, Gloria Talbott (Themselves).

SYNOPSIS

In this installment, the history of Scream Queen is covered (and uncovered).

REVIEW AND NOTES

Whether they are in their nightgowns being chased up a tree by a werewolf, or hacking their rivals apart with chainsaws, the Scream Queen has been a staple of horror films since the very beginning of the genre. This particularly entertaining installment of the series covers them from beginning to the latest (at the time) generation, from Brigitte Helm to Fay Wray through Evelyn Ankers and Beverly Garland to Linnea Quigley — although the inclusion of Brigitte Helm (from the silent film *Metropolis*) rather begs the question, "If no one can hear you scream, can you still be a scream queen?" Caroline gets to elaborate on her left-out-in-the-rain moment from *Dracula A.D. 1972*; Beverly

OTHER WORKS: Film & TV—*Eurotika!* (1999) / *Inside* The Spy Who Loved Me (2000)

Garland is wonderful, describing the experiment victims in *The Alligator People* as looking like they had "urinals on their heads"; and monster fan Hugh Hefner points out the lack of sexual equality in monster movies.

Eurotika! (television documentary series, 1999; 12 episodes) Boam Productions

"Blood and Sand: All You Ever Wanted to Know About Spanish Horror Films" (Episode #11, December 12, 1999)

Episode Crew: Producers-Directors-Writers: Andrew Starke, Pete Tombs; Film Editor: Andrew Starke; Title Art: Birago Balzano; Sound: Paul Cotterell; Camera Operators: Merrill Aldighieri, Ben Howard, Andrew Starke; Rostrum Camera: Ken Morse; On-Line Editor: Simon Richards; Titles: Adam Gaywood, Steve Tolfrey.

Episode Cast: Amando D'Ossorio, Orchidea de Santis, Daniela Giordano, Jorge Grau, Jose Ramon Larraz, Daniel Lesoeur, Paul Naschy, Caroline Munro (Themselves).

SYNOPSIS

The history of the Spanish horror film as seen through the eyes of some of its most important participants.

REVIEW AND NOTES

Every episode of this short-lived, very informative weekly television series dealt with a different theme (the films of Jean Rollin, the films of Jess Franco, the films of Michael Reeves and so forth). Caroline wasn't what you'd call a mainstay of Spanish horror, but she did make films with both Paul Naschy and Franco, so she made her contribution. The episode also features the father of the *Blind Dead* series, Amando D'Ossorio.

Inside The Spy Who Loved Me — 2000, MGM Home Entertainment, video documentary short film

Episode Crew: Producers: John Cork, David Naylor, Bruce Scivally; Field Producer (London): Dave Worrall; Field Producer (Rome): Mary Benedicta Cipolla; Director-Writer: John Cork; Film Editor: Dave Goldstein; Makeup: Joannel Clemente, Abigail Graves, Jodi Lynn Malitsky, Marilyn Rieul; Sound: Louis Borgia, Francesca Forletta, George Ann Muller, Geoff Neate, Dave Rody, Doug Smith, Chris White; Sound Mixer: Michael J. White.

Cast: Patrick Macnee (Narrator); Ken Adam, Barbara Bach, Dana Broccoli, Robin Browne, William P. Cartlidge, Lewis Gilbert, John Glen, Charles Juroe, Curt Jurgens, Richard

OTHER WORKS: Film & TV—*VH-1 Where Are They Now?* (2000)

Kiel, Katharina Kubrick Hobbs, Peter Lamont, Valerie Leon, Alec Mills, Roger Moore, Caroline Munro, Ron Quelch, Steven Saltzman, Sue St. John, Rick Sylvester, Victor Tourjansky, Michael G. Wilson, Christopher Wood (Themselves).

SYNOPSIS

A behind-the-scenes look at the making of the tenth James Bond movie, featuring archival footage and interviews with key actors, actresses, and technicians.

REVIEW AND NOTES

A well-done 41-minute documentary on *The Spy Who Loved Me*. One particularly interesting nugget of hitherto-unknown information is that no one could figure out how to light the sub pen set effectively until the problem was solved by an uncredited Stanley Kubrick. The famous Lotus was actually seven different models (and one an actual model), each one performing a specific function for the shot in which the action occurs. It also explains why this was the first Bond to be produced by "Cubby" Broccoli alone, rather than in his famed partnership with Harry Saltzman; Saltzman was forced to sell his half of the 007 franchise because of mounting debt due to family health problems (his wife's cancer and his own depression) and bad investments.

The only actor who gets any significant interview time is Roger Moore; still-stunning Caroline is on screen for only a few minutes, giving an account of how she was cast in the film: "I did a poster campaign in the '70s and early '80s, and the character that was portrayed on the posters was quite a strong character ... I wore a wetsuit and I carried a knife, so she was quite strong. And supposedly 'Cubby' saw this image of this strong woman, and he said, oh, you know [*adopts a gruff, showbiz tone*], 'I'd like to see her, send her to my office,' so that's what he did." As this is pretty much how she came to be employed at Hammer, it's a wonder she ever even had to employ an agent, seeing as her billboards did all the talking.

VH-1 Where Are They Now? (television documentary series, 1999–2002; 57 episodes) VH-1 Television

"Video Vixens" (Episode #16, July 28, 2000)
   Episode Crew: Producer: Riley McCormick; Voiceover Engineer: Jason John Cicalese.
   Episode Cast: James Curreri (Narrator), Caroline Munro, Amelia Kinkade, Betsy Lynn George, Jeana Tomasina, Rana Kennedy, Sharise Neil (Themselves).

SYNOPSIS

Former music video sex symbols bring viewers up to date on their current professional and personal lives.

OTHER WORKS: Film & TV—*The Joe Spinell Story* (2001)

REVIEW AND NOTES

This short-lived series explored a different genre or theme for each show (Superheroes, New Wave, Hair Bands, Child Stars), interviewing stars who became famous in that genre or theme and asking about their current state of affairs (so to speak). This show focuses on women whose faces and figures were perhaps more familiar to music-video viewers than their names. A whole new generation learned the name of Caroline Munro, whose face and form they had thrilled to in videos by Adam Ant and Meatloaf (see last section). Jeana Tomasina was a former Playmate and was one of the Muses in "Legs," "Sharp-Dressed Man," and "Gimme All Your Lovin'" by ZZ Top. Amelia Kinkade appeared in videos by Stray Cats, Cher, and the Scorpions, among others. Betsy Lynn George gained notoriety by doing a striptease in "Cradle of Love" by Billy Idol; Rana Kennedy likewise became infamous for the "Poison" video by Alice Cooper, which was censored, not because of the blue thong she wore but because that was the *only* thing she wore.

The Joe Spinell Story— 2001, Blue Underground

Crew: Executive Producers: Jay Douglas, William Lustig; Producers: David Gregory, Lizette Pena; Associate Producer: Luke Walter; Director: David Gregory; Music: Robert Bayless, Mark Raskin; Photography: Raechel Legakes; Film Editors: Mike Murphy, Mary Ann Skweres; Assistant Editor: Deonna Boman.

Cast: Joe Cirillo, Tony Conforti, Kate Forster, Robert Forster, Buddy Giovinazzo, Sonny Grosso, Patrick Jude, William James Kennedy, William Lustig, Richard Lynch, Jason Miller, Caroline Munro, Frank Pesce, Grace Raimo, Thomas C. Rainone, John Scott, Luke Walter (Themselves).

SYNOPSIS

An informative, touching, and entertaining documentary portrait of the late, great character actor featuring individuals who knew and worked with him.

REVIEW AND NOTES

As Bugs Bunny would say, "What a unique character!" Spinell was a native New Yorker and a hemophiliac who loved his mom, loved to drink and smoke dope, and, most of all, loved movies. Caroline describes him on the set of *Maniac*: "He was a wild one; yes ... he absolutely lived life to the full in every which way, especially when he was doing this character. Some nights he actually wouldn't sleep, he'd go out ... he'd say, 'Well, I've got to do this, I've got to look right for the next morning,' and he did, by golly ... he looked a bit rough sometimes when he'd come in, in the morning."

Though *Maniac* is a slasher genre classic, Caroline doesn't include it in her list of favorites: "It was quite a brutal film, quite a raw film, of which many have sort of come along after that ... I can't say I like the film, but it was very powerful."

She also shares some thoughts on *The Last Horror Film*:

> Because of the success of *Maniac*, we thought, well, it seems to be quite a winning formula, the two of us together, and we liked to tour together.
>
> It was done very impromptu, because we were doing the Film Festival, and a lot of the scenes couldn't be set up at all, so we had to just go with what was happening and make very—you know, a lot of ad-libs going on.
>
> Joe brought himself to that. He designed the set, he designed his bedroom, he designed it—he put every picture up the way he wanted it, he designed the color of his room, he knew exactly what this person would need as this kind of obsessed fan with this woman. When we were there filming, it was extraordinary; he really did party a lot then during that time.
>
> Definitely not the tightest production ... it was a long production, I know I was absolutely exhausted; we went to Cannes, and we went to Geneva, and I think some of it was shot in New York.

If Joe's last name (Spagnuolo) seems slightly familiar, it's because it pops up in the sports pages every football season; his distant cousin Steve Spagnuolo is a professional football coach.

Once Upon a Time in Europe— 2001

Crew: Producer: S. Gibbings; Directors: Manel Mayol, Carles Prats; Writer: Joan Ferrer; Music: Salvador Rey; Photography: Pere Ballesteros, Angel Puig; Film Editor: Lolo Munoz; Art Director: Frank Plant; Costume Designer: Maria Domingo; Makeup Artist: Silvia Parra; Sound: Josep Perales; Production Coordinator: Patricia Lora; Production Assistant: Frankie Colome; Auto-Cue Operator: Fatima Casas; Researcher: Rafael Dalmau.

Host: Christopher Lee

Cast: Carlos Aguilar, Alessandro Alessandroni, Dario Argento, John Barry, Martine Beswicke, Erika Blanc, Barbara Bouchet, Arthur Brauner, Mario Caiano, John Cater, Damiano Damiani, Tonino Delli Colli, Amando de Ossorio, Jacques Deray, Fernando Di Leo, Sergio Donati, Eduardo Fajardo, Jess Franco, Christopher Frayling, Riccardo Freda, Caron Gardner, Gianni Garko, Guiliano Gemma, Jose Giavonni, Uschi Glas, Jorge Grau, Antonio Isasi-Isasmendi, Marianne Koch, Michael Latimer, Carlo Leva, Antonio Margheriti, Eugenio Martin, Sergio Martino, Ennio Morricone, Patrick Mower, Caroline Munro, Paul Naschy, Rosalba Neri, Franco Nero, Ingrid Pitt, Wolfgang Preiss, Lina Romay, Carlo Rustichelli, Aldo Sambrell, Conrado St. Martin, Janette Scott, Julio Sempere, Sergio Sollima, Bud Spencer, Jack Taylor, Tonino Valerii, Florestano Vancini, Horst Wendlandt, Virginia Wetherall.

SYNOPSIS

A history of European genre films and filmmakers focusing on the period from the late 1950s through the mid–1970s.

OTHER WORKS: Film & TV—*GMTV* (1993–2010) / *Blood* (2002) / *Bond* (2002)

REVIEW AND NOTES

Towards the end of the 1950s, there was an exponential increase in the number of countries that produced genre films. This documentary looks at the European boom, which was influenced and encouraged by the revolutionary techniques and ideas of the French New Wave and British Free Cinema, which produced films, filmmakers and stars whose influence still resonates in present-day films.

GMTV (UK television series, 1993–2010) October 15, 2002

Caroline appeared on this award-winning British television morning show.

Blood Craving— 2002, After Midnight Entertainment

Crew: Producer-Director-Screenplay: Jeffrey Arsenault; Film Editor: George Cruz; Casting: Diane Bonsignore; Sound: Brian Miklas; Camera Operator: Frank Kaplan; Lighting Designer: Eric J. Xie.

Cast: Tiffany Helland (Jillian), Francesco J. Caputo (Gustavo), Leslie Slemp (Victoria), Israel Monrroy (Angel), Frances Lozada (First Victim), Michael Naselli (Second Victim), Julio Rivera (Third Victim), Caroline Munro (Herself).

Bond Girls Are Forever— 2002, Planet-Grande Pictures, Metro-Goldwyn-Mayer (MGM), documentary for American Movie Classics

Crew: Executive Producer: Eamon Harrington; Executive Producer: Jessica Falcon; Producers-Writers: Maryam d'Abo, John Watkin; Associate Producer: Kate Harrington; Supervising Producer: John C. Fitzgerald; Co–Executive Producers: Gillian Gordon, Howard Rosenman; Director: John Watkin; Photography: Brian Pratt; Film Editors: Kevin Bourque, Harry Watson; Executive in Charge of Production: Nancy McKenna; Production Manager: Carol-Ann Plante.

Cast: Maryam d'Abo (Herself-Host-Narrator), Maud Adams, Ursula Andress, Halle Berry, Honor Blackman, Samantha Bond, Lois Chiles, Judi Dench, Jill St. John, Carey Lowell, Roger Moore, Luciana Paluzzi, Rosamund Pike, Jane Seymour, Michelle Yeoh (Themselves).

OTHER WORKS: Film & TV—*James Bond* (2002)

SYNOPSIS

A documentary containing interviews and archival footage of the "Bond Girls."

REVIEW AND NOTES

This is a slickly produced film companion to the book of the same name, also done by Maryam d'Abo. It's compelling because of the always-compelling Bond Girls, but ultimately a bit disappointing because it is so d'Abo-centric: footage which could have been utilized interviewing women like Caroline Munro or Shirley Eaton is spent on shots of Ms. D'Abo walking in the park, chatting or shopping, as well as being on screen for all of the interviews. The interviews range from the first Bond Girl, Ursula Andress, to that year's model, Halle Berry, but the scope is not as inclusive as that would suggest. The '60s and most of the '70s are skirted over rather breezily in favor of the more recent Bond Girls, when, according to the narrative, they became more assertive and action-oriented rather than mostly damsels in distress (Pussy Galore was a damsel in distress?).

James Bond: A BAFTA Tribute—2002, British Broadcasting Corporation (BBC)

Crew: Executive Producer: Beatrice Ballard; Producer: Arabella McGuigan; Director: Stuart McDonald; Writer: Steve Punt; Lighting Director: Mark Kenyon; Composer (James Bond Theme): Monty Norman; Stage Manager: Caroline Caley; Researcher: Tim Harcourt.

Cast: Michael Parkinson (Host), Shirley Bassey, Ken Adam, Maud Adams, Ursula Andress, Michael Apted, Vic Armstrong, David Arnold, John Barry, Halle Berry, Honor Blackman, Samantha Bond, Barbara Broccoli, Pierce Brosnan, Martin Campbell, Robert Carlyle, Lois Chiles, John Cleese, Sean Connery, Maryam d'Abo, Timothy Dalton, Judi Dench, Shirley Eaton, Fiona Fullerton, Lewis Gilbert, John Glen, Julian Glover, Tom Jones, Richard Kiel, Peter Lamont, George Lazenby, Christopher Lee, Cary Lowell, Lulu, George Martin, Lois Maxwell, Roger Moore, Caroline Munro, Rosamund Pike, Colin Salmon, Vincent Schiavelli, Keely Shaye Smith, Jane Seymour, Toby Stephens, Lee Tamahori, Michael G. Wilson, Rick Yune (Themselves).

SYNOPSIS

A gala tribute to the Man with the Golden Franchise.

REVIEW AND NOTES

BAFTA stands for the British Academy of Film and Television Arts, and is unique in that these sort of lavish affairs are generally tributes to living people, and not fictional characters. But Bond is not your typical fictional character. Dame Shirley Bassey is still beautiful and her voice had not lost a bit of its ability to produce spinal chills. Roger

Moore has a wonderful line about why he stopped playing Bond: "Well, they ran out of villains who looked old enough to be knocked out by me." Host Michael Parkinson seems obsessed with asking on stage about the details of guests' love scenes. Caroline, like most of the guests, is only on stage for a few minutes, but at least she's spared the embarrassment of Parkinson asking her about a love scene.

The Beauty Behind Faceless — 2004, Fever Dreams

Crew: Executive Producer: John Sirabella; Producer-Interviewer: Carl Morano; Director–Supplement Producer: William Hellfire; Editor–Graphic Animator: Christian Alexander Moran; Post-Production Manager–Camera: Scott Marchfeld; Post-Production Supervisor: Sean Molyneaux; Assistant Editor: Naneen Paglieri; DVD Author: Stephen Poole; Production Assistant: Zoe Moonshine; Photographs: Lucas Baibo.
Cast: Caroline Munro

SYNOPSIS

Caroline discusses her role and co-stars in *Faceless*, and also briefly touches on a number of her other roles and proposed roles.

REVIEW AND NOTES

This DVD extra was produced by many of the same technical crew members responsible for *Flesh for the Beast*. This was their introduction to Caroline, which resulted in her cameo in that film. Although primarily focused on *Faceless*, the lengthy interview is career-spanning and informative. She even admits that, although she had certainly heard of him, she had never actually seen any of Jess Franco's films before she made *Faceless*, and at the time of the interview, still hadn't seen any others. But she does promise to get around to it!

Caroline Munro: First Lady of Fantasy — 2004, Strange Media, Fan Club Video

Crew: Producers: John Scoleri, Steffan Schulz; Director/Film Editor: Steffan Schulz; Photographs: John Scoleri, Caroline Munro, Tami Hamalian, Jerry Mendoza; Special Thanks: Stan Stice, Jerry Mendoza, Jimmy Gillis, Jayne Crimin, Tami Hamalian, Caroline Munro.
Cast: Caroline Munro (Herself).

SYNOPSIS

A feature-length, career-spanning interview with Caroline.

REVIEW AND NOTES

Available only through her fan club, this 90-minute documentary is the definitive look at Caroline: an oral history of her life and career from the very beginning to the year it was filmed. In one amusing sequence, she calls *Flesh for the Beast* "Feast for the Beast." It includes many extras: a complete list of her films with selected clips; select television appearances and commercials; her music videos with Adam Ant and Meat Loaf; "Growing up with Caroline," a slideshow by Tami Hamalian with captions, a photo gallery and fan club information.

Crumpet! A Very British Sex Symbol— 2005, Scarlet Television

Crew: Producer-Director: John Moulson; Executive Producer: Paula Trafford; Executive Producer (BBC Scotland): Alan Tyler; Idea: Julie Burchill, Jane Garcia; Camera Operator: Den Pollitt; Sound: Steve Earle; Film Editor: Mark Wharton; Dubbing Mixer: Hanna Fairclough; Colorist: Ray King; Researchers: Caron Miles, Emma Holtham; Production Coordinator: Erinn Campbell; Production Manager: Karen Bonnici; Development Consultant: Katie Lander.

Cast: Tony Livesey (Host), Austin Little (Young Tony), Robin Askwith, Alexandra Bastedo, Jonathan Benton-Hughes, Honor Blackman, Carol Cleveland, Lynsey De Paul, Shirley Eaton, Julie Ege, Dr. Germaine Greer, Dylan Jones, Valerie Leon, Jeremy Lloyd, Barbara Lord, Linda Lusardi, Caroline Munro, Leslie Philips, Ingrid Pitt, Wendy Richard, Ned Sherrin, Madeline Smith, Sally Thomsett, Sue Upton, Dee Dee Wilde, Barbara Windsor, Shirley English, Charles Hawtrey, Sid James, Joan Sims, Kenneth Williams (Themselves).

SYNOPSIS-REVIEW-NOTES

Charming, funny, wistful and (above everything else) unashamedly sexy, this documentary explores the heyday, the evolution and appeal of British "crumpets" (British slang for a "tasty" beautiful woman), a very special breed of sex symbol. Typical Hollywood glamour was not the crumpets' appeal; they were the girl next door who, as former *Daily Sport* and *Sunday Sport* editor-in-chief and managing director Tony Livesey notes, never seemed to live next door; an obtainable unobtainable beauty. From the *Carry On* films through Bond Girls, Hammer glamour, Monty Python, Page Three Girls and Benny Hill, not a stone is left unturned, not a skirt unlifted.

Introduced by Livesey as "part of the fabric of British life," Caroline recalls her big break as the Lamb's Navy Rum Girl: "It was like a sailor's drink, it was a dark rum for men ... and they wanted to change the image, and the first picture — which was seen as pretty daring — was a tattoo; so I have a tattoo on my shoulder of a ship, so that was really 'woo-Hoo,' quite racy in those days ... and my goodness, the sales of rum shot up!" She also remembers her "missed" opportunity with *Playboy* magazine: "It's funny because I was offered *Playboy*, and my grammy, who was in her eighties, she said, 'Oh, do it, do it,' because they offered quite a nice little bit of money, but I just didn't want to do it."

The Witch's Dungeon: 40 Years of Chills— 2006, Colorbox Studios, Video Documentary

Crew: Producer-Director-Film Editor: Dennis Vincent; Videographers: Dennis Vincent, John Elton Floyd; Second Unit Videographer: Skip Wilder; Writer (Narration): Tomi Saviste; Music: Kurt Coble, Dennis Vincent; Assistant Editor: John Bartucca.

Cast: Steven Savino (Narrator), Kyle Smith (Young Cortlandt Hull), Forrest J Ackerman, Karen Allen, Ricou Browning, Bob Burns, Veronica Carlson, Ron Chaney, Ben Chapman, Kurt Coble, June Foray, Dwight Frye Jr., Basil Gogos, Charles Herbert, Sara Karloff, Christopher Lee, Bela Lugosi Jr., Caroline Munro, Cassandra (Elvira) Peterson, Bobby "Boris" Pickett, Rex Reason, Michael Ripper, Daniel Roebuck, Tom Savini, Richard Sheffield, Dick Smith, Dee Wallace-Stone, John Zacherle, Todd Feiertag (Themselves).

SYNOPSIS

A guided tour through America's longest-running classic movie monster museum.

REVIEW AND NOTES

Cortlandt Hull is the great-nephew of Henry Hull, the star of *WereWolf of London* (1935), and is a native of Bristol, Connecticut, where the Witch's Dungeon is located. It opened in 1966; Cortlandt's father Robert helped him build the Swiss chalet–style building, which measures 40 ¥ 17 feet. The museum is only open on weekend evenings in October. Caroline is on the advisory board and has also been connected with a number of special functions at the museum. As opposed to most of the guests, who get extensive interview segments, Caroline is only around for a few minutes: "Hello, this is Caroline Munro. I'm absolutely delighted to be on the board, now, of the Witch's Dungeon. I've been made a member, and I'm absolutely thrilled; I really highly support this organization, and hopefully you do, too. I look forward to seeing all of the progress in the near future.... There's some fantastic stuff, as you can see behind me ... please look out for it and support it ... we need it."

The Fanex Files: Hammer Films— 2008, Midnight Marquee Productions, Longthrow Multimedia International

Crew: Producers: Jeff Herberger, Gary J. Svehla, A. Susan Svehla; Co-Producer: George Stover; Director-Writer: A. Susan Svehla; Director-Editor-Camera: Jeff Herberger; Trailers:

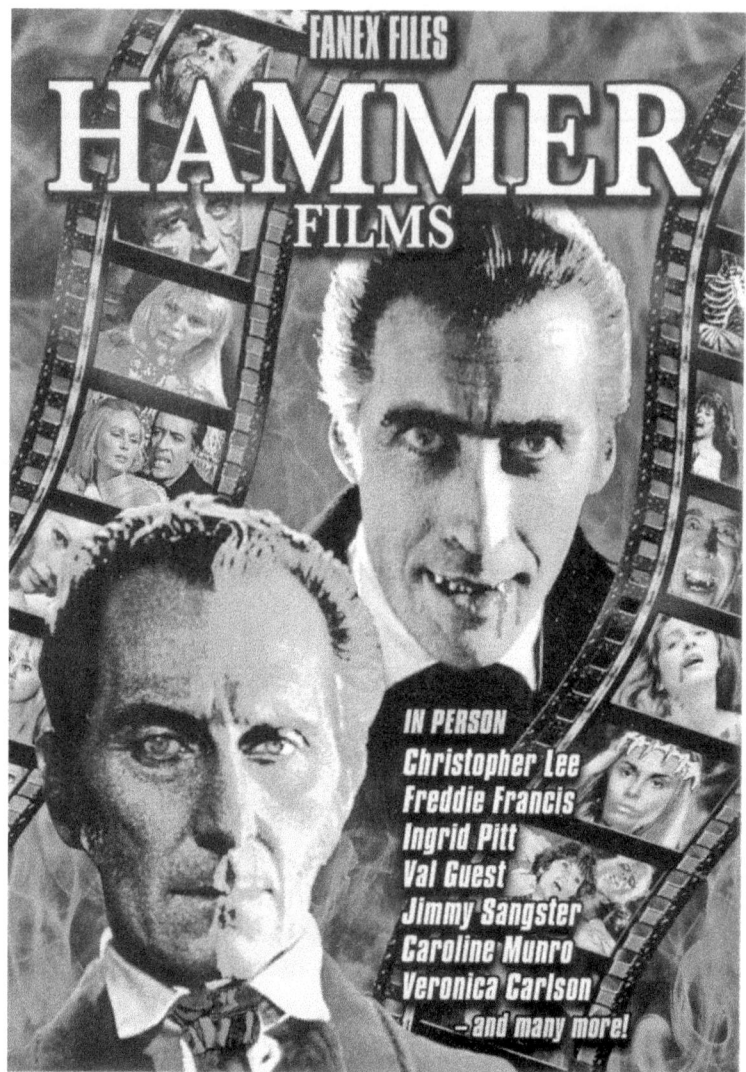

Interviews with Caroline and a heaping helping of Hammer stars are featured in this documentary culled from the glory years of the Fanex convention (courtesy Gary J. Svehla).

George Stover; Music: Smartsound Publishing Inc.; Special Thanks: Martine Beswicke, Veronica Carlson Love, Sue and Colin Cowie, Bobby Ellis, Pam Francis, Bruce Hallenbeck, Tom Johnson, Christopher Lee, Dick Klemensen, Suzanna Leigh, Bill Littman, Denis Meikle, Caroline Munro, Barry Murphy, Ted Newsom, Ingrid Pitt, Tom Proveaux, Jimmy Sangster, Barbara Shelley, Yutte Stensgaard, George Stover, Virginia Wetherall.

Cast: Tom Proveaux (Narrator); Christopher Lee, Veronica Carlson, Ingrid Pitt, James Bernard, Val Guest, Jimmy Sangster, Freddie Francis, Caroline Munro, Virginia Wetherall, Michael Ripper, Barbara Shelley, Yutte Stensgaard, Joyce Broughton, Aaron Christensen, Dwight Kemper, Jon Kitley, Streebo Majic, Gary Svehla (Themselves).

OTHER WORKS: Film & TV—*The Man Who Saw Frankenstein Cry* (2010)

SYNOPSIS

The history of legendary Hammer Films as seen through the eyes of some of its most significant participants, in interviews from the legendary Fanex convention.

REVIEW AND NOTES

Probably the definitive Hammer documentary, done by one of the definitive sets of voices in fantasy film fandom, Gary and Susan Svehla. They founded and publish the seminal *Midnight Marquee* magazine, as well as publish a very fine line of genre books, and were responsible for the ten-year run of the seminal Fanex convention, whence these interviews come. But it's not just a series of interview clips; the personal appearances are interwoven with a visual and audio history that's as in-depth as anything ever been done, with loads of film clips, trailers, photos, and one-sheets in sections that feature Hammer's dynamic duo of Cushing and Lee, Michael Ripper, other series and one-off films, Hammer Scream Queens, a tribute to Amicus, and Hammer's Final Years. In the moving tribute to "Props" Cushing (so nicknamed for his propensity for springing unrehearsed and unscripted props on the director and crew), Caroline describes him with real affection, and the bond that developed between them: "[W]e did a lot of scenes in *At the Earth's Core*, and I felt he was very supportive for me. Yes, actually, I suppose he became like my grandfather, he felt like my grandfather ... I could go to him and say, 'Well, what do you think about this, Peter?' and he would say, 'Well ... well my child...' and he had his little white gloves on [for smoking, so that his hands would not be nicotine-stained on screen], and he'd say, 'Well, I think perhaps —' cause, you know, he knew I was relatively inexperienced — I'd done bits and pieces, but I was working with him and Doug [McClure], and of course, they were old hands at it, and he gave me great guidance through the situations. But he was very comforting to me, because my grandfather died during the making of the film, and ... his wife had died, so he knew ... what grief was. He was a lovely, lovely gentleman."

That's the only interview clip of Caroline, but don't watch it just for her — all of the guests shine in this richly detailed labor of love. It brings back a flood of memories, not just of Hammer, but for those who are no longer with us, and for the much-loved Fanex conventions themselves.

The Man Who Saw Frankenstein Cry— 2010, SciFiWorld Entertainment, Waldemar Media, La Cruzada Entertainment

Crew: Executive Producer-Art Director: Luis Miguel Rosales; Producers: Jose Luis Aleman, Sergio Molina; Director-Writer: Angel Agudo; Music: Enrique Garcia; Photography: Aitor Uribarri; Film Editor: Oscar Martin; Second Unit Director: Perry Martin; Graphics:

OTHER WORKS: Film & TV—*Cinema 3* (1984–present)

Javier Yanez Sanz; Art Key: Raul Gil Toural; Sound Editor: Benny Gil; Production Assistant: Angel Luis Sucasas; Translator: Elena Romea; German Translator: Daniel Mendez Kunschke; Thanks: Rick Baker, Paco Cabezas, Geraldine Chaplin, Juan Miguel Cobos, Roger Corman, Fernando Cortizo, Wes Craven, Olvido Gara, Stuart Gordon, Mike Hostench, Sir Christopher Lee, Eugenio Martin, Christian Molina, Mariano Ozores, Juan Pinzas, Ruben Iniguez Perez, Carlos Javier Rodriguez, Elena Romea, Daniel Romero, Eli Roth, Tim Sullivan, Tony Timpone, Guillermo Del Toro, Mario Vaquerizo, Rob Zombie; Special Thanks: Mirek Lipinski.

Cast: Mick Garris (Host); Joe Dante, John Landis, Emilio A. Pina, Caroline Munro, Jorge Grau, Del Howison, Jose Antonio Perez Giner, Angel Luis De Diego, Antonio Mayans, Javier Aguirre, Jose Luis Aleman, Javier Botet, Maria Jose Cantudo, Nacho Cerda, Laura De Pedro, Donald F. Glut, Miguel Iglesias, Victor Matellano, Bruno Molina, Sergio Molina, Elvira Primavera, Angel Sala (Themselves).

SYNOPSIS

A video documentary on the life and times of Spain's greatest horror star, Paul Naschy.

REVIEW AND NOTES

This affectionate, moving tribute to Paul Naschy was co-produced by his son, Sergio, who appeared in six of Naschy's films, including *Howl of the Devil* with Caroline; she and Emilio Pina, who is now a successful producer, are on hand from that film as well. Jose Giner produced a number of Naschy's films, including *Horror Rises from the Tomb*, *House of Psychotic Women*, and *Vengeance of the Zombies*; he also produced the last "Blind Dead" film, *Night of the Seagulls*, and was executive producer of the first, *Tombs of the Blind Dead*. Javier Aguirre was the director on *The Hunchback of the Morgue* and *Count Dracula's Great Love*; Maria Cantudo had been his co-star in *Horror Rises from the Tomb*. Joe Dante and John Landis discuss Naschy's influence on their own werewolf movies *The Howling* and *An American Werewolf in London*, respectively. Naschy was nicknamed "The Boris Karloff of Spain," which is actually somewhat of a disservice, as Naschy was so much more than just an actor; he had experience in nearly every facet of filmmaking: producer, director, writer, etc., and his devotion to the genre was unparalleled. He passed away in 2009, and nobody ever cast a longer Werewolf's Shadow.

Cinema 3 (spanish television series, 1984–present)
Televisio de Catalunya

Episode #373, October 16, 2010

Episode Crew: Executive Producer: Laura Cuadrado; Producer: Joan Pavon; Director: Jaume Figueras; Writer: Begona Garcia Pla.

OTHER WORKS: Film & TV—*Anna and the Killer* (2010) / *The Life of Death* (2010)

Episode Cast: Jaume Figueras (Host); Montse Llussa, Crisol Tua (Voices), Ivana Baquero, Luiso Berdejo, Paco Cabezas, Mario Casas, Fernando Cayo, Andrew Garfield, Barbara Goenaga, Felix Gomez, Macarena Gomez, Kellan Lutz, Eugenio Mira, Christian Molina, Guillem Morales, Caroline Munro, Tetsuya Nakashima, Olivier Pictet, Marc Recuenco, Fergus Riordan, Vicente Romero, Belen Rueda, Aaron Sorkin, Daniel Stamm, Pablo Martin, Manuela Velles, Miguel Angel Vivas (Themselves).

NOTES

Sometimes it's on once a month, sometimes three times, sometimes none, but the Spanish version of *Entertainment Tonight* (featuring show biz news and interviews) has endured for nearly 30 years.

Anna and the Killer with Caroline Munro— 2010, Red Shirt Pictures

Crew: Executive Producers: Gregory Chick, William Lustig; Director–Film Editor: Michael Felsher; Photography: Bob Omer; Production Coordinators: Mike Baronas, Art Ettinger; Special Thanks: Jane Crimin, Aine Leicht.
Cast: Caroline Munro, Art Ettinger (Themselves).

SYNOPSIS

An interview with Caroline devoted primarily to her experiences during the making of *Maniac*.

REVIEW AND NOTES

A 13-minute DVD extra that can be found on Blue Underground's 30th anniversary release of *Maniac*. The bulk of the interview questions concern *Maniac*, although a few other films (*Dracula A.D. 1972*, *Slaughter High*, *The Last Horror Film* and *Faceless*) are touched upon.

The Life of Death— 2010, Brimstone Media Productions

Crew: Producer-Director-Editor: Kevin J. Lindenmuth; Music: Seasons of the Wolf.
Cast: Caroline Munro, Debbie Rochon, David Crumm, Lloyd Kaufman, Bob Fingerman, Jack Ketchum, Keith R.A. DeCandido, Tom Sullivan, Scooter McCrae, Sasha Graham, Tony Timpone, Don May Jr., Art Regner (Themselves).

OTHER WORKS: Film & TV—*Lamb to the Slaughter* (2011)

SYNOPSIS

A documentary that explores how death is perceived by a wide spectrum of media personalities, and whether or not that perception has any effect on how they conduct their lives and go about their work.

REVIEW AND NOTES

A wide spectrum indeed: David Crumm is a spiritual journalist; Kaufman the delightfully mad mastermind behind Troma; Bob Fingerman is a respected comic-book author-artist (*Minimum Wage*). Authors are represented by Ketchum ("Off Season," "The Girl Next Door," and "Red") and DeCandido, who has done media tie-ins for numerous series, including *Star Trek* and *Doctor Who*. Tom Sullivan was the special effects makeup artist for *The Evil Dead* and animator for *Evil Dead II*, and Scooter McCrae was the director and writer of *Shatter Dead*. Tony Timpone was the longtime editor of *Fangoria*, and Art Regner is a legendary Detroit sportscaster. Debbie Rochon got her start in *Ladies and Gentleman: The Fabulous Stains*. Asked how she'd like to die, Caroline echoes most of the other interviewees: "Please, God, you want it to be quick, obviously, and as painless as possible and, er ... and also not too soon!"

Lamb to the Slaughter: The Scream Queen Career of Caroline Munro— 2011, High Rising Productions, Arrow Video

Crew: Producer-Director: Calum Waddell; Producer–Film Editor: Naomi Holwill; Special Thanks: Alan Brice, Almar Haflidason.
Cast: Caroline Munro.

SYNOPSIS

Caroline recollects a number of her best known films in this 26-minute short.

REVIEW AND NOTES

Lamb to the Slaughter is a fairly well-produced special extra feature that was produced for the UK DVD of *Slaughter High*. Caroline talks about her "Scream Queen" roles in *Dracula A.D. 1972*, *Maniac*, *The Last Horror Film*, *Faceless*, and, of course, *Slaughter High*; she spends as much time discussing *Maniac* and *Faceless* as she does the main feature. Caroline is a "Scream Queen" from the days when the term actually meant something, like somebody who had actually appeared in theatrically released movies, rather than just strippers who don fangs and sell sexy photos at conventions. The most amusing moments are when Caroline characterizes Naomi from *The Spy Who Loved Me* as "a bit naughty," calls *Starcrash* a "Spaghetti *Star Wars*," and describes the *Last Horror Film* scene where she runs across the lobby in nothing but a towel "not a pretty sight at all"—even though, for a great many of her fans, it has to be the best scene in the film!

Ray Harryhausen: Special Effects Titan—2011, Frenetic Arts, Ray and Diana Harryhausen Foundation

Crew: Producer-Music: Alexandre Poncet; Co-Producer: Tony Dalton; Director-Writer-Film Editor: Gilles Penso.

Cast: Ray Harryhausen, Steven Spielberg, Simon Pegg, Tim Burton, Peter Jackson, James Cameron, Guillermo del Toro, Terry Gilliam, Jean-Pierre Jeunet, John Landis, Joe Dante, Vincenzo Natali, Caroline Munro, Henry Selick, Peter Lord, Rick Baker, Nick Park, Ray Bradbury, Douglas Trumbull, Martine Beswicke, Christopher Young, Dennis Muren, Phil Tippett, Steve Johnson, Randall William Cook, Andy Jones, Robert Zemeckis, Ken Ralston, Colin Arthur, Greg Broadmore, Vanessa Harryhausen, Tony Dalton (Themselves).

SYNOPSIS

From the Ray & Diana Harryhausen Foundation:

This is the definitive documentary about Ray Harryhausen [with] interviews with the great man himself, shot over five years.... For the first time, Ray and the Foundation have provided unprecedented access to film all aspects of the collection including models, artwork and miniatures, as well as Ray's private study, where he designed most of his creations, and his workshop where he built them. In addition the documentary will use unseen footage of tests and experiments found during the clearance of the LA garage.... This definitive production will [also] illustrate the influence that Ray's work has had on filmmakers during the past 50 or so years."

REVIEW AND NOTES

This documentary has not yet been released as of press time, but the trailers certainly are mouth-watering. Interviewee James Cameron says, "*The Terminator* owes its roots to the skeleton fight in *Jason and the Argonauts*, which I saw when I was seven years old. We all owe Ray a great debt." According to Peter Jackson, "If it hadn't been for Sinbad and *Jason and the Argonauts* and *Mysterious Island*, there would be no *Lord of the Rings* and no *King Kong* remake." Similar praise flows from Steven Spielberg, Tim Burton, Terry Gilliam and a host of others. Caroline and Martine Beswicke relate their experiences facing Ray's creatures.

Advertising and Music

— Advertising —

In addition to her acting roles in film and television, Caroline also carved out a solid body of work in the advertising field. The most long-running, successful, and prominent were the print ads and billboard ads for Lamb's Navy Rum; it was on one of these billboard ads that she was spotted by Sir James Carreras, who soon signed her up at Hammer. Her other ad work includes:

Babycham (television commercial).
Manikin Cigars (television commercial).
Woodpecker Cider (television commercial).
Dr. Pepper (television commercial; Caroline appeared as a three-legged bartender — "I only have two, really, folks!" — in the *Star Wars*–inspired "Space Cowboy").
Fry's Turkish Delight (television commercial with future James Bond George Lazenby when his primary occupation was male model). "One of the earliest ones was done with George Lazenby ... we did a commercial in southern Spain for Fry's Turkish Delight.... George was, for about three years, 'Mr. Big Fry'; he had to carry about this whacking great box on his shoulder that said 'Big Fry' on it...."
Noxzema Shaving Cream (television commercials). Caroline appeared in two for Noxzema, following Farrah Fawcett. "Great Balls of Comfort" and "Auntie Friction" were banned in the South because Caroline did naughty things with her eyes.
Picnic Chocolate Bar (television commercial).
Consulate Cigarettes (television commercial, directed by Ridley Scott).
Gancia Wine (television commercial).
Inter-Continental Hotel Group (television commercial).

A photograph from the ad campaign that launched Caroline's movie career.

OTHER WORKS: Advertising and Music

— Music —

Caroline has also been associated with the music biz, both as a performing and recording artist. In 1967, she ventured into the pop singles charts with "This Sporting Life" ("Tar & Cement" was the flipside) for Decca, which has been collected for posterity in the digital age as part of MSI Distribution's *Dream Babes* series (Vol. 2, *Reflections*). "Tar & Cement" is a wistful slice of English pastoral rock *à la* the Kinks' "Waterloo Sunset," while "This Sporting Life" rocks hard and heavy, and no wonder — the session musicians employed are Eric Clapton on guitar, Jack Bruce on bass, and Ginger Baker on drums, soon to be collectively known as Cream, and Steve Howe of prog-rock powerhouse Yes. In 1984, she signed up with Gary "Cars" Numan's Numa Records and released the infectious, electronic dance-pop single "Pump Me Up." It didn't make much of a splash, due mostly to poor promotional efforts on the part of the label. The flipside of "Pump Me Up" was a slow, moody piece called "The Picture"; both songs were written and produced by Numan, who also contributes keyboards and backing vocals. She also provided vocals and lyrics for the song "Warrior of Love," which was used in the film *Don't Open Till Christmas*. The song has never had an official release as a single or part of an album.

She has also performed in videos by both the king of bombast, Meat Loaf ("If You Really Want To") and former Malcolm McLaren protégé Adam Ant ("Goody Two

Caroline on the cover of an album of covers that would never have recovered its costs had she not been on the cover.

155

Other Works: Interviews, Articles, Pictorials and Covers

Caroline graces the cover of her own single, the extended club version of "Pump Me Up," done in collaboration with Gary Numan.

Shoes"). "Goody Two Shoes," from the album *Friend or Foe* and written by film buff Ant and Marco Pirroni, was the much bigger hit of the two; it was #1 in the UK singles charts for two weeks in 1982, and was later #1 in Australia. It was Ant's first (and biggest) hit in the US, reaching #12. In the video, Caroline plays a prim and proper journalist who finishes the song taking a walk on the wild side with Ant. Meat Loaf saw her in the Adam Ant video and signed her up for the video of "If You Really Want To," *Midnight at the Lost and Found*. Not even Caroline as a seductive vampire (finally!) could help it chart any higher than #59 in the UK. Caroline has even been the subject of at least one rock 'n' roll song, "Caroline Goodbye" on the 1971 LP *One Year*, the first solo album by Colin Blunstone, former lead singer of the legendary Zombies; it concerns the breakup of their relationship. She was also the cover model on a few nondescript compilation albums in the '70s. And in another instance of photograph-only appearance, she was featured in such a capacity in the *Space: 1999* episode "The Séance Spectre" (Season 2, Episode # 20, August 18, 1977).

Magazine Interviews, Articles, Pictorials and Covers

— Interviews —

Chiller Theatre No. 4, 1996.
Cinema Retro (UK/US) No. 6, 2006: "The Legend of Casino Royale from Book to Screen."

OTHER WORKS: Interviews, Articles, Pictorials and Covers

Empire (UK) No. 94, 1997, "(Where Are They Now?) Buxom Beauty," Jake Hamilton.
Fangoria No. 4, February 1980, "A Talk with Caroline Munro"; No. 102, May, 1991, "Ripped Off in Rome," Steve Swires.
Filmfax No. 83, March 2001, "The Cinemazing Career of Caroline Munro: From Sinbad's Sexy Shipmate and Center of the Earth centerfold to Interstellar Amazon and Beyond!," Michael Stein; No. 117, 2008.
Forrest J Ackerman's Monster Land No. 6, December 1985.
Gorezone No. 6, 1989, "Caroline Does Splatter," Steve Swires.
Little Shoppe of Horrors No. 18, September 2006, "The Ladies of Hammer, Part VI — Caroline Munro," Bruce G. Hallenbeck.
Saturday Express (UK), June 4, 2011, "(Whatever Happened To?): Caroline Munro."
Starburst (UK) No. 24.
Starlog No. 57, April 1982, "Caroline Munro: Fantasy Films' First Lady," Steve Swires; No. 130, May 1988, "Caroline Munro: Starting Over," Steve Swires.

— Articles —

Bizarre (UK) No. 26, December 1999, "Hack and Slash with the Screen Goddesses."
Famous Monsters of Filmland No. 155, July 1979, "*Starcrash*"; No. 182, April 1982, "Caroline Munro: Beauty among the Beasts."
Fangoria No. 7, 1980, "How to make a *Maniac*."
Femme Fatales vol. 6, no. 1, July 1997, "Caroline Munro: Her Liaison with Hammer Vampires Kindled a Career as a Femme Fatale," Ted Newsom; Vol. 9, no. 4/5, September 2000, "Hammer Heroines/Caroline Munro," Fred Szebin.
Films Illustrated (UK), August 1981.
Film Review (UK), May 1975.
Knave (UK) vol. 15, no. 6, June 1983, "The A-Z of Bond Girls," Tony Crawley.
Oui vol. 2, no. 4, April 1973, "New Sex Symbol Discusses Leeks," Richard Roraback.
Space Wars vol. 3, no. 1, March 1979, "The Adventures of Stella Star," A.B. Whiteman.
Starburst (UK) No. 38, "Caroline Munro — Top Fantasy Female Stars in New Horror Film."
Questar No. 7, June 1980: "Portrait: Caroline Munro, Sci-Fi's Queen of Space."

— Pictorials —

ABC Film Review (UK), February 1972 (centerfold photo).
Adam vol. 12, no. 11, November 1968, "Portfolio."
Celebrity Skin vol. 1, no. 1, 1979, "Fantasy Body."

What reader of Adam wouldn't be tempted by this Eve? One of Caroline's two covers for the long-running men's magazine.

Celebrity Sleuth vol. 2, no. 5, 1989, "*The Spy Who Loved Me*'s Naomi"; Vol. 6, no. 4, 1993, "Fantasy Hall of Fame #1—Caroline Munro."
Femme Fatales vol. 1, no. 2, 1992.
Film Review (UK), October 1974; August 1976.
High Society, November 1984, "Scream Queens—Hot Shots of Horror Movies' Sexy Stars."
Mediascene No. 27, 1977; No. 37, 1981.
Penthouse, July 1977.
Prevue No. 63, February 1986.

OTHER WORKS: Interviews, Articles, Pictorials and Covers

Although she never posed for *Playboy*, Caroline was no stranger to the world of men's magazines. This was the second of her two covers for *Adam*.

— Magazine Covers —

Adam vol. 12, no. 11, November 1968 (front and back covers); Vol. 13, no. 6, June 1969.

Cinema (Italy) No. 7, 1978.

Fangoria No. 4, February 1980 (front cover inset photo).

Film, Szinhaz, Muzsika ("Film, Theatre and Music") (Hungary) No. 48, 1967 (back cover).

Filmfax No. 83, March 2001, cover painting of Caroline as Margiana from *The Golden Voyage of Sinbad* by Harley Brown; No. 117, 2008 (front cover inset).

OTHER WORKS: Interviews, Articles, Pictorals and Covers

Forrest J Ackerman's Monster Land No. 6, December 1985 (front cover inset photo).
International Film Collector (UK) No. 22, June 1978.
Little Shoppe of Horrors No. 18, September 2006, front cover painting of *Captain Kronos, Vampire Hunter* stars by Bruce Timm; No. 22, March 2009, back cover painting of *Dracula A.D. 1972* cast by Bruce Timm.
Mediascene No. 37, 1981.
Starburst (UK) Nos. 24, 38.
Starlog Poster Magazine vol. 6, Summer 1986.

BIBLIOGRAPHY

Books

Briggs, Joe Bob, *Profoundly Disturbing: Shocking Movies That Changed History!* New York: Universe, 2003.
Brosnan, John. *James Bond in the Cinema.* London: Tantivy Press, and South Brunswick, NJ: A.S. Barnes, 1972.
Frank, Alan, *Horror Movies.* London: Octopus Books, 1974.
Hearn, Marcus. *Hammer Glamour.* London: Titan Books, 2009.
Holston, Kim, and Tom Winchester. *Science Fiction, Fantasy and Horror Film Sequels, Series and Remakes: An Illustrated Filmography, with Plot Synopses and Critical Commentary.* Jefferson, NC: McFarland, 1997.
Hunter, Jack. *House of Horror: The Complete Hammer Films Story.* London: Creation Books, 1994.
Johnson, Tom, and Deborah Del Vecchio. *Hammer Films: An Exhaustive Filmography.* Jefferson, NC: McFarland, 1996.
Kinsey, Wayne. *Hammer Films: The Bray Studios Years.* Richmond, Surrey: Reynolds & Hearn, 2002.
_____. *Hammer Films: The Elstree Studios Years.* Sheffield: Tomahawk Press, 2007.
Marrero, Robert G. *Vampires: Hammer Style.* Key West: RGM Publications, 1982.
Maxford, Howard. *Hammer, House of Horror: Behind the Screams.* Woodstock, NY: Overlook Press, 1996.
Meikle, Dennis. *A History of Horrors: The Rise and Fall of the House of Hammer.* Rev. ed. Lanham, MD: Scarecrow Press, 2009.
Naschy, Paul. *Paul Naschy: Memoirs of a Wolfman.* Baltimore: Midnight Marquee Press, 2000.
Parish, James Robert, and Steven Whitney. *Vincent Price Unmasked.* New York: Drake, 1974.
Sheppard, David. *On Some Faraway Beach: The Life and Times of Brian Eno.* London: Orion, and Chicago: Chicago Review Press, 2009.
Seuss, Dr. *Green Eggs and Ham.* New York: Beginner Books, 1960.
Winder, Simon. *The Man Who Saved Britain: A Personal Journey into the Disturbing World of James Bond.* New York: Farrar, Straus and Giroux, 2006.

Periodicals

Castle of Frankenstein Nos. 19, 21, 24, 1972, 1974.
Chicago Sun-Times.
Cinefantastique Vol. 3, no. 2, 1974.
Famous Monsters of Filmland Nos. 106, 155, 182, 1974, 1979, 1982.

Fangoria Nos. 4, 7, 102, 1975, 1986
Femme Fatales Vol. 6, no. 1; Vol. 9, no. 4/5, 1997, 2000.
Filmfax No. 83, 2000.
FXRH Vol. 1, no. 4, 1974.
Gorezone No. 6, 1989.
Halls of Horror No. 20, 1978.
House of Hammer Nos. 1, 2, 1976.
Little Shoppe of Horrors Nos. 18, 22, 2006, 2009.
Los Angeles Times.
Monster Fantasy No. 1, 1975.
Monsters of the Movies No. 4, 1974.
MonsterScene No. 10, 1997.
Movie Monsters No. 1, 1974.
Rue Morgue No. 90, 2009.
Scarlet Street No. 15, 1994.
Starlog Nos. 57, 130, 1982, 1988.
Variety, 1971.

Websites

Internet Movie Database (www.imdb.com).
Margiana: Caroline Munro and *The Golden Voyage of Sinbad* (http://www.margiana.freeservers.com/index.html).
Wikipedia (Wikipedia.org).

INDEX

Numbers in ***bold italics*** indicate pages with photographs.

The Abominable Dr. Phibes (film) 18–24
The Absence of Light (film) 110–116
Adam Ant 155–156
American International Productions 23
Amicus Film Productions 64
Anna and the Killer with Caroline Munro (documentary short) 151
At the Earth's Core (film) 58–64
El Aullido del Diablo (film) 93–95
The Avengers (TV series) 73

Baker, Tom ***49***, 51
Bates, Ralph 57
The Beatles 15
Beswick, Martine 137
Blood Craving 143
Bond, James 10, 69–72
Bond Girls Are Forever (documentary) 143–144
Broccoli, Cubby 140
Burroughs, Edgar Rice 61, 63

Captain Kronos — Vampire Hunter (film) 38–46
Caroline Munro — First Lady of Fantasy (documentary) 145–146
Carreras, Sir James 29
Casino Royale (film) 7–12
Cater, John 36, ***44***, 45
Cinderella: The Shoe Must Go On (TV movie) 91–92
Cinema 3 (TV series) 150–151
Clemens, Brian 45, 51
Collins, Joan 55, 57
Cozzi, Luigi 101, 102
Crumpet! A Very British Sex Symbol (documentary) 146–147
Cue Gary (TV series) 127
Cushing, Peter 28, 36, ***61***, 62, 128, 149

Demons 6: De Profundis (film) 99–103
The Devil Within Her (film) 54–58
Dile, Gary 114
Dr. Phibes Rises Again (film) 31–38
Doctor Who 62, 91
Domestic Strangers (film) 109–110
Don't Open Till Christmas (film) 122–124
Dracula A.D. 1972 (film) 24–31

Eldorado (film) 116–117
Eurotika! (TV documentary series) 139

Faceless (film) 95–98
Famous Monsters of Filmland (magazine) 37, 52, 75, 77, 87
Fanex Convention 148, 149
Fanex Files: Hammer Films (documentary) 147–149
Flesh and Blood: The Hammer Heritage of Horror (documentary) 131–133
Flesh for the Beast (film) 105–109
Franco, Jesus 97

G.G. Passion (film) 6–7
GMTV (TV series) 143
The Golden Voyage of Sinbad (film) 46–54
Gortner, Marjoe 78

Hamalian, Tami 88
Hamill, Mark 52, 121
Hamilton, Judd 15, 76, 79, 87
Hammer Films 27, 40 41, 132, 134
Harryhausen, Ray 49–53, 153
Heroes of Comedy (TV documentary series) 135–136
The Horror of Hammer (documentary) 133–134
The Howerd Confessions (TV series) 64–65

I Don't Want to Be Born see *The Devil Within Her*
Inside the Spy Who Loved Me (documentary) 139–140

Jagger, Mick 7, 31
James Bond: A BAFTA Tribute (TV special) 144–145
Janson, Horst 39
Joanna (film) 12–13
The Joe Spinell Story (documentary) 141–142

Kiel, Richard 70
Kraft Music Hall Presents: The Des O'Connor Show (TV series) 120–121

Lamb's Navy Rum 29, 154
The Last Horror Film (film) 85–88
Law, John Philip ***50***, 51
Lee, Christopher 25, 28, 29, 137
Leon, Valerie 68, 72
Lewis, Fiona 13
The Life of Death (documentary) 151–152
Lustig, William 84, 85

Maigret (TV movie) 98–99
The Man Who Saw Frankenstein Cry (documentary) 149–150
Maniac (film) 79–85
McClure, Doug ***61***, 62
Meat Loaf 155, 156
Mitchum, Chris 98
MonsterScene (magazine) 23, 35
Moore, Roger 71, 145

Naschy, Paul 94, 95, 150
The New Avengers (TV series) 72–74
Night Owl (film) 129–130

Once Upon a Time in Europe (documentary) 142–143

163

Index

100 Years of Horror (documentary series) 136–139

Price, Vincent 21, 35, 37

Ray Harryhausen: Special Effects Titan (documentary) 153

The Seventh Annual Science Fiction Awards (TV special) 121–122
Slaughter High (film) 88–91
Smoke Over London (film) 5–6
Spinell, Joe 78, 82–83, **84**, 86–87, 141–142

The Spy Who Loved Me (film) 65–72
Starcrash (film) 74–79
Stellar Quasar and the Scrolls of Dadelia (film) 117–118
Sweating Bullets (TV series) 103–104

A Talent for Loving (film) 13–15
This Is Your Life (TV series) 128
3-2-1 (TV series) 124–127
Thriller Zone (film) 134–135
To Die For (film) 104–105
Turpin (film) 116

The Vampire Interviews (documentary) 130–131
VH1 Where Are They Now? (TV documentary series) 140–141

Welles, Orson 9–10
Where's Jack? (film) 15–18
The Who 24, 119, 120
A Whole Scene Going (TV series) 119–120
The Witches' Dungeon: 40 Years of Chills (documentary) 147
World of Hammer (documentary series) 128–129

The Zombies 156

www.ingramcontent.com/pod-product-compliance
Ingram Content Group UK Ltd.
Pitfield, Milton Keynes, MK11 3LW, UK
UKHW050523150426
5217IPUK00026B/1764